THE JEWISH MARRIAGE CONTRACT

A Study in the Status of the Woman in Jewish Law

BY

LOUIS M. EPSTEIN, A.M., D.H.L.

Rabbi Congregation Kehillath Israel
Brookline, Massachusetts

THE LAWBOOK EXCHANGE, LTD.
Clark, New Jersey

ISBN 978-1-58477-464-8 (Hardcover)
ISBN 978-1-61619-511-3 (Paperback)

Lawbook Exchange edition 2005, 2015

The quality of this reprint is equivalent to the quality of the original work.

The Lawbook Exchange, Ltd.
33 Terminal Avenue
Clark, New Jersey 07066-1321

Please see our website for a selection of our other publications and fine facsimile reprints of classic works of legal history:
www.lawbookexchange.com

Library of Congress Cataloging-in-Publication Data

Epstein, Louis M., 1887-1949.
The Jewish marriage contract: a study in the status of the woman in Jewish law / by Louis M. Epstein.
p. cm.
Originally published: New York: Jewish Theological Seminary of America, 1927.
Includes bibliographical references and index.
ISBN 1-58477-464-9 (cloth: alk. paper)
1. Ketubah. 2. Marriage (Jewish law) I. Title.

KBM572.E67 2004
296.4'44—dc22 2004053816

Printed in the United States of America on acid-free paper

THE JEWISH MARRIAGE CONTRACT

A Study in the Status of the Woman in Jewish Law

BY

LOUIS M. EPSTEIN, A.M., D.H.L.

Rabbi Congregation Kehillath Israel
Brookline, Massachusetts

NEW YORK
JEWISH THEOLOGICAL SEMINARY
OF AMERICA
1927

The Century Press Boston, Massachusetts

ברגשי כבוד ואהבה הנני מקדיש

את הספר הזה

תולדות הכתובה בישראל

ראשית פרי עמלי, להורי היקרים

הרב הגדול מהור' עזריאל בהר' יהודה ליב

והרבנית מבת' מרת רבקה בתר' ניסן

עפשטיין

מורי ומדריכי אשר שאיפת חייהם היתה לגדלני על ברכי התורה לחנכני להיות מוקיר ומייקר כל הקדוש לעמנו ולשתות בצמא את דברי חכמינו זכרונם לברכה. תום דרכיהם ואהבתם לתורת ד' סללו לפני דרך ישרה לשאיפותי אני. ד' הטו"ב יאריך ימיכם, הורי ומורי החביבים, בכל טוב, אמן.

המחבר

A KETUBAH OR MARRIAGE WRIT PHOTOGRAPHED FROM A MANUSCRIPT IN THE JEWISH THEOLOGICAL SEMINARY LIBRARY

PREFACE

It is not mere accident that the Hebrew word, Torah, denotes both learning and law. Speaking for my own day, I am impressed with the fact that among Jews living in a distinctly Jewish environment the feeling is general that only he is a scholar who masters the law. Nor does that seem to be a feeling peculiar to our own day; that same feeling is predominant in the entire three thousand years' chain of the records of the Jewish past. Fully appreciative though I am of the great minds that have been consecrated to the fields of Jewish history and Hebrew philology and like investigations, I cannot challenge in myself — ancient that I am! — an admiration of halakic scholarship exceeding that of any other kind of learning. Jewish law is the essence of Judaism as well as its most faithful record. The Law is to the Prophets, the halakah is to the agadah, the responsum is to the piyyut what fact is to interpretation or what text is to comment. Until the facts have been fully established, therefore, their interpretation must remain of lesser importance.

It must be admitted that the popular mind is more attracted to the agadah than to the halakah. This must not be taken, however, as a verdict in favor of the former as against the latter. Rather it is due to the fact that a certain technical training and intellectual equipment are necessary for the understanding of the subject matter of the halakah. Were the halakah presented in popular form, I have no doubt but that it would supersede the agadah in popular interest. What makes it difficult to present halakic material in a form suitable for the general reading public is the fact that our sources must be submitted to textual criticism before we can glean the information we seek; and textual criticism is not the most engaging reading matter even for the scholar, much less for the layman. To overcome in a measure this difficulty, I have attempted to maintain a clear division in this work between the text of the book and the notes. In the former I have attempted to give a continuous account of our subject and in the latter I have included all the technical discussions.

The subject of "The Jewish Marriage Contract" should prove of interest to the reader not only because the position of woman has engaged the attention of present day social and political leaders, Jewish as well as non-Jewish, but also because it represents a section of the law which has special interests peculiar to itself. It constitutes within itself a combination of civil and ceremonial law, it mirrors Judaism in its inner rather than outer relations, and more than any other section of the law, it has defied the ravages of time and hostile conditions, remaining inviolable and fully valid to this day.

It was my intention at first, when I began collecting material, to treat the entire field of the Status of the Woman in Jewish Law in a single volume in which the Marriage Contract would form one chapter. I discovered early enough that the one chapter on the Marriage Contract was expanding into a whole book, and I later discovered that I would have to curtail the material and abbreviate the treatment of the work in order to make it possible to fit even the smaller subject into the form of an average sized book.

I am pleased to acknowledge my profound gratitude to my teacher and friend, Professor Louis Ginzberg, of the Jewish Theological Seminary, for the advice, guidance, suggestions and corrections that he generously gave me in the preparation of this work. From him I have learned during my student days the critical method of investigation into rabbinic sources, to him also I have turned ever since for encouragement and aid in all my scholarly endeavors. In so far as this work has any merit, it reflects the assistance given to me by my beloved teacher. My friend, Rabbi Abraham Burstein of New York, has helped me in the correction of the copy and in the preparation of the index and in many other personal ways, and I acknowledge my debt of gratitude to him. Professor Harry A. Wolfson, of Harvard University, Cambridge, and Professor Adolph Büchler, of Jews' College, London, have shown a kindly interest in this work and have offered many helpful suggestions. I also wish to record my indebtedness to the authorities of the British Museum, the Cambridge University Library, the Bodleian Library, to Haham Doctor Moses Gaster, to Elkan N. Adler, Esq., and to Mr. David Sassoon, for permission to use their libraries and to consult their manuscripts, and to the Chief Rabbi of Great Britain, Doctor Joseph H. Hertz for helping me to obtain that permission. And to the encouragement and suggestions of Doctor Cyrus Adler, President of the Jewish Theological Seminary of America and of my teachers and friends on its Faculty, Professor Alexander Marx and Professor Israel Davidson and of a host of friends in the American rabbinate, I owe much of the good that may be found in this book.

May I also record affectionately the debt I owe to my wife, Minnie Hannah, for her coöperation with me in innumerable ways in the compilation of this work which from its very inception she and I planned together?

Brookline, Mass., Tishri, 5688

ABBREVIATIONS

BGE Beitrage z. Geschichte d. bibl-talmud. Eheschliessungsrechts, Jacob Neubauer.
CH Code Hammurabi, ancient Assyrian code of laws.
EH Eben Ha-ezer, fourth volume of the code of R. Joseph Caro.
GES Zur Geschichte d. Ehegüterrechts b. d. Semiten, L. Freund.
Jer. Jerushalmi, ed. Krotoschin, cited by folio and column.
JE Jewish Encyclopedia.
JQR Jewish Quarterly Review.
KBD Ketubat benin dikrin.
KBN Ketubat benan nukban.
MGWJ Monatschrift f. d. Geschichte u. Wissenschaft d. Judenthums.
RABJH R. Elazar b. Joel Halevi, German Talmudic commentator.
RABD R. Abraham b. David, Spanish rabbinic authority, known as critic of Maimonides.
RDBZ R. David b. Zimra, Egyptian Talmudic scholar.
REJ Revue des Etudes Juives.
RG Rabban Gamaliel, Tanna.
RIBSH R. Isaac b. Sheshet, Spanish rabbinic authority.
RID R. Isaiah di Trani, called R. Isaiah, the First, Italian rabbinic scholar.
RITBA R. Yomtov of Seville, Spanish Talmudic commentator.
RSBG Rabban Simeon b. Gamaliel, Tanna.
RSBA R. Solomon b. Adret, Spanish scholar, author of responsa and Talmudic Novelae.
RSBM R. Samuel b. Meir, French tosafist and Talmud commentator.
SBS Simeon b. Shetah, Tanna.
SKAW Sitzungsbericht d. kaiserliche Akademie d. Wissenschaften, philosoph.-historische Klasse.
Tos. Tosifta.
TShBZ Teshubot Samson b. Zemah, responsa by R. Samson b. Zemah, an Algiers rabbinic authority.
WZKM Wiener Zeitschrift f. d. Kunde d. Morgenlandes.
ZVR Zeitschrift f. Vergleichende Rechtwissenschaft.

TABLE OF CONTENTS

Lien of Ketubah not effective against movable property — Movable property by way of immovable — Both movable and immovable property — The geonic enactment — The effect of the enactment — The formula: Even from the cloak on my back — The formula: Property that I did acquire or that I shall acquire — The formula: Out of the choicest of my property — The guarantor for the Ketubah — Formulae intended to guard against *Asmakta* — Precaution against *Moda'a* — Composite lien formula.

CHAPTER XVI — PAYMENT 255

The need to present the Ketubah document with the demand for payment — Administering an oath to the woman demanding payment of her Ketubah — The vow as a substitute for the oath — The sale of the husband's property for the payment of the Ketubah — Priority of claim as between Ketubot and notes of indebtedness — Cases where priority does not apply — The lien not applied to cover other Ketubah terms but mohar, mattan and dowry — The execution of the clause providing support for the wife — Burial and ransom — Alimentation of the widow — *Ketubat benan nukban* — *Parnasah* — *Ketubat benin dikrin* — Priority of claim among the several Ketubah provisions.

CHAPTER XVII — SPECIAL CLAUSES 269

Characterization of special clauses — Special clauses in the matter of succession — Providing against polygamy and against objectionable female slave — Domicile — Providing that the wife shall be freed from oath or vow — Support of step-daughter — Care of husband's children — Providing for divorce only with the wife's consent and in a Jewish court — Providing against the danger of desertion — Proper care of the wife's dowry — Observance of religious rites — Agreements as to religious rites in marriages between Karaites and Rabbinites — Reflection in the Ketubah of social conditions.

THE JEWISH MARRIAGE CONTRACT

CHAPTER I

THE KETUBAH AND ITS FUNCTION

There are three interested parties to a marriage contract, the husband, the wife, and the State. In modern days, the State's interest is so paramount that it completely overshadows the other two. The State binds and the State releases the bond. It not only sets the standards for marriage relations, but it also effects the union itself. As it issues a decree of divorce, so it validates a marriage. Modern marriages, therefore, have no need and practically no room for a marriage deed, or a written marriage contract.

The more ancient systems of law, while recognizing the State's share in a marriage bond, permit the center of the romantic circle to be occupied by the bride and the groom or their guardians. Ancient law is more true to the conception—valid even in modern terminology—that marriage is a voluntary transaction between two parties, a male and a female. Jewish law, for instance, does not recognize a decree of divorce of any court without the act of divorcing carried out by the husband. It is the husband who divorces, not the court. Equally, it is the husband who marries, not the court. Therefore, for many centuries, Jewish marriages were negotiated by means of marriage deeds. The deed, or as it is called כתובה, sets down the terms of the marriage contract. The practice of writing a marriage deed still obtains among Jews today, but its importance in the marriage has been lessened by the influence of the statutory marriage of modern law, that is, the marriage whose foundation is social legislation or statute rather than contract. Still, the Ketubah is with us today as a survival of an ancient institution, and submits itself readily to a historical and analytical examination.

The Ketubah presents a variety of interests, mirrors segments of life, and records a fairly long span of the Jewish past. It is not the document of the wealthy or the scholar or the prince. It is the home companion of every Jew everywhere.[1] But above all these interests, there is the interest that scholars should have in its central theme, the legal relations of marriage, the marriage contract. To one who seeks to grasp the character of the Jewish marriage, there is no better approach to it than by way of the study of the Ketubah. It is not sentimental, it is not rhetorical, it is not subjective. It is a legal document embodying the essential points agreed upon by the parties and sanctioned by the law as to the manner of their living together as husband and wife.

Only the Ketubah, with an insignificant companion, the Tena'im, or the writ embodying the terms of the engagement, have survived to our day. During the Talmudic period and for a number of centuries following it, there existed many other instruments connected with marriage, and the scribe's business was apparently more flourishing. The *Ketab kiddushin,*[2] more popularly termed *Shetar kiddushin,*[3] had its own place in the marriage; so did the *Shetar erusin u-nesu'in,*[4]

[1] Cf. *The Ketubah,* M. Gaster, Rimon Publishing Co., 1923.

[2] J. Gittin 44c, 45d; Deut. R. 3:12.

[3] M. K. 18b, etc.

[4] Kid. 9b; Ket. 102b; B. B. 167b. Amoraim believe this writ to be synonymous with *Shetare Pesikata.* Some commentators (Cf. *Shitah mekubezet* Ket. 102b) believe that it repre-

accounted to be synonymous with the *Shetare Pesikata.*[5] During the Geonic period and after it, a number of other writs were added or reconstructed and presented in legal form for the use of scribes.[6]

Both in Talmudic and post-Talmudic literature, however, the ketubah is the most prominent of the marriage instruments. A whole tractate of the Talmud bears that name, and it is probably the most widely studied part of the entire Talmud. Despite the tradition of the rabbis which ascribes greater antiquity to the *Shetar Kiddushin*—which tradition I shall attempt in due course to discredit—the ketubah seems to be the oldest Jewish marriage contract. In pre-rabbinic times, it is referred to as *S'far Intu*[7] and in a Greek text as *Syngraphe.*[8] The Rabbis also sometimes speak of it as *Sefer Ketubah*[9] or *Shetar Ketubah,*[10] but its popular name in the Talmud is just *Ketubah.* By this name it is designated in traditions of great antiquity, such, for instance, as have been transmitted by R. Simeon II b. Gamaliel[11] and his contemporary, R. Joha-

sents two contracts, the pesikata and the ketubah. In view of the halakah cited in B. B. ibid., it is hardly possible that the *Shetar erusin u-nesuin* would represent such two divergent instruments, for the *pesikata* is made out in the interest of the husband, the ketubah in the interest of the wife.

[5] Kid. 9b, etc.

[6] Cf. Fischer, *Urkunden in Talmud.* See *Sefer Ha-shetarot,* R. Judah Barceloni, ed. Halberstam, Berlin, 1898.

[7] Assuan Papyri, F;4.

[8] Tobit 7:13, according to Text A. Other texts add modifying words. Cf. Fritzsche, *Libri Apokryphi,* a. l.

[9] Mishna Jeb. 15:3 (117a); Eduyot 1:12; Tos. Ed. 1:6; Jer. Jeb. 14d. This follows the Biblical terminology of *Sefer Keritut* (Deut. 24:1) and *Sefer Ha-miknah* (Jer. 32:10).

[10] Ket. 104b.

[11] Tos. San. 7:1. The emphasis in this tradition on caste and purity puts it back in Temple days. Cf. Buechler, *Familienreinheit und Familienmakel,* Schwartz's *Festschrift,* pp. 133 ff. See also Geiger, *Urschrift,* pp. 114 ff.

nan b. Zakkai,[12] both of the first century of the common era, and their master, Hillel the Elder.[13]

The word "ketubah" means literally a written instrument,[14] and hence the reason for its application to the marriage deed. But because the marriage deed contained a number of clauses of conveyances and guarantees, it was not uncommon to speak of any of the clauses as ketubah, and so we have *ketubat isha,* meaning maintenance of the widow,[15] or *ketubat b'nan nukban,* guaranteeing support to the orphaned girls, or *ketubat b'nin dikrin,* certain guarantees to male children in the matter of succession to their parents' property. More specifically is the term ketubah often used as synonomous with *mohar,*[16] or marriage price, or with dowry,[17] because of the prominence of these elements in the marriage deed. When, therefore, the word "ketubah" appears in some clause in the marriage deed, and some of these clauses are of very great antiquity, going back even to Simeon b. Shetah of the first century before the common era, there is no way of determining whether the instrument itself or its provisions are meant.[18]

[12] Ket. 66b. "I remember that I signed the ketubah of this woman."

[13] Tos. Ket. 4:9; B. M. 104a; Jer. Jeb. 14d. "Bring me your mothers' ketubot."

[14] And is applied sometimes to a realty purchase deed. Cf. Jer. Jeb. 14d.

[15] Tos. Ket. 12:2.

[16] Mekilta Ex. 22:16; Jer. Ket. 27d. Among the Karaites, the ketubah is often called *Shetar Ha-mohar* and it is so called also in *Ketubah Jerushalemit,* ed. Berliner, in *Kobez'al Yad* IX.

[17] Jeb. 38a. Ket. 80b. It also designates general arrangements of property grants and guarantees between husband and wife, Cf. Sab. 130a.

[18] "The male children which thou shalt have by me shall inherit thy ketubah," or the Judean formula, "Thou shalt dwell

The function of the ketubah in our day is practically no other than to perpetuate an ancient tradition. Its effectiveness in actual questions of law, even Jewish law, is very slight, since it is stereotyped and reduced to the very minimum of specifications. Every ketubah is exactly like every other ketubah. In former days, its effectiveness as a document of rights and guarantees was real. But, as far back as the days of the tannaim of about the beginning of the second century, it did nothing more than that. It played no part in the consummation of the marriage. The marriage was valid or invalid on its own merits, regardless of the validity of the ketubah. The clause in the ketubah, reading, "Be thou my wife according to the law of Moses and Israel," was taken to be a record of the marriage—not a pronouncement of marriage.

If a writ was used for the consummation of the marriage, it was not the ketubah but the shetar kiddushin. In the minds of the later rabbinic authorities, the two instruments were distinct from each other. The shetar kiddushin was a simple, stereotyped declaration of marriage, given to the bride at the time of the betrothal, and useless after being received by her. It probably read: "I, so-and-so, do hereby betroth thee, so-and-so, according to the law of Moses and Israel." [19]

in my house and be supported out of my estate during thy widowhood until the heirs pay thee thy ketubah" (Ket. 52). The formula of SBS reads "All my property shall be a lien for the payment of thy ketubah" (Ket. 82b).

[19] This formula is a composite of two formulae found in the Talmud. The first one (Kid. 9a) is cited in a beraita as a comment on the first mishna of Kiddushin, reading "Thy daughter be consecrated to me, thy daughter be betrothed to me, or thy daughter be my wife." That this beraita is a late one is seen from the fact that it adds that the parchment bearing the inscription need not be worth a peruta—revealing that the discussion between the Hillelites and the Shamites as to whether

The ketubah was neither simple, nor stereotyped, nor a declaration of marriage, nor even necessarily given to the bride at the time of betrothal,[20] and was always retained by the wife as a memorandum of guarantees, until they were fully met and the ketubah was cancelled.

This distinction between the two instruments is not known in earlier rabbinic sources,[21] and ample ground is given for the suspicion that originally the ketubah and the shetar kiddushin were one, thus giving the ketubah the additional function of consummating the marriage itself. Philo, speaking of marriage conveyance by deed, describes the instrument as containing

a peruta or a dinnar is the marriage coin was already settled in favor of the Hillelites. The second formula is quoted in the Palestinian Talmud in the name of R. Johanan, reading, "I, so-and-so, do hereby betroth thee, so-and-so." See Jer. Kid. 63d, Jer. Erubin 21b. The words, " according to the law of Moses and Israel," are added on the basis of their appearance in our present ketubah and in the ketubah cited by Hillel and in the marriage formula of the Book of Tobit.

It is the simplicity of the shetar kiddushin which accounts for the Talmudic discussion whether the shetar made for one woman may be used for another (Kid. 9a). Even the date was not inserted in the shetar kiddushin as known in amoraic days (Jeb. 31b).

[20] Which matter will be taken up separately later.

[21] Cf. Freund, *Zur Geschichte der Eheguterrechts bei den Semiten,* (GES) p. 7, note 2.

It is true, the beraita, Kid. 9a, cited in note 19, wishes us to believe that the shetar kiddushin is meant by the word "shetar" in the first mishna of Kiddushin, which mishna is, of course, very old. One has cause to doubt the historical correctness of such an assumption. Between the mishna of Kiddushin and this beraita, a period of approximately five hundred years passed, of activity in law among Jews, in which there is practically no mention of the shetar kiddushin. How can that be explained except by the assumption that the "shetar" of the mishna is more akin to the ketubah than the shetar kiddushin?

the names of the bride and the groom and the agreements pertinent to the marriage.[22] Again, that which is technically termed ketubah and has the nature of the ketubah in that it serves the purpose of a memorandum of guarantees, is taken up by Hillel the Elder as the pivotal document upon which to determine the legitimacy of children by a certain marriage.[23] Evidently, the shetar kiddushin of Philo was also the ketubah, as the ketubah of Hillel was also the shetar kiddushin, leading us to the conclusion that originally both instruments were one.

Having established this point, we are in a better position to understand another but closely allied phase of the development of the ketubah. Rab, the first of the amoraim, at the beginning of the third century, is the first one to speak of "a place where the writing of the ketubah is not in vogue." [24] R. Meir, his predecessor by two generations, who probably noticed a tendency among the people to submit to ketubah-less marriages,[25]

[22] Special Laws, I, 107; III, 72.

[23] Tos. Ket. 4, 9; B. M. 104a; Jer. Jeb. 14d. "The Alexandrian Jews would betroth their brides, and at the time of the nuptials others would come and snatch away the brides. The scholars wanted to declare their children illegitimate, whereupon Hillel the Elder said to them: 'Bring me your mothers' ketubot.' When they did so, he found in them the reading 'When thou art come unto me by nuptials, shalt thou be my wife, etc.' On this ground were the children declared legitimate." See appendix A for further interpretation of this text.

[24] Ket. 89a. Mishna Ket. 51a, taken by Neubauer *Beitrage zur Geschichte d. biblisch-talmud. Eheschliessungsrechts*, Leipzig 1920 (BGE) p. 238, to represent a ketubah-less marriage, is not necessarily correct. It seems rather to refer to the omission of the mohar clause.

[25] This tendency seems to have been the result of the persecutions begun in Hadrianic days, when every public act of Jewish religious significance was being suppressed, and it was unsafe to preserve and even to make out written documents of

declares, "It is forbidden to every man to live with his wife without a ketubah even for one hour." [26] Furthermore, a tradition runs through rabbinic literature that a ketubah-less marriage is not a legal marriage at all. The midrash cites a parable of the bride of a king who was found unfaithful, and to save her from a death penalty, the paranymph tore her ketubah, saying, "Rather that she be considered unmarried." [27] Of the

a religious character such as the ketubah. See Freund, GES p. 9, note 4; Fischer, *Urkunden,* p. 73.

[26] B. K. 89a.

[27] Exod. Rabbah ad 32:11; 34:1. This parable and its application to Moses's breaking of the Tablets of the Law do not present a very clear motive. Either the marriage was to be annulled or the evidence was to be destroyed or an opening was to be made for the bride to hide her guilt by the plea of ignorance of the penalty for unfaithfulness. The last is not to be taken seriously, for it is used by the Rabbis as the only alternative out of two evils, namely that the marriage bond between Israel and God is dissolved or that Israel should be destroyed. It cannot count as a motive in the tearing of the ketubah in our parable. Of the other two motives, Neubauer chooses the latter, that of hiding evidence (See BGE, p. 239, note 1.). This interpretation is not impossible, but not quite fully bearing out the suppositions of the story. The supposition is that the marriage was a public marriage like the giving of the law on Sinai. Evidence, therefore, is not limited to the ketubah. The supposition further is that the bride has one choice out of two evils, either to be put to death for unfaithfulness or to lose her property and guarantees by tearing her ketubah. Now, how would the destroying of the ketubah save her from death? The answer is, she would be treated as unmarried. In other words, though publicly married, she would still be unmarried so long as the ketubah was not written.

The one exception that may be made to the evidence from this midrash that the ketubah determined the legitimacy of the marriage among Jews, is the hypothesis of Ziegler that these parables represent non-Jewish life. See Ziegler, *Koenigsgleichnisse in Midrash.*

Unlike the evidence from this midrash, little proof may be

piety of a certain Egyptian Jewish community, it is told that a bride and groom were captured and mated together by their captor, but they abstained from marital relations because a ketubah was not made out.[28] R. Meir submits a tradition that "a wife has a ketubah, a concubine has not;"[29] R. Judah says, a con-

found in the Talmudic account of the destroying of many ketubot in Nahardea on the basis of a declaration issued by Rab Judah, that a certain family which had intermarried with freeborn families was discovered to be slaves (Kid. 70b.). Here the destroying of the ketubot was not to be the source of the annulment of the marriages, but the effect.

[28] Gittin 57a. The feeling against intercourse between bride and groom before a ketubah is made out is also reflected in a discussion between R. Ami and his colleagues on the question whether the first intercourse may be had on the Sabbath (Ket. 7a). It can only be explained by the lingering tradition of earlier days. While originally without the ketubah the marriage was not legal, in the course of development the feeling at least remained that no intercourse should take place without a ketubah.

[29] Jer. Ket. 29d. Freund (GES, p. 9) takes this statement of R. Meir literally, that the writ is necessary to make a marriage legal. Neubauer, (BGE, p. 240) argues that not the writ is the question, but the standard obligation, which is often termed by the Rabbis "ketubah." The possibility of Neubauer's interpretation cannot be excluded on evidence from the text itself. The argument against it is strongest in the parallelism between Jewish law and Babylonian law on this subject. Babylonian law has two kinds of concubines, the slave-wife and the *sugetu* or wife, freeborn but of lower order. Cf. Freund, GES, p. 4, note 2. R. Meir takes the *Pilegesh* as the *Amah* of the Hebrew (So also taken by the Karaites; see *Gan 'eden, Nashim,* end of chapter 16), to be the slave-wife, without the writ, without dowry from her father or mohar from her husband. R. Judah takes the Pilegesh to be equal to the *sugetu* of the Babylonians, with mohar from her husband and dowry from her father and therefore a writ of guarantees, but without the other terms of the ketubah, such as provisions for the widow and the orphaned children, and the like.

Our proof from the statement of R. Meir that the ketubah

cubine also has a ketubah, but the ketubah clauses are not specified in it;[30] Rab modifies the tradition somewhat, saying "a wife has a ketubah and marriage, a concubine has neither." [31] Rab, who knew of legal ketubah-less marriages, had to compromise with the older tradition by declaring that legality depends upon ketu-

was essential for the legitimacy of a marriage is valid according to either interpretation, if we view this matter from a sociological point. According to R. Meir, the legitimate wife does always have a ketubah, the concubine—even according to Neubauer's interpretation—has not. True, scholars may differentiate between the ketubah as necessary for legitimacy and the ketubah as a mere fact but not legally necessary. The popular mind, however, does not indulge in such distinctions. What would such a condition mean when the ketubah is practically necessary but theoretically unnecessary? It would simply tell the story that the people preserved consciousness of an older tradition, while the law ushered in a new conception and a change of tradition. If this be so, we would only have to conclude that the time when the ketubah was recognized by the law as a necessity for the legitimacy of a marriage was somewhat prior to the time of R. Meir.

[30] Jer. ibid. According to Neubauer (l.c.) this statement means that a wife has a claim on mohar and other marriage terms of the ketubah; a concubine has a claim on mohar but on nothing else. The statement of R. Judah is not pertinent to our question, and therefore no more need be said on it than what has been said in the previous note. As an explanation of the Biblical *pilegesh*, R. Judah's statement that the *pilegesh* has mohar or a ketubah is hard to understand, in view of his teaching that mohar is altogether post-Biblical (Ket. 56b).

[31] San. 21a. Rashi to Gen. 25:6 omits the word *kiddushin* in Rab's statement, making Rab's statement equal to that of R. Meir. Nahmanides corrects Rashi. Maimonides (Melakim 4:4) has our reading. Aptowitzer (WZKM, XXIII) corroborates the Rashi omission of the word *kiddushin*. To my mind, Rashi's reading is either an old scribal error, or, if intended by Rashi, it was done for the purpose of explaining the term *pilegesh* in the case of Abraham's wives, where *kiddushin* was not yet in vogue. (See Yad, Ishut, 1:1.)

bah plus marriage formalities.[32] But the older tradition seems definite, that a ketubah-less marriage represents concubinage. That tradition must be as old as the ketubah itself and its origin is probably Babylonian, for Hammurabi (2200 B. C.E.) rules in his code, "If a man take a wife and do not arrange with her the proper contracts, that woman is not a legal wife." [33]

The early ketubah, then, had its function of legalizing a marriage. It was not only present at every wedding, but it was legally necessary with every marriage of the first order. In this respect it superceded even a combination of the later ketubah and the later shetar kiddushin, for both of these even in combination are not, according to later law, essential to the legitimacy of a marriage.

And, with this conclusion, we feel compelled to read into the first mishna of kiddushin this very old tradition, that "A woman is acquired by three means, ... by money *and* by a writ *and* by intercourse." [34]—not, as the later halakah read, "either by money, or by a writ, or by intercourse." [35] In support of the former interpretation of this very old mishna,[36] we have the tradition among the Karaites,[37] and we have the record of a marriage described in the Book of Tobit in which

[32] See Freund l. c. and Aptowitzer, ibid.

[33] Code Hammurabi 128, also 137, 145, 170, and 171.

[34] Kid. 2a.

[35] Formulated first by R. Hiya, of the last generation of the tannaim. Tos. Kid. 1:2; Jer. Kid. 58b. Mek. ad Exod. 21:7, Sifre Deut. 24:1 cannot be taken as proof of R. Hiya's interpretation of the mishna, for they may speak of the validity of either element in a marriage combining the three together.

[36] The age of this mishna is evident from the fact that it is treated as a text in a discussion between the Shamaites and the Hillelites in the same mishna.

[37] *Gan 'Eden, Nashim,* 6. *Aderet Elijah, Nashim,* 1. See also Gaster, Karaitic ketubah, MGWJ. 54, p. 578.

the three elements together form the marriage ceremony. Again, this first mishna of Kiddushin is followed by another mishna describing the manner in which realty is conveyed, "by money, by a deed, and by use," and here the concluding halakah of the amoraim requires at least money and deed in every legal transaction of realty.[38] The conveyance of property recorded by Jeremiah, was carried out by means of all the three elements combined.[39] It seems, therefore, that both mishnas intended to teach that a combination of three elements, money, writ, and use was necessary to conclude a conveyance, whether of realty or of a wife.

The development of this phase of the ketubah, its function, from that of a marriage deed to a memorandum of guarantees, has its root not in the ketubah itself but in the development of the marriage scheme as a whole. The Jewish marriage was consummated originally in one single event. As a recent writer puts it, it was a cash transaction—the money for the bride paid and the bride delivered. But in Biblical times we already hear of two separate marriage functions, betrothal and nuptials. Legally this division of the single marriage event into two meant only a postponement of the delivery of the bride to her husband. Betrothal, or *erusin,* represented the full consummation of the marriage. From that moment on, the betrothed or *arusah* was in every respect the wife of her husband. Nuptials, termed *huppah* or *nisu'in,* had no legal sig-

[38] Kid. 26a. See further where the opinion of Rab is quoted that in all realty transactions, *kesef* and *shetar* must be present to make the conveyance valid, unless it be a gift or a bad bargain. In the former case no money is paid; in the latter case no writ of conveyance is needed for the purchaser's protection.

[39] Jer. 32: 9-10.

nificance whatever, save a slight change in the punishment prescribed for unfaithfulness. In tannaitic days, this Biblical marriage scheme prevailed, and common usage allowed a year to lapse between betrothal and nuptials.

It was not unnatural, however, for a social feeling to come into being in the course of time that the bride is not really a wife until she has entered her nuptials. Although unfaithfulness of the betrothed may be treated as severely as or even more severely than adultery, nonetheless, the betrothed was in her father's house looking forward only to a future common life with her husband. As this social feeling grew the law kept thinning the bond of betrothal and enlarging the bond of nuptials. Nuptials became a real legal factor in the marriage. The *arusah* was more and more recognized by the law as belonging to her father's household rather than that of her husband. Thus, to annul her vows, father and groom had to act in consonance.[40] If the groom was a priest and the father an Israelite, she ate of her father's bread, not of the holy bread of her husband.[41] If both were priests, the father, not the groom, was permitted to defile himself in connection with her burial.[42] The father was heir to her possessions, not the groom, if she died during the period of betrothal.[43] The husband's privilege of using the income on his wife's property or his right to her earning was declared as applying only to the wedded wife, not the betrothed.[44] Likewise his obligations, sustenance,

[40] Nedarim 10, 1(66b).
[41] Ket. 48a-b; 57a-b.
[42] Sifra ad Lev. 21, 2-3.
[43] Ket. 89b, etc.
[44] Ket. 46b. See also Jeb. 31b.

ransom, burial,[45] mohar,[46] mattan,[47] and the specific ketubah clauses of *bnan nukban*[48] and the lien[49] did not apply to the betrothed.[50] Evidently, the law has consistently operated in the direction of minimizing the importance of betrothal in every aspect of the marriage relation, save that of unfaithfulness. That is, the legality of the marriage alone was determined by the betrothal, but nothing more than that. Out of the entire ketubah only one clause was effective at the time of betrothal, the marriage clause, "Be thou my wife according to the law of Moses and Israel." This brought about a betrothal, that is, an establishment of a legitimate marriage in which the ketubah was of no legal value. Under such conditions, what could be more natural than to consider the ketubah as in no way connected with the legitimacy of a marriage, and to substitute for a while an "abbreviated ketubah" containing only the marriage clause—which is really what the shetar kiddushin amounts to. The latter, being only a substitute and an invention of late origin, could not rise to the original importance of the ketubah of being a necessary element in a legal marriage. The shetar kiddushin remained optional and unimportant in marriages; the ketubah became dissociated from the consummation of the marriage, and remained merely a memorandum of obligations assumed by the husband.

With these changes in the marriage itself and the consequent changes in the function of the ketubah, we get a better light on the story of how the ketubah was

[45] Ibid. See also Ket. 67a.

[46] Yad, Ishut 10, 11 based on Ket. 89b.

[47] Ket. 5, 1(54b); Ket. 54a; 56a.

[48] Ket. 54a.

[49] Ket. 43b-44a.

[50] In this connection Cf. Appendix A.

shifted from betrothal to nuptials. It was already pointed out by scholars[51] that from many a tannaitic source it is evident that the ketubah was customarily written at the time of betrothal, despite the fact that the amoraim seem unable to find such evidence.[52] There can be no doubt that this represents the original usage, since originally the ketubah and the shetar kiddushin were one, and the ketubah was essential for the legitimacy of a marriage. But, as may well be expected, since the terms of the ketubah were shifted from betrothal to nuptials, the problem arose how to continue writing the ketubah at betrothal when its terms apply no longer to betrothal. It was not so easy to change an old usage even to conform with the newer law. The old vogue continued despite the steady progress of the new law, and down to the end of the tannaitic period the ketubah was still customarily made out at betrothal. The Alexandrian Jews, seeing the inconsistency of writing at betrothal an instrument whose terms did not apply until nuptials, invented a new phrase to be inserted in the ketubah, "when thou comest into my house," by way of introduction to the terms of the ketubah, making the ketubah specifications apply to nuptials even though the instrument was written at the betrothal.[53] The Palestinian Jews permitted no such innovation, but left it to the old usage and the new law to settle the conflict between themselves, with the result that in amoraic days it was a matter of local option whether to write the ketubah at betrothal or nuptials.[54] The general practice was to write it at nup-

[51] Ket. 43b, 53a , Jeb. 29b, 43b, Jer. Ket. 30b, etc. Cf. Büchler, *Das juedische Verlobniss*, in Israel Lewy's *Festschrift*, pp. 122-129.

[52] Ket. 89b.

[53] Cf. Appendix A.

[54] Kid. 50b. The case cited above of bride and groom in cap-

tials.[55] The separation of betrothal from nuptials, however, broke down during the Middle Ages, because people were too poor to arrange for two separate feasts, and to this very day the two are celebrated together and the ketubah is written in connection with that single event.[56]

tivity who abstained from intercourse because they had no ketubah (Gittin 57a) probably represents an instance where the ketubah was written at nuptials.

[55] Ket. 7a. The Talmud assumes that previous to nuptials there would be no ketubah, and proposes this fact as an objection to nuptials on the Sabbath.

[56] Yad, Ishut 10, 7; *Machzor Vitri,* p. 588.

CHAPTER II

The Antiquity of the Ketubah

Our investigation in the previous chapter led to the conclusion that the original ketubah combined the ketubah and the shetar kiddushin. The history of the ketubah must therefore pass on from the ketubah to the shetar kiddushin and vice versa, without allowing the distinctions which the later halakah drew between them.

Of course, the Talmud holds them distinctly separate, and ascribes a separate history to each of them. It considers the shetar kiddushin older and believes it to be Biblical in origin. Though the Bible does not mention a marriage instrument, since it prescribes divorce by writ, the rabbis argue quite logically, that it must have known also of a marriage writ. Acquiring a wife and releasing her must be executed by similar processes.[1] This argues for the Biblical origin of the shetar kiddushin, not the ketubah. As for the latter, the Talmud seems to grant its existence as a non-Jewish institution even in pre-Mosaic times,[2] as is corroborated by Code Hammurabi,[3] but as a Jewish institution it is declared to be post-Biblical.[4] Within this period, there are differences of opinion as to the approximate date. Some set it at the

[1] Kid. 5a, 16a, based on Deut. 24, 2.

[2] This is reflected by the statement of R. Meir (Jer. Ket. 29d) that concubinage is marriage without ketubah, also by the implication of the following statement, "Noahides write no ketubot for males" (Chulin 92b).

[3] C. H. 128.

[4] Sabbath 14b, etc.

very beginning, considering the ketubah an institution of the "Men of the Great Synagogue,"[5] others set it at its last possible limit, as an ordination of Simeon ben Shetah of the first century B. C. E.[6]

An independent inquiry into the antiquity of the ketubah requires us to examine the two earliest rabbinical references to it. The first mishna of Kiddushin, of which mention has been made before, reads: "A woman is acquired by three means, . . by money, by a writ, and by intercourse." The antiquity of this tradition is evident by the fact that the Shamaites and the Hillelites discuss the required amount of the money, later in the same mishnah. If our assumption is correct that this mishna requires all the three means together to legalize a marriage, it must belong to the period when betrothal and nuptials had not yet become definitely distinct from each other, for it would presuppose cohabitation between the betrothed couple. If our assumption is wrong, and the mishnah requires only one of the three means for the consummation of a marriage, its antiquity is still evident, for it would have to be placed at such a time when marriage in its savage form, by cohabitation, without further ceremony, was socially common and legally sanctioned.[7] As a

[5] Rabbi Isaac b. Sheshet (RIBaSh) Responsa, 153. Maimonides (Yad, Ishut 10, 7 and 16, 3) states simply that the ketubah is a rabbinical institution, and adds (ibid. 16, 9) that its terms go back to enactments of the Sanhedryion. Cf. Chernowitz, *Hashiloah*, Vol. 7, p. 484.

[6] See Ket. 82b, and S. P. Rabinowitz, notes on Graetz's *History of the Jews* (Hebrew) Vol. 1, p. 453.

[7] Cf. Neubauer, BGE, p. 35. This author chooses the last alternative, that either one of the three elements is sufficient to establish a marriage, and on this basis he concludes that *Die Mischna ist allein aus dem traditionellen Erinnerungsvermoegen an ein weit zurueckliegende Periode zu erklaeren wo die Eheschliessung ueberhaupt nur aus einem einzigen rechtswesentlichen Vorgang bestand.*"

choice between these two suppositions, the latest date that may be assigned to this mishna is that of the Book of Tobit, where betrothal and marital union are described as taking place at the same time; in other words, belonging to the pre-Maccabean period.[8]

The traditional view as to the history of the ketubah is stated in the Talmud in the following passage.[9]

[8] See Simpson, *Introduction to the Book of Tobit,* in Charles' edition of the Apocrypha.

[9] Ket. 82b. In order to make the reader's task lighter, I have omitted discussion of the details of the text in the book itself, and beg leave to deal with them in the notes.

a) "In olden times they would *write,* etc. . . . " is emended by the tosafists and R. Hananel to read, "In olden times they would *give.*" The emendation was felt necessary in order to show the difference between this first stage and the last, the enactment of Simeon b. Shetah. In other words, these commentators believe that the enactment of Simeon b. Shetah introduced the writing of the ketubah. That this is not correct is sufficiently proven in the first place by the text itself; in the second place, by the fact that we are in possession of ketubot prior to Simeon b. Shetah. In my interpretation I leave the word "write," but I interpret it to mean that it was recorded in the ketubah as *having been given.* Friedmann in *Iggeret teshubah 'al debar hakketubah* has come to conclusions similar to mine in many points of interpretation of this text, but he is forced to the emendation of *give* in the place of *write.*

b) "But they would grow old and would not marry wives." Who would grow old and refuse to marry, and why? Rashi says the girls would grow old, refusing to give themselves in marriage without proper security for their mohar, and hence the men would not marry. This interpretation is assented to by Tosafot. Its weakness, however, is apparent. It would imply a change in the noun, they (wives) would grow old, and they, (husbands) would not marry. It would require emending the verb, *grow old,* to suit the feminine plural. It would not explain how this condition was improved by the second stage, if it prevailed in the first stage. Freund, GES, p. 27, is inclined to believe that this part does not belong to the original tradition at all, because it

"Rab Judah says, in olden times they would write two hundred zuzim for a virgin and one hundred for a widow, but they would grow old and would not marry wives. Whereupon Simeon ben Shetah came and instituted that all the husband's property should be a lien for her ketubah. The following tannaitic tradition supports it. In olden times they would write two hundred zuzim for a virgin and a hundred for a widow, but they would grow old and would not marry wives. Whereupon, it was instituted that it should be kept in her father's house. Yet, if he became wroth with her, he would say to her, Go to thy ketubah. It was, therefore, further ordained that it be put in the house of her father-in-law. Rich women would make of it gold and silver baskets, poor ones would make of it brass grape containers. Still in a fit of anger, he would say to her, Take thy ketubah and go. Thereupon came Simeon ben Shetah and instituted that he write her,

is not found in Tosifta and Jerushalmi. Aptovitzer, WZKM, XXIII, p. 398, contends that it does belong to the original tradition; so does Fischer, *Ukrunden*, p. 77, note 4. I take this phrase to be genuine and perhaps even the oldest part of the tradition, for the motives of the changes in the rest of the tradition are moral, to discourage divorce; the motive here expressed is economic, the costliness of marriage. This phrase, then, records that the original giving of two hundred zuzim was a burden on the men who would postpone marriage.

c) "In the house of her father-in-law" is synonymous with in trust of her husband, and corresponds exactly to the Palestinian tradition "that her ketubah be with her husband." In the halakah we often find the antithesis between property "of her father's house" and "of her father-in-law's house" (See Ket. 66b).

d) "Brass grape containers" is the reading of R. Tam. Probably the original had only the word *'Abit* to which commentators added modificatory phrases. The root of *'abit* probably means articles given as pledge for loans. (Deut. 24, 10).

'All my property be security for the payment of her (thy) ketubah'." [10]

The text presents many difficulties, which are due in a measure to its evident antiquity. It becomes some-

[10] This tradition contains two, that of Rab Judah and that of the Beraita. Added to the Tosifta and the Jerushalmi, we have four traditions in all. To me they appear as one, with omissions in some that are not to be taken seriously. The fullest account is given in our beraita here, to which, however, must be added one stage mentioned in the Jerushalmi which is omitted in our Beraita. The Beraita has: a) Cash to the father of the bride, b) the father only a trustee for the bride, c) the husband a trustee for the bride and he may buy household articles for the mohar, d) SBS's enactment. Jerushalmi omits the first stage (a) but instead divides the third stage (c) into two, namely c) the husband a trustee for his wife and d) he may buy household articles for the mohar. The composite of the Babli and the Jerushalmi beraitot gives me the four stages prior to SBS, which I have outlined: a) Cash to the father, b) father as trustee, c) husband as trustee, d) used for household articles; and thereupon the enactment of SBS. Rab Judah and the Tosifta give only the two important stages, leaving out the others. The former gives the first and the last of the Babli, the latter gives the first and last of the Jerushalemi.

My conclusion that four stages are here recorded prior to Simeon b. Shetah, all falling within the period when the writing of the ketubah was in vogue, may be challenged by the retort that my entire foundation is the word "write" used in the Babli to record the first stage. My answer is, the equivalent to the word "write" is also used in the Tosifta and the Jerushalmi in connection with the first stage, namely, "ketubah." Secondly, "Go to thy ketubah" is put in the husband's mouth as a possible expression prior to SBS, by the Babli and Jerushalmi and the Mishna (Ket. 80b). Third, the impression is definite in all texts that SBS did not introduce the writing but a clause. If the writing of a document is not assumed in the first stage, but is assumed in later stages, the rabbis would have been guilty of gross neglect to have failed to tell us when and why the writing was introduced and whether it encouraged or discouraged marriage.

what more complicated by the presence of two other texts of the same tradition. The Tosifta[11] submits this brief summary: "In olden times when her ketubah was at her father's house, it was easy for him to divorce her. Therefore, did Simeon ben Shetah institute that her ketubah be with her husband and that he write, 'All my property be lien and guarantee for the money of thy ketubah'." The Palestinian Talmud has a lengthier and somewhat modified account of the same tradition.[12] "In olden times, her ketubah was entrusted to her parents and he found it easy to divorce her; and then it was ordained that her ketubah be with her husband, yet he could easily divorce her. Then it was instituted that a man buy for his wife's ketubah cups and dishes and bowls . . . Following upon this came the enactment that a man should use his wife's ketubah in business, for, as he uses his wife's ketubah in business and loses it, he will find it difficult to divorce her. This is what Simeon ben Shetah instituted . . . that a man put his wife's ketubah into his business."

Despite the apparent difficulty of the texts, it is comparatively easy to get their story. The several texts must be taken together, to yield a composite account of the stages that led up to this enactment of Simeon b. Shetah. They deal with the mohar, two hundred zuzim, which the groom had to pay to the father-in-law for the hand of his daughter, and which was set down in writing in the ketubah. At the very beginning, the Talmudic tradition relates, the payment of the two hundred zuzim which was recorded in the ketubah was a cash payment to the bride's father, who pocketed it for his own use. That made marriage quite a burden on young men, with the result that marriage

[11] Tos. Ket. 12, 1.
[12] Jer. Ket. 23b-c.

was delayed. An inducement was offered the young man, that the father would hold that money merely as trustee for the bride. It meant a good deal to the groom to know that what he paid down went to his wife and not to his father-in-law. Ultimately, it meant, either he or his children would get it back as heirs. That, however, did not remedy the situation completely. After all, the young man had to part with the two hundred zuzim. Another inducement was offered, that he, the groom himself, be the trustee of the money for his bride. It was not to be expected, though, that for very long the custom would persist in demanding a husband in moderate circumstances to keep two hundred zuzim idle as a trust for his wife. It had to yield to the next stage, of permitting the husband to buy with the money household articles, which were kept intact as embodying the wife's two hundred zuzim. But all told, it still meant that the young groom had to have two hundred zuzim in his possession before he proposed marriage, and after marriage he had to submit to a luxury of expensive household goods, when he needed more important things. Then came Simeon b. Shetah with his enactment that the wife lend the money to her husband and he be permitted to use it in his business, on the condition that he guarantee the payment of it by all the property he might possess. In other words, the mohar was no longer paid but promised, and the promise substantiated by a lien clause in the ketubah.

The motive for the several changes here traced, it will be noticed, is given as purely economic, to make marriage economically easier. It must be admitted that this motive is read only between the lines of the texts. The Babylonian text alone gives the clue to it by saying, "They would grow old and would not marry wives." The explicit reason for the changes is, "that the husband find it difficult to divorce his wife." After he had already paid the mohar to the father-in-law and had nothing to lose or to gain, as in the first stage, he could easily send his wife away, if he began to dislike her. It was not so easy to seek a divorce, when, as in the second stage, she had her own two hundred zuzim which he would lose by divorcing her. It was still harder to give up that two hundred zuzim when he himself was trustee of it, as in the third stage. When household articles were bought, as in the fourth stage, divorce would mean giving up beautiful and costly things. Finally, with Simeon b. Shetah's enactment, divorce would mean paying a mohar of two hundred zuzim, which without divorce he might possibly never have to pay. And with this last stage mohar becomes actually a divorce penalty upon the husband and very effective in checking divorces.

It is not hard to notice the parallelism between the economic and the moral motives of these changes in the usage concerning the mohar as an element in the ketubah, and one is easily impressed that these different stages do not represent theoretical outlines but real social conditions with which the law had to cope. Hence our natural conclusion must be that this tradition treats of four distinct social changes, and four definite changes in legislation prior to Simeon b. Shetah, all of them falling within the period when the writ was already in use. No one can tell how much time would be needed for the historic process representd in those four changes of legislation prior to Simeon b. Shetah. Perhaps by means of the ketubah, we are here linking up with the latest of the Biblical authors.

Of pre-rabbinic days, we have two literary records as evidence for the antiquity of the ketubah. The Book of Tobit describes the giving of Sarah, the daughter of Raguel, in marriage to Tobias, the son of Tobit, in the following passage: "And he (Raguel) called his daughter Sarah, and took her by the hand and gave her to be wife to Tobias and said, Behold, take her to thyself after the law of Moses and lead her away to thy father. And he blessed them and called Edna his wife and he took a book and wrote an instrument and sealed it. And they began to eat . . . . and when they had finished their supper, they brought Tobias in unto her.[13] It can easily be seen, as scholars have long pointed out[14] that a marriage instrument is here recorded, and in view of our assumption that the original marriage contract and ketubah were one, the further question whether we would call that instrument in the Book of Tobit a ketubah or not is of no moment to us.[15] The author of the book would have us believe that he depicts conditions of the days of Shalmanesser of Assyria (727 B. C.). In the opinion of the leading scholars, however, the book was written about the date 200 B. C. E., and its description of the marriage helps us, therefore, to trace the ketubah back at least to that date.

[13] Tobit, 7, 13-15, 8, 1.

[14] Fritzche, *Handbuch zu d. Apokryphen II*, Leipzig, 1853, p. 54; Strack u. Zoekler, *Commentar z. d. heligen Schriften.* Kautzsch, Book of Tobit (German).

[15] That it does represent the ketubah is maintained by Graetz, *Das Buch Tobit*, MGWJ, 1879, p. 447; D. Kaufmann, *Zur Geschichte der Ketubah*, MGWJ, 1897, p. 213; F. Rosenthal, *Vier Apokryphische Buecher*, Leipzig, 1887, p. 132. That it does not represent a ketubah is argued by Rosenmann, *Studien z. Buche Tobit*, Berlin, 1894, p. 18; Neubauer, BGE, pp. 240-41. The argument against it being a ketubah is based on the supposition that the distinction between the shetar kiddushin and the ketubah is very ancient, which supposition is itself untenable, as has already been pointed out.

The second pre-rabbinic record of a ketubah among Jews dates back to the fifth century B. C. E. In various manners the ketubah and some of its terms are mentioned in the group of Aramaic Papyri discovered at Assuan and Elephantine,[16] and Papyrus G of the Assuan Papyri,[17] is itself a ketubah of a couple married according to Jewish rites[18] about 420 B. C. E. It reads as follows:

"On . . . . (date) . . . . . of the King, said Ashor the son of Teos, builder to the king, to Mahseia, an Aramaean of Seyne belonging to the quarter of Warizath, saying: I came to thy house that thou give me thy daughter Miphtahya to wife. She is my wife and I am her husband from this day and forever. I have given thee as a marriage settlement for thy daughter Miphtahya the sum of five shekels royal standard; it is accepted by thee and thy heart is content therewith. I have delivered unto the hand of thy daughter Miphtahya as money for an outfit . . . . . . (sum) . . . . . .[19] I have delivered unto her hand

[16] Assuan Papyri, ed. Sayce and Cowley, Nos. G. and F.; Elephantine Papyri ed. Sachau, Nos. 28, 35, 47.

[17] *Aramaic Papyri Discovered at Assuan,* ed. A. H. Sayce and A. E. Cowley, London, 1906. *Aramaic Papyri of the Fifth Century B. C.* ed. A. E. Cowley, Oxford, 1923. Articles discussing Papyrus G are found by L. Freund, WZKM, Vol. 21, p. 171; J. N. Epstein, *Jarbuch d. jued-lit. Gesellschaft* VI, p. 395: Funk, ibid. Vol. VII, p. 378; Fischer, ibid. Vol. VIII, p. 371.

[18] As-hor is Egyptian, Miphtahya is Jewish, but there are internal evidences to show that they married under Jewish jurisdiction. See introduction to Papyrus G. in Sayce and Cowley edition.

[19] "Thou has delivered unto the hand of thy daughter . . . . Thou hast delivered unto her hand . . . . " is the translation of Freund, but Cowley in his edition of 1923 rejects this translation because the total includes the mohar and must have been

. . . . (things enumerated) . . . , all the money and the value of the goods amounting to . . . . (sum) . . . There is accepted by me and my heart is content therewith . . . . . (things valued singly) . . If tomorrow or any other day, As-hor shall die having no issue whether male or female by Miphtahya his wife, Miphtahya shall have full right[20] over the house of As-hor and his goods and chattels and all that he has on the face of the earth without exception. If tomorrow or any other day Miphtahya shall die having no issue whether male or female by As-hor her husband, As-hor shall be heir to her goods and her chattels. If tomorrow or any other day, Miphtahya shall stand up in the congregation and say: I divorce As-hor my husband, the price of divorce shall be on her head; she shall return to the scales and she shall weigh for As-hor the sum of five shekels (6 ?) and two d., and all which I have delivered unto her she shall give back,[21] both string and thread,[22] and she shall go away whithersoever she will and no suit or process shall ensue. If tomorrow or any later day As-hor shall stand up in the congregation and[23] say: I divorce my

given, like the mohar, by the groom. It represents, therefore, not nedunya but mattan.

[20] Freund bids us take notice that "shall have full right" is not equal to "be heir" later. In other words, the wife can have only right of domicile, the husband is heir in the absence of children. See Freund, GES, p. 46.

[21] Freund translates, "and all which she brought with her she shall take away."

[22] The word *Cham* has no translation in the Sayce and Cowley edition. I have rendered it by "string" in accordance with Perles, (Schwartz *Festschrift,* Wien 1917, p. 299), who takes it to mean a leather strip of slight value, possibly used as a shoelace.

[23] Divorce in public or in court is not required by the Talmud. Here we have the original mention of a divorce in a

wife Miphtahya, her marriage settlement shall be forfeited, and all that I have delivered unto her she shall give back,[24] both string and thread, in one day at one time, and she shall go away whithersoever she will so that neither suit nor process shall ensue. And if he shall rise up against Miphtahya to drive her away from the house of As-hor and his goods and his chattels, he shall pay the sum of 20 kebhes and this deed shall be annulled;[25] and I shall have no power to say: I have another wife than Miphtahya and other children than the children which Miphtahya shall bear to me. If I shall say I have children and a wife other than Miphtahya and her children, I shall pay to Miphtahya the sum of 20 kebhes royal standard, and I shall have no power to take away my goods and my chattels from Miphtahya. And if I shall have removed them from her . . . . (erasure) . . . . I will pay Miphtahya the sum of 20 kebhes royal standard. Nathan the son of Ananiah has written this deed at the dictation of As-hor, and the witnesses thereto are Penuliah the son of Jezaniah, Jezaniah the son of Uriah, Menachem the son of Saccur; Witnesses."

Perhaps we might bring the ketubah down to a greater antiquity than even that indicated by the papyri, by turning to the Bible for further information on the subject. There is no definite mention in the Bible of a marriage writ, but as was previously said, the

congregation. *Targum Jonathan* (ed. Ginzburger, Deut. 24, 1) echoes this lingering tradition in requiring *beth-din* for divorce.

[24] Freund translates, "and all that she brought with her she shall take away."

[25] The Sayce and Cowley edition reads in line 31 ויעמד which would mean "and this deed shall hold good for her," but in the Cowley edition, the reading is ויעדי changing the meaning to "and this deed shall be annulled." See the author's note on p. 50 in the latter edition.

rabbis feel certain that a marriage writ was known in Bible days, in as much as a writ of divorce was known. The divorce is recorded in Deuteronomy in the following passage: "When a man had taken a wife and married her, and it came to pass that she found no favor in his eyes because he hath found some uncleanness in her, then let him write her a bill of divorcement and give it in her hand and send her out of his house." [26] On the basis of this passage, the probability is very strong and the logic compelling that in Deuteronomic days the writ was already employed in Israel both for the dissolution as well as for the contraction of marriage. That one writ and not the other was adopted by Jews is very unlikely. And if one were adopted, it would in all likelihood be the marriage writ alone rather than the bill of divorce alone.[27]

The Bible also records another writ, the deed for the sale of realty. Jeremiah himself is the purchaser of a field, and he gives an account of the transaction in the following words, "And I bought the field from Chanamel, my uncle's son . . . . . and I weighed out unto him the money, seven shekels and ten pieces of silver. And I wrote it in a deed and sealed it and had it certified by witnesses, and weighed the money in balances." [28]

The kinship of the marriage deed to the deed of

[26] Deut. 24, 1-3.

[27] Papyrus G, for example, which represents a marriage writ, still speaks of divorce as being concluded by standing up in the congregation and saying: "I divorce my wife . . . . " without mention of any writ. If this is not merely an omission, it supports a suggestion made by Professor Louis Ginzberg, that the Deuteronomic law of the bill of divorcement prescribes the writ only for the purpose of testimonial, in order that she may be taken by another husband.

[28] Jer. 32, 8-12.

sale of realty is not quite as evident as the relation between the marriage deed and the bill of divorcement. Yet the rabbis frequently notice an inner relation between the two.[29] When the legal aspect of marriage is taken into account, regardless of whatever may be its moral or romantic coloring, it becomes evident that there is little difference between the conveyance of a field and the conveyance of a daughter in marriage. Marriage represents purchase. Legally it stands directly in line with the purchase of a slave or a field and is consummated by one legal formality.[30] Hence, one concludes with a fair degree of confidence that in Jeremiah's time (sixth century B. C. E.) not only was the deed for the sale of realty known, but even the marriage writ was in vogue.

Let it be added that if the opinion of Biblical critics be correct that the Book of Deutronomy is a product of the time of Josiah (seventh century B. C. E.), then the two parallel writs, the bill of divorcement and the deed for the conveyance of realty, converge to approximately the same historical period, and unite in their evidence for the existence of the marriage deed at about the end of the First Commonwealth.

There is decidedly no evidence in the Bible of the existence of a writ in connection with marriage prior to this date. On the contrary, the evidence is against it. Dramatic effect is much sought in the narrative of the marriage of Isaac to Rebecca. Many a detail finds a place in the Biblical record of that marriage. Not

[29] Cf. Kid. 4b, deriving the marriage by coin from the purchase of realty by Abraham, also Kid. 9a, where the Talmud is puzzled to understand why the marriage deed and the deed of realty are not exactly alike. Cf. Billauer, *Grudzuege d. babyl.-talmud. Eherechts,* Berlin, 1910, pp. 9-23.

[30] Cf. the first five mishnayot of Kiddushin.

a word about a writ. Jacob's marriage first to Leah and thereafter to Rachel involves misrepresentation and deception. Why not refer to the stipulations in the writ? Jacob and Laban have a heated controversy between them, when the former leaves the house of the latter. Questions of dowry are involved. The ketubah is not brought in as testimony. They conclude by an oath covenanting that, "If thou shouldst afflict my daughters or if thou shouldst take other wives beside my daughters, when there is no man between us; see God is witness between thee and me" [31]—a clause later found in the ketubah—yet the oath is recorded on a heap of stones, not on a writ. The Book of Ruth takes all the pains necessary to describe in full the conveyance of Ruth to Boaz, without admitting any writing into the ceremony. Nor is a writ recorded in the marriages of Samson and of David, nor does any prophet use the marriage writ in any of his similies of Israel's betrothal to God.

We must conclude, therefore, that the writ in general and the marriage writ in particular are not original Jewish institutions. Originally they belong to Babylonia, mother of commerce and commercial deeds in antiquity. Jewish contact with Babylonia was necessary in order to introduce the writ in Judea. This contact came about in a political and commercial way during the last century of the first Commonwealth, and with it came the adoption of the ketubah, among other writs, by the Jews.

[31] Gen. 31, 50.

CHAPTER III

Formalities and Construction

To the modern mind a written contract suggests itself as made out in duplicate. Since all contracts imply agreements between two parties and mutual guarantees between them, it is naturally supposed that two copies of the instrument are made, one for each of the parties. This is not the case with the Jewish marriage contract. Only one ketubah is written. Then the question arises who writes the ketubah and who holds it.

The general rule has it that the grantor writes the instrument and gives it to the grantee. In the case of a marriage deed, however, the terms grantor and grantee are not very clear. Yet, because the woman always needs more defence against the violation of her personal rights than the man and the marriage writ offers her that defence, the law places the husband in the position of the grantor and the wife in the position of the grantee. Therefore, the wording of the ketubah betrays the husband's authorship and it is upon him that the obligation of paying the scribe falls.[1]

But to say that this rule holds good in all cases is not quite correct. The grantee is sometimes the author of the instrument, not the grantor. And this exception to the rule is rooted in the history of the writ. The writ came into use among Jews at an age when covenants were made in accordance with certain social formalities. The object of the convenanting symbol was a stone or a sheep or a garment or what not. When the

[1] B. B. 167b; Yad, Ishut, 10, 7.

writ was introduced, in the minds of the people, it represented simply another object by which covenants might be carried out. The writ was, therefore, a form of covenant, and, as may be expected, all social formalities that belonged to the ancient covenant went over into the writ.

As for the ancient covenants, one gets the impression that it did not matter who carried out the covenanting ceremony, the grantor or the grantee. In the covenant between Abraham and Abimelech[2] to confirm the former's claim on a certain well, Abraham, who is the grantee, arranges the seven flock of sheep. On the other hand, in the covenant of friendship between David and Jonathan, the latter being superior and therefore the grantor, is the one to initiate the covenanting ceremony.[3] The Book of Ruth tells us: "Now this was formerly the custom in Israel at a redeeming and at an exchanging, to confirm anything, that one pulled off his shoe and gave it to the other, and this was the manner of testimony in Israel."[4] This Biblical passage evidently teaches that either one of the parties may give the shoe to the other. The rabbis seek to determine who gives and who receives the shoe, but without success.[5]

[2] Gen. 21, 30. In the case of the covenant between Laban and Jacob by the former setting up a heap of stones, there is no telling which was considered from the Biblical view point the grantor and which the grantee. Cf. Gen. 31, 52.

[3] I Samuel, 18, 4.

[4] Ruth 4, 7.

[5] B. M. 47a. Let it be noticed that three questions remain open in this connection. First, in the case of the ancient custom mentioned in the Book of Ruth of giving the shoe, who gave the shoe? There is no evidence from the Bible itself. The rabbis offer no evidence in the matter either. Second, in the case of Boaz, who followed out the ancient custom, the question asked

This indifference of the law to the matter of whether the grantor or the grantee initiates the covenant is carried over faithfully into the writ. Contracts of sale of realty are always made out by the seller; yet, in the Biblical record of such a contract, Jeremiah,

is, did Boaz or the redeemer take off his shoe? This is the object of discussion among the tannaim. They come to no conclusion, and any conclusion they might reach would not be of great significance, since the custom is referred to as already archaic in the time of the author of the Book of Ruth. One evidence is being offered on behalf of the theory that Boaz was the one who took off the shoe from the redeemer, or that the redeemer gave the shoe to Boaz. For, this case is similar to the case of *Halizah* described in Deut. 25, 9, where the redeemer's shoe is pulled off, as a token that his right of redemption is taken away from him. By this instance, we judge, when the redeemer scorns the duty and privilege of redemption, the shoe is taken off violently; when he transfers that privilege, he gives the shoe voluntarily. This theory would bear out the general rule that the grantor is by custom the one to certify his grant, by covenant symbol first, and later by writing the deed. The third question that is opened in this connection is how to carry out the ceremony of *Kinyan Sudar* or *Halifin,* which the rabbis infer from this passage in the Book of Ruth. This question never suggested itself to the tannaim, because *Halifin* is an amoraic institution unknown to them. As the term indicates, *Halifin* or exchange, in tannaitic days, was a cash transaction, "exchanging a cow for an ox" (Kid. 28a), not a symbolic exchange. The tannaim did know of a symbolic payment as a substitute for cash in the case of purchase, but did not go so far as to apply this symbolism in the case of exchange. The reason is simple. Commerce through buying and selling developed rapidly, and with it the legal forms of conveyance, but exchange was not quite so frequent an occurence on the market, and therefore its legal form remained in the primitive stage, that of actual exchange. It was not until the amoraic days that the law was forced to adopt new forms for exchange, when one of the parties did not have the object of exchange with him. Therefore, the law permitted the one who could not at the moment give up the thing he promised in exchange to give a symbol of his object, a piece of garment. Hence the view of Rab, that the buyer gives the object, which

who is the buyer, makes out the deed. In like manner, ketubot, as we said, are made out by the husband; yet the marriage writ recorded in the Book of Tobit is made out by the bride's father, not the groom.[6] Quite in accord with this historic background, therefore, the mishna teaches that "The woman may write her own divorce and the husband may write his own receipt for the ketubah, for the instrument is validated solely by the attest of the witnesses."[7]

is accepted by the halakah, (Cf. R. Hananel and Alfasi, a. l.) is historically correct. This *Halifin* having been introduced in transactions of exchange, it was found later convenient to carry it over into all forms of commerce, for every conveyance, and became the *Kinyan Sudar*; for, after all, every purchase is an exchange of a kind, an exchange of money for an object. The fact that *Kinyan Sudar* is a very late institution explains why it was not employed in marriages, for the marriage institution is too conservative to adopt new forms of conveyance readily. The Talmud (Kid. 3a) gives another reason why *Kinyan Sudar* is not valid in marriages. Rashi, correctly, finds the Talmudic reason unnatural, and forces himself into still greater difficulties.

[6] The peculiar parallelism between the purchase of Jeremiah and the marriage of Tobias, in both cases the deed written by the one who is declared by usage and by law the grantee, no doubt is striking. Professor Ginzberg is inclined to believe that in that ancient past, the bride's father was really by usage expected to write the deed. To this I cannot agree, because the papyri deeds are all made out by the husband and the seller. There is only one other explanation that may be offered for the account of the Book of Tobit, and that is that the marriage recorded there savors of the levirate element; and in levirate marriages the groom does not give a ketubah, the old ketubah remaining valid. Wherefore the deed would have only the marriage formula, and for the marriage formula alone, the bride's father, who is the grantor, is the one to write the deed. That, however, would leave the Jeremiah purchase unexplained, besides the fact that it is in itself a vulnerable theory. See L. Ginzberg, *Compte rendu des Melange Israel Lewy*, Paris, 1914, p. 16.

[7] Gittin 22b.

The above conclusion would lead us to believe that the law was also indifferent to the wording of the deed. If the buyer wrote the contract, he would write "I, so-and-so, bought from thee, so-and-so . . . . ." and if the seller wrote it, he would write "I, so-and-so, sold to thee, so-and-so . . . ." In like manner, in marriage writs, the husband may write "I, so-and-so, marry thee, so-and-so . . . . " and if the wife wrote it, she would write "I, so-and-so, am married by thee, so-and-so . ." Possibly this is the strict legal side of the question. A remnant of this law is left in a Palestinian tradition, which reads: "The formula for the sale of a daughter as slave-wife is: I, so-and-so, sold my daughter to so-and-so; the formula for marriage is: I, so-and-so, gave my daughter in marriage to so-and-so. R. Haggyi asked R. Jose, if he might alter the formulae and say: I, so-and-so, bought the daughter of so-and-so, or I, so-and-so, married the daughter of so-and-so? The latter answered: What of it!"[8] It is evident from this text, however, that as a matter of fact the writ always spoke for the grantor, the seller, or the bride's father. That the instrument should represent the buyer is a mere legal hypothesis. This is practically true of all instruments known to us. Regardless of who writes it, the instrument speaks on behalf of the grantor.

The only exception to this rule is the shetar kiddushin. While the Palestinian tradition submits the formula for the shetar kiddushin to be, "I, so-and-so, gave my daughter in marriage to so-and-so," in accordance with the general rule that the grantor speaks through the instrument, the Babylonian Talmud insists that the formula should read, "I, so-and-so, married the daughter of so-and-so."[9] All mediaeval deeds follow the

[8] Jer. Kid. 59a.

[9] Kid. 9a.

Babylonian tradition. How shall we understand the discrepancy between the Palestinian and Babylonian traditions, and since the Babylonian tradition prevailed, how shall we understand its deviation from the rule that the grantor is represented by the deed, not the grantee?

The Babylonian amoraim themselves seek to give an explanation for this irregularity. They say: "Behold, this deed (shetar kiddushin) is unlike the commercial deed; there the seller writes . . . . . here the husband writes, Thy daughter be married to me . . . Said Raba, this is the custom."[10] This answer to the question sounds like an evasion of the issue, but it really is not. It contains an admission that there is nothing in the law to account for this irregularity. We should add, in accordance with our investigation, that the law is really indifferent to the question of whether the grantor or the grantee speaks through the instrument. This formality, says Raba, goes back to custom. And this is the custom, as we can now see it. The shetar kiddushin was part of the ketubah. In the ketubah, the husband is considered the grantor, for evident reasons that have been mentioned above. Hence, when the shetar kiddushin became a separate instrument, it continued in form as it had been hitherto, with the husband as the grantor—though, with reference to the isolated marriage clause, the husband was the grantee, not the grantor. Therefore Raba is correct; the tenacity of custom accounts for the fact that the husband who is the grantee makes out the shetar kiddushin.

[10] Kid. ibid. Rashi renders Raba's answer, "This is Mosaic law," and Professor Ginzberg (*Compte rendu,* ibid.) finds support for this view from Kid. 16a. I follow Tosafot. See discussion in Friedmann, *Iggeret Teshubah.*

To recapitulate, there is no legal significance to the authorship of any instrument, but custom has, for very logical reasons, given the grantor the duty of making out the instrument. The seller is the grantor in commercial transactions. The husband is the grantor in the original ketubah, and continued to be treated as the grantor in the later ketubah. The husband, however, is the grantee in the shetar kiddushin, but because the shetar kiddushin is an outgrowth of the original ketubah, he remained the author of it by historic usage despite the rules of logic.

The latest development of this matter is much simpler than its history. The shetar kiddushin is hardly ever used. Theoretically, in accordance with the Babylonian tradition, it should be written by the husband. The ketubah, stripped of its covenanting character, a bare testimonial of guarantees, represents neither the wife nor the husband, but the witnesses. They speak through the instrument, giving their testimony in writing of the agreements reached by the parties. From the middle ages, therefore, to this very day, the ketubah is made out by the witnesses, fully in accord with the mishnaic rule that "Contracts are validated solely by the attest of the witnesses."

Any language may be employed in the writing of the ketubah as well as any other deed, so long as falsification is guarded against.[11] Despite this halakah, however, and despite the vicissitudes marking Jewish life, the ketubah has consistently been written in Aramaic, except for some isolated cases, and except for the Samaritans and the Karaites, who write their ketu-

[11] Gittin, 10b, 87b; Yad, Gerushin 4, 11 and *Magid* commentary thereto, Ishut 3, 8; Cf. Fischer, *Urkunden*, p. 8.

bot in Hebrew.[12] That Aramaic was given preference to Hebrew in the writing of deeds is due to the international character of Aramaic at the time when the writ was adopted by the Jews, and to the gradual intrusion of Aramaic into Judea at the time of the Restoration.[13] Hebrew was preserved as the tongue for things sacred and Aramaic for things secular.[14]

[12] The exceptions here referred to are several phrases in Hebrew of which we treat in the later notes; also a ketubah in Hebrew published by A. Berliner in *Kobetz 'al Yad* IX, designated as *Ketubah Jerushalmit;* and a *shetar erusin* in Hebrew published by Israel Levy in REJ, Vol. 49, p. 301. For the Samaritan and the Karaitic ketubot, Cf. Gaster in MGWJ, Vol. 54, pp. 518 ff. Cf. also Luncz, *Jerushalayim*, Vol. 6, p. 237.

[13] In Isaiah's time Aramaic was not yet known to the Jews, but it made its way into Judea through the contact between Syria and Palestine politically and commercially, through the influx of Jewish colonists from Babylonia, at the time of the Restoration, where they had dwelt in the "Aramaean quarter," and through the mixture of a Samaritan element in the Jewish population. See Zunz, *Gottesdienstliche Vortraege*, p. 8.

[14] See Zuns, ibid. note D. Cf. San. 21b: "The Israelites chose for themselves the Syrian script and the holy tongue, and left to the *hedyotot*, the Hebrew script and the Aramaean tongue. Who are the *hedyotot*? Said R. Hisda, the Samaritans." The correctness of R. Hisda's interpretation cannot be doubted, but it is too narrowly limited. *Hedyotot* means in general "secular," and is applied to distinguish the secular from the sacred. Thus the secular writ is distinguished from the holy writ by the use of that term. Tos. Ket. 4, 9; B. M. 104a, speak of the *hedyot* tongue" in application to deeds. Cf. *Shita mekubezet* ad B. M. 140a. Cf. also Friedmann, *Iggeret Teshubah*, p. 33, 39-43. In the same sense must the word *hedyotot* be taken in Tos. Sab. 13, (14), 1; Sab. 116b; J. Sab. 15c: "Reading scripture is prohibited on the Sabbath on account of documents of *hedyotot*. Rashi (Sab. 116b) says, it refers to correspondence; a tosafist argues that it refers to notes and deeds. I feel convinced that *hedyotot* here means "secular" and refers to any secular reading. Cf. Greek version of Ben-Sira, 56, 26.

It seems that at some time there was an attempt on the part of the rabbis, in loyalty to their national tongue, to turn the writ into Hebrew. That effort concentrated mostly in Palestine;[15] it met with some success in the case of the later and the native Jewish writ, the shetar kiddushin;[16] but it also left its traces on the other writs.[17] All told, however, it failed, and even the slight measure of success that it did have was limited to the Hebraizing of the one conveyance clause out of all the clauses of the several writs.

The text of the ketubah may begin with a preamble, which is generally set apart from the ketubah itself. The preamble may vary in length from a simple *"Mazol tov"* or good luck, through a variety of Biblical verses expressive of felicitations to bride and groom, to a lengthy poem in payyetanic style dealing with the

[15] The evidence for this effort is found in the remnants of Hebrew phrases in deeds. Now, two explanations are possible. Either, as we say here, the attempt was made in rabbinic days to go back to Hebrew, succeeding only slightly, or the Hebrew phrases remained from pre-ketubah times, when these formulae were used orally in the native tongue. I reject the second alternative, because of the fact that the Hebrew used in these deeds is not a Biblical Hebrew but a late rabbinical Hebrew. Thus for marriage, the term קדש instead of לקח or היה לאשה is used; for divorce מגורשת and מותרת are used and never the Biblical שלח. That the effort was strongest in Palestine is not only a conjecture but also supported by the fact that a Judean ketubah phrase, quoted in the Mishna עד שירצו היורשין ליתן לך כתובתך is given in Hebrew. On the basis of this phrase, Fischer (*Urkunden*, p. 10 and note 3) believes that in Judea the entire ketubah was in Hebrew. This is not quite likely, for it is implied in the mishna that the Judeans employed the other phrases of the ketubah in no manner different from the standard, which is given in Aramaic. See Ket. 52b.

[16] Kid. 9a: בתך מקודשת לי וכו' or Jer. Kid. 59a: אני פלוני קדשתי בתו של פ'.

[17] E. g. Kid. 9a: שדי מכורה לך

purpose of creation, the advantages of marriage, the beauty of the bride and the stateliness of the groom, invoking blessings upon the union, the couple, their parents, the scholars of the community, the gaon and the exilarch, and indulging in many other flourishes within the limits of—if indeed there be a limit to—poetic license. If the poet was a graphic poet, he wrote his verses in caption or border designs on the ketubah; if he was not gifted with the graphic art, he just wrote his poem, satisfying himself with an ornamental letter here and there. The lengthier preamble is a characteristic of the oriental ketubah; perhaps lengthiest of all is that of the Samaritan writ; while the European ketubah is comparatively simple —a neat border design, sometimes artistic, and a Biblical verse to introduce the ketubah text.

The ketubah text itself begins with the date. The law prescribes the mention of the date at the beginning of the deed in all private writs, and at the end in court writs.[18] The ketubah, though it has the status of a court decree,[19] is by its nature a private writ, and therefore has the date at the beginning. The omission of the date is possible, according to the amoraim, in the shetar kiddushin[20] but not in the ketubah, because all realty sales made by the husband following the date of the ketubah are subject to the lien of the ketubah. For this reason, falsification of the date invalidates a ketubah, more particularly, antedating a ketubah.[21]

The date is given in terms of the day of the week,

[18] Cf. Fischer, *Urkunden*, p. 15 and note 2.

[19] Gittin, 18a. Cf. *Hagahot Maim.* Yibbum 4, 33, quoting RABJH.

[20] Jeb. 31b; *Eben Haezer* (EH) Kid. 32, 4.

[21] Cf. *Hoshen mishpat, Halvaah,* 43, 5.

the month, the year, and the era.[22] An old usage in Jerusalem also required naming the hour.[23] The era is variously counted by Jews. In time of national independence, they counted it by their kings or important events in their history.[24] When under subjection, they counted by the foreign kings as token of their allegiance.[25] For the subject of the ketubah, two eras are important, the era of creation and the Seleucid era (311-312 B. C. E.), the former used by Western Jews, the latter the official era for dating deeds among the Jews of the East, and hence termed the *minyan shetarot*." [26] Since the days of David ben Zimra (15th century), however, the Oriental Jews have also adopted the era of creation.[27]

The place follows the date. Like the latter, it appears at the beginning of a private contract and at the end of a court decree, and in the ketubah it appears at the beginning. The place is geographically described, by the name of the town, or in addition, its neighboring town; by landmarks, more especially riv-

[22] Tos. B. B. 11, 2. Cf. Pesikta, ed. Buber, pp. 52-53 and notes 178-179. The marriage of Ahasuerus and Esther is accounted legal because a *gamixon* was made out containing the date and era, as it is written: In the tenth month which is the month of Tebet, in the seventh year of his reign (Esther 2, 16). Numb. R. 1, 5, gives a fuller account of the manner of dating: Write here the date of the week, the year, the month, the day of the month, and the era. Cf. *Nahlat Shiv'ah*, 12, 4.

[23] Ket. 93b, 94b.

[24] The following eras are found: Creation, Exodus, Solomon's Temple, Persian and Babylonian dynasties, Seleucid, Simon the Hasmonean, Destruction of First Temple, Destruction of Second Temple. Cf. Fischer, *Urkunden*, pp. 17-25.

[25] Gittin, 80a.

[26] Other eras have been used by Jews, among them the era of Napoleon Bonnaparte (See Adler in JE s. v. Ketubah).

[27] See Azulai, *Shem haggedolim*, s. v. David'n Zimra. The Yemenites, however, still use the *minyan shtarot* largely.

ers and ocean, and country. Detailed geographic specifications are required by the Talmud in the case of the divorce, but not in the ketubah.[28] During the middle ages, however, it must have been understood that the same requirement held good for all other deeds, including the ketubah. The Jews of Europe, nevertheless, have for several centuries satisfied themselves with just naming the town and perhaps also the country in their ketubot.[29]

After the ketubah records the date and place, it gives the names of bride and groom.[30] In recording the formula for the shetar kiddushin, the Babylonian Talmud omits the mention of names, prescribing, however, that the scribe shall have in mind the parties for whom he writes the deed;[31] while the Palestinian Tal-

[28] Gittin 27a, B. M. 18a, 20a.

[29] Cf. *Nahlat shiv'ah,* 12, 16. He takes the detailed geographical description as a distinct Sephardic custom. At the present time, there is yet a good deal of these geographical details in the Italian Ketubah. Elkan N. Adler in JE s. v. Ketubah, cites ketubot wherein Paris is described by the Seine and the Bievere, London by the Thames and the Walbrook.

[30] In the earlier ketubot, the principal names are those of the groom and bride's father, because the latter had the legal power to give his daughter in marriage. The bride herself in those instances is named secondarily. In the later ketubah, though, the bride and the groom are the contracting parties.

[31] Kid. 9a-b, *Sefer Hashetarot,* p. 11, EH, Kiddushin 32, 4. The Babylonian omission of the names in the record of the shetar kiddushin is taken to be significant, indicating that according to the Babylonian Talmudic law the names may be omitted. RShBA, Responsum 420, argues, on the other hand, that the omission in the Talmud is not to be taken as an indication that omission in the deed is permitted. I am inclined to agree with him, in view of the Palestinian tradition. The Talmudic omission is to be taken only as a defective report, and is perhaps due to the fact that the shetar kiddushin was more or less theory to them. Cf. Jeb. 31b, showing that marriage by shetar

mud records the names of bride and groom also in the shetar kiddushin.[32] The names of the bride and the groom and their parents, and sometimes their grandparents, are given.[33] Further identifications are often given, such as their places of residence, occupations, tribal descent, and other marks and appellations. In the Orient, in general, and among the Samaritans, in particular, glorious, fantastic titles are prefixed to the names. In geonic times, with the aristocracy of learning, such titles were given only to scholars. Ultimately, victory was on the side of simplicity and democracy in writs. The European ketubah today prefixes to the names of the parties Hebrew titles corresponding to "Sir" for a layman and "Rabbi" for a scholar, and the names are given in the briefest traditional form, "so-and-so, the son of so-and-so."

Next in order is a series of clauses whose content will be treated later, but of whose form a word may be said here. The original ketubah was framed either in first person, "I agree to do thus by thee," or in third person, "X agrees to do thus by Y." As we have seen above, the ketubah has finally come to be a written testimony of the witnesses. Therefore, the witnesses sometimes quote the parties directly, sometimes indirectly, and sometimes speak for themselves in direct testimony. Thus, for illustration, they state: "And thus he said to her: Be thou my wife according to the law of Moses and Israel . . . . . . and she was satis-

kiddushin was unusual. Cf. note of Elijah Wilna ad EH Kiddushin, 32, 4, *Magid*, Ishut, 3, 4.

[32] Jer. Kid. 59a, Jer. Erubin 21b, Exod. R. 46, 4.

[33] Gittin 88a; such is also the requirement among the Sephardim and the Samaritans today. A certain amount of care in spelling the names is also prescribed by later law. Cf. *Nahlat Shiv'ah*, 12, 18.

fied and became his wife . . . . . . and we saw that the dowry came into his possession . . . . "

When the terms of the ketubah are all recorded in the several clauses, the scribe is instructed to conclude the writ in a certain specified manner. The concluding formalities are important from the point of view of the law, because they guard against additions by one party without the knowledge of the other or the witnesses. Two prescriptions in this matter were made by the tannaim, that the end of the text summarize the contents of the contract, and that the witnesses sign close to the last line.[34] The amoraim added further precaution, that part of the summary—and nothing else—be on the last line[35] and that following the summary a concluding formula be used, "Established and certified."[36] While this law applies to contracts generally,

[34] The summary is reported in B. B. 165b. In the divorce, the summary is probably represented by the words: "And this is what you have from me, a writ of separation and an instrument of release and a bill of divorcement, that you may go and marry any man you wish." (Gittin 85b) The law that witnesses must sign close to the last line is given in beraita B. B. 162a. Fischer (*Urkunden*, p. 27) believes that the summary occurred only in the simple contract, not in the 'folded deed.' I can find no proof of it in the sources.

[35] That the summary and nothing else be put in the last line, and should any new matter be taken up, that new matter is wholly disregarded, is what I understand by the statement of R. Johanan, B. B. 161b at the bottom. Tosafot's attempt to make the view of R. Johanan agree with earlier customs is futile.

[36] "Established and certified," not known to the tannaim but mentioned by the amoraim, B. B. 160b. That this phrase is used only in "folded deeds" (Tosafot B. B. 162a) and that it is used only when the summary is not given (ibid. and RShBM 162a s. v. אמר) is not conclusive by any means. It is maintained by some that the words "Established and certified" must fill up the entire last line. This is incorrect also, for many ketubot

the ketubah is no exception, and therefore contains at the end, reaching down to the last line, ". . concerning everything that is written and specified above[37] . . . . and all is hereby established and certified." [38]

The signature of witnesses follows the text of the ketubah. The shetar kiddushin, from the point of view of later halakah, need not have the attest of witnesses,[39] but it is essential for the ketubah. The earlier requirement, however, for the attest of witnesses was not that they sign the deed, but be named as those who were present at the transaction. In Papyrus G, as in other papyri deeds, there is no difference between the handwriting of the deed and the attest of the witnesses. Apparently the scribe wrote the witnesses' names.[40] It was a rabbinic enactment, reported in the

and other deeds that have come to my notice disregard this law entirely. Cf. Fischer, *Urkunden*, p. 27, note 3, who follows Tosafot in error.

[37] This entire concluding formula is amoraic, since it concludes the testimony, וקנינא that the witnesses have performed the *Kinyan Sudar*, which we said above was an amoraic institution. B. M. 47a cites part of this testimony in the name of an amora. What the tannaim employed as a concluding summary I do not know. There is no contract extant of tannaitic times and the Papyri contracts need no concluding formulae, because, as will be shown later, in those days the witnesses did not sign but testified orally, when necessary. The words "concerning everything that is written and specified above," are considered a repetition of the contents of the writ and part of this occurs on the last line. Cf. RShBM, 161b at the bottom.

[38] Some ketubot add some other synonyms of "certified"; e. g. the Sephardic ketubah: שריר ובריר ובהיר אמת ויציב ונכון וקיים

[39] See Kid. 9a. The passage in Kid. 48a reading בשטר שאין עליו עדים does not refer to the shetar kiddushin. Cf. also *Hagahot Maim.*, Ishut 3, 3; Isserlis EH 32, 4; Tosafot Jeb. 31b, Mordecai and *Nimuke Joseph* thereto.

[40] In the Book of Tobit we either have an autographed instrument—or if witnesses were present, there is no mention of

mishna, that made it obligatory on witnesses to sign their names, "for the convenience of the public." [41] The

their signing the instrument. In Kautzche's *Apokryphen* Vol. 1, p. 142, Loehr reads Tobit 7, 11 literally: *bis ihr* (*sie*) *darstellt und euch* (*als Zeugen*) *mich stellt.* This verse may indicate the presence of witnesses. Further, Raguel's calling Edna his wife in connection with the writing of the deed may be for the purpose of witnessing. The expression in 7, 14, "and he sealed it," may also be an indication of the presence of witnesses. None of these, however, say anything about the witnesses signing. The word *hatam,* to seal, means either the presence of witnesses, or writing the concluding formula, or making it a "folded deed." Cf. B. B. 180b.

The one evidence that may be offered against our assumption that originally witnesses did not sign the deed is that of Jeremiah, 32, 12: "And I gave the deed . . . . before the eyes of the witnesses that had signed (*Ha-kotebim*) the deed . . . " In answer to this I would only say that by a slight change in the vocalization we have *Ha-ketubim,* that are written down, instead of *Ha-kotebim.* The reading *Ha-ketubim* finds support in a number of texts. See Ehrlich, *Mikro kipeshuto,* a. l. Even the Massoretic reading is not altogether conclusive evidence, for as the Talmud puts it, it was a special case intended for durable testimony (B. B. 28a). R. Elazar who maintains עדי מסירה כרתי cannot agree to the proposition that the signature of witnesses is recorded in the Bible. He must either read *Ha-ketubim* or must accept the second explanation, as Rashi (Gittin 36a s. v. 'לרא). A suggestion is made that R. Elazar deals with divorce only but admits that witnesses signed other deeds in Biblical times. This suggestion is not tenable, because the very question דאוריתא הוא (ibid) implies a parallelism between divorce and other deeds insomuch as the entire halakah treats the divorce as in no way different from the other instruments, and R. Elazar's view is interpreted by the amoraim explicitly to include other deeds also. Cf. Gittin 22b and 86b.

[41] Gittin 34b. I wish to emphasize that this is the natural explanation of the mishna. This is also the view of the mishna held by R. Elazar, who insists that the important witnesses are those who are present at the transaction. The attempt on the part of the amoraim to make the view of R. Meir agree with this mishna is futile because the two represent

public convenience here referred to is this. Under the old system, the witnesses had to testify in person, if any contract was repudiated; while under the new system, their handwriting, if known to the court, was testimony for the validity of the contract. This enactment dates back certainly to Temple days, either to Rabban Gamaliel I (First century C. E.) or to one of his ancestors.[42]

The effect of this enactment on the people is noticeable through the halakah. Literacy became necessary in the commercial world. You could not be a witness unless you could sign your name. Therefore, "originally only priests, levites, and those who intermarried with priests signed ketubot,"[43] they being as a rule the literates. Therefore also, the earlier authorities permit-

different strata of the halakah. Their attempt also to make the beraita, Gittin 36a, agree with the mishna is far fetched. The former deals with the question of a full signature, the latter with the requirement of the witnesses signing. Mishna Gittin, 86a gives clearly R. Elazar's interpretation of the enactment as we have presented it here.

[42] This enactment is placed in the mishna at the end of the enactments of R. Gamaliel I and before the enactment of Hillel, mentioned there. Rashi maintains that this belongs to RG. R. Tam believes that it does not belong to RG. (See Tosafot Gittin 36a s. v. והעדים where, by the way, the tosafist confuses R. Gamaliel I with the R. Gamaliel II). Notice should be taken of the fact that the last enactment of RG cited in this series of mishnas deals with the ketubah, not with the divorce, as the others do. This enactment deals with the divorce. If it were also an enactment of RG, why was it not placed among the other enactments on the divorce? If the enactment was not by RG it must have been by one of his antecedents, for it was certainly known in Temple days. Thus R. Johanan b. Zakai signed a ketubah (Ket. 66b); aristocratic people in Jerusalem were signing ketubot (Mek. ad Exod. 23, 1; Gittin 87b; Tos. San. 7, 1).

[43] Tos. San. 7, 1.

ted witnesses who could not sign their names to use stencils, and R. Simeon b. Gamaliel permitted it only for divorces.[44]

The signature of witnesses was destined to go through another stage of development. Under the old system, the contracting parties and the witnesses had to meet together in one place in order to carry out the full process of contract writing. The witnesses heard the agreements entered into by the parties, they were named in the deed in that capacity, and they saw the culmination of the transaction in the delivery of the deed. Supposing one of the parties could not come to the place where the other was, then the transaction could not be carried out. With the development of commerce such a condition became intolerable. Even morality required the recasting of this law, for was not the case often that of a husband who wished to divorce his wife or a wife who wished to be freed from her husband who had gone away to a distant land? How was that case, for instance, among many others of like nature, to be solved? The enactment that witnesses must sign the writ did not solve it. It sometimes saved the trouble of going to the place where the parties were having a court hearing on the validity of the contract, but they had to be present at the transaction in order to be witnesses at all.

The law sought a solution to this difficulty in a legal analysis of the function of the witnesses. The witnesses seemed to have two distinct functions. They witnessed the transaction, i. e. the negotiations between the parties, the giving of the money, if it was a sale, the conveying of the object, and finally the delivery of the deed. So far they are *'ede mesirah*, witnes-

[44] Gittin 19b.

ses to the transaction culminating in the delivery of the writ. But the witnesses also signed the writ, and thus made the deed a deed instead of a piece of parchment. In this particular function, they were *'ede hatimah,* witnesses to the writ. In the first stage, when witnesses did not sign, this distinction was impossible; but with the new enactment, the law could easily distinguish between the one function and the other. True, both were traditionally performed by one set of witnesses, but why not divide them between two sets of witnesses? By this means, transactions could be carried out across any distance. The grantor could make out the writ with the help of the *'ede hatimah,* send it on to the grantee who could accept it and thus conclude the transaction in the presence of the other set of witnesses, the *'ede mesirah.*[45]

With this breaking up of the function of the witnesses and introducing the *'ede hatimah,* it came about that the witnesses who signed the writ did not see the transaction at all. Therefore, the "pure minded" of Jerusalem, it is reported, hesitated to put the word "Witness" after their signatures on deeds, because witness to them meant being present at the transaction, which was not the case.[46] Evidently, the older feeling was that the real witnesses were the *'ede mesirah,* the view maintained by R. Elazar, but the newer tendency in the law was to make room for a valid instrument, regardless of the condition of the transac-

[45] This presupposes recognition by the law of the status of the "agent" (שליח). The conception of the agent, however, also arises with the need of carrying out transactions across a distance. We know of an enactment of R. Gamaliel in connection with the delivery of a divorce by an agent (Gittin 32a) but the conception of *'ede hatimah* is apparently not known to him.

[46] Gittin 87b.

tion, and therefore to call him a witness who validates the contract—the view of R. Meir, the opponent of R. Elazar.[47]

As to the number of witnesses that is required for writs, it is hard to say what was the upper limit, for we often find many named as witnesses. The lower limit seems to be, as Deuteronomy has it, "two or three."[48] The older sources seem to require at least three witnesses,[49] but the later halakah has established the ruling that two are required for the simple writ and three for the "folded deed."[50]

The attest of the witnesses in the older writs reads: "Witnesses thereto, so-and-so, son of so-and-so, . . . witnesses." The later formula was: "I, so-and-so, son of so-and-so, signed as witness." Probably on account of difficulty in finding men who would write with fluency, the older law permitted abbreviating the signature, writing only the first half or the second half of the signature, but during the second century witnesses were already required to sign their names in full.[51]

[47] Gittin 36a, etc. According to Alfasi (a. l.) R. Meir recognizes only the witnesses who are signatories to the deed, while R. Elazar recognizes either set of witnesses. Cf. Yad, Gerushin 1, 16.

[48] Deut. 19, 15. Cf. Makkot 5b.

[49] So it is in Papyrus G, and so it is reported in the Testament of Abraham.

[50] B. B. 160b.

[51] This is the intention of the report in Tos. Gittin—at the end—cited Gittin 36a. It corresponds exactly to the case cited in Gittin 87b of a signature reading only "I, so-and-so, witness" or "son of so-and-so, witness." The interpretation of Rashi that this Tosifta guards against the omission of the name altogether is hardly correct. The enactment that witnesses must sign their full names is cited in the name of R. Gamaliel in the Babylonian Talmud and in the name of R. Simeon b. Gamaliel in the Tosifta. It certainly is not R. Gamaliel I (as Tosafot

However, some famous amoraim used only a design for their signatures.[52]

takes it) but it may be Rabban Gamaliel II, possibly RG the Third. It looks, though, that the Tosifta reading of R. Simeon b. Gamaliel is correct and he is the one whom we find dealing with the problem of the illiteracy of the witnesses as shown above.

[52] Gittin 36a.

CHAPTER IV

The Marriage and the Mohar Clauses

Heretofore we have been dealing with the external matters of the ketubah. We now approach its content, the clauses. Certain clauses are common to all ancient, oriental peoples;[1] they are three in number.

1. The marriage clause, expressed in a certain sanctioned formula.
2. A declaration that the mohar was paid and received.
3. Enumeration of the dowry received by the husband.

   To these, Papyrus G adds four more clauses.

4. The clause of succession, if no issue remain.
5. Conditions of divorce.
6. Fines for mistreatment, or expulsion from the house.[2]
7. Limitations to and fines for polygamy.

   The rabbinic ketubah, with additions and modifications, contains:

1. The marriage clause, with the Jewish formula.
2. A promise to pay the mohar and mattan.

[1] Cf. L. Freund, GES, whose comparative study includes contracts from Babylonia, Assyria, pre-Islamic Arabia, Egypt and Judea, basing himeslf on Kyr. 183 (V. Marx, *Die Stellung d. Frau in Babylonien*) Demotic Documents, ed. Spiegelberg (*Receuil de travaux relatifs a la philologie et l'archéologie*, Vol. 192) Papyrus Strassburg 56 dated 117 B. C. E., ed. Spiegelberg, under the title *Der Papyrus Libby* (*Schriften d. Wissenschaftliche Gesellschaft z. Strassurg*, 1907, Vol. I, pp. 9 f.) and Papyrus G.

[2] This clause occurs also in the Ptolemean texts of Spiegelberg.

3. Enumeration of the dowry, its value.
4. The clauses of succession.
5. Conditions of divorce and the disposition of the property of the pair.
6. Mistreatment or expulsion—not a ketubah clause, but a statute.[3]
7. Limitations to and fines for polygamy.
8. A promise to give the wife food, clothing, medicine, ransom, burial, and marital satisfaction.
9. A promise to pay her debts—not definitely a ketubah clause.
10. An order to support the wife and the minor daughters out of the estate after his death.
11. A lien on his property for the fullfillment of the ketubah terms.
12. Special clauses.

These twelve items represent a composite outline of the ketubah clauses, with which we must deal individually and separately, each one having a history of its own and a halakic development peculiar to itself.

The marriage clause is the legal or social formula for concluding the marriage. We get our information about this formula from three sources, the traditional oral marriage formula, the ketubah marriage clause, and the shetar kiddushin marriage pronouncement.

Before the ketubah or any writ was employed by Jews, social custom had already established certain definite formulae for marriage declaration. Even after the deed was introduced, and no matter what marriage

[3] The statute here referred to is that of "Rebellion" (*mored*). This seems to be the closest substitute for the case of expulsion. It became a statute rather than a ketubah clause because it had to provide for different possibilities of mistreatment which the ketubah probably could not enumerate.

writs were employed, the marriage formula had to be orally pronounced. We have no definite record of the marriage formula used in Bible days, but it appears that "be a wife to" (היה לאשה) was in one form or another part of the marriage pronouncement. It further appears that the formula was in most or in all cases recited by the bride's father, not by the groom. Thus Laban says to Eliezer, "Behold, Rebecca is before thee, take her and go, and she *be wife to* thy master's son."[4] The Book of Tobit gives a fuller oral marriage formula: "Take her to thyself after the law of Moses," —and here too the pronouncement is made by the bride's father. The Talmud requires the husband to pronounce the formula, and its formula is, "Behold, thou art consecrated unto me," or "Behold, thou art betrothed unto me," or "Behold thou art my wife."[5] הרי את מקודשת לי, הרי את מאורסת לי, הרי את לי לאנתו

[4] Gen. 24, 51. This expression occurrs again and again in the Bible.

[5] The requirement that the husband pronounce the formula is based on the conception that the husband must do the marrying, as it is written (Deut. 22, 13) "If a man marry a wife," not if a wife marry a man. Cf. Kid. 2b, 5b, 6a.

These formulae are probably the most common among the many others mentioned in the Talmud. Cf. Kid. 5b, 6a. The term קנויה cited Kid. 6a seems to represent an older form (לישנא דאוריתא) —See Kid. 2b.—which was no longer popular in later days. The oral marriage formula of the Karaites is based on the terms לקח and קנה. Cf. Harkavey, *Zikron larishonim,* II, pp. 113, 119.

The most popular formula was הרי את מקודשת לי and that has remained in use today. Tosafot Kid. 2b interprets *mekudeshet* to mean set aside, "for marriage makes the woman an object of prohibition to the world." Blau (*Zur Geschichte d. juedische Eherechts,* Schwartz *Festschrift,* pp. 200-203) suggests that the word *mekudeshet* originates from priestly marriages. I should like to add another suggestion. The marriage ceremony itself was first known as *kiddushin,* even as the tractate of the Talmud is so named because it deals with marriage.

These Talmudic formulae, however, must be taken as incomplete, omitting the last half. The full formula read: "Behold, thou art consecrated unto me according to the law of Moses and Israel."[6] הרי את מקודשת לי כדת משה וישראל. And this is the marriage pronouncement employed by Jews to-day.

This name has some connection with the marriage blessing recited over a cup of wine and reading אשר קדשנו even as the blessing over wine on the entrance of the Sabbath or holiday is called *Kiddush* or the prayer over the new moon, designated as *Kiddush Lebanah* or *Kiddush Hahodesh* or the reciting of the verse, "Holy, holy, holy is the Lord of hosts . . . " is termed *Kedusha.* Is it not possible that on account of the blessing the ceremony of marriage was called Kiddushin and from the name of the ceremony was derived the formula, הרי את מקודשת? Nevertheless, there is no escape from the conception of holiness implied in marriage. However, it should not be taken in the negative sense, that the wife becomes prohibited to others but in the positive sense, that she is dedicated, purified, permitted, an object of sanctioned contact to her husband. This is what Tosafot calls the literal meaning of the term.

[6] The Talmud never cites this part of the formula, namely, "according to the law of Moses and Israel," in connection with the oral pronouncement. On this basis, Z. Frankel, *Grundlinien d. mosaisch-talmudischen Eherechts*, p. 25, note 4, maintains that it was not used with the oral formula until the time of the tosafists. Tosafot Ket. 3a, is what Frankel has reference to, and that authority takes this phrase to be a stipulation that the marriage is validated on the condition that it meet with the approval of the sages who represent the law of Moses and Israel. Cf. also *Nahlat Shiv'ah* 12, 18 and *Sefer ha-hinuk,* 552. The omission of this phrase is not only to be noticed in the Talmud, but also in Saadyah (*Sha'are Zedek,* 18b) and Maimonides (Yad, Ishut, 3, 1-2). I maintain that they are all omissions in the record for the sake of brevity, but were used in the oral formula even in tannaitic days. I cannot see how the ketubah would record the marriage clause differently from its use among the people, except insofar as it preserved the older Aramaic forms, for the phrase, "according to the law of Moses and Israel," has been used in the ketubah since the days of Hillel, as will be seen later. Besides, the marriage formula in Tobit also contained this phrase. See Friedmann *Iggeret Teshubah,* p. 45.

The marriage formula of the shetar kiddushin is practically the same as that of the oral pronouncement, according to records in the Babylonian Talmud. The Palestinian Talmud cites it in the following form: "I, so-and-so, married so-and-so." [7] Here, too, it is to be understood that it concluded with the phrase, "according to the law of Moses and Israel."

The marriage declaration in the ketubah was originally, as found in Papyrus G: "She is my wife and I am her husband from this day and forever." [8] Four centuries from the time of the papyri pass without further record as to the marriage clause. Then we find the clause cited by Hillel in the form: "Be thou my wife according to the law of Moses and Israel." [9] And thereafter, for almost two thousand years, Jews have employed this formula for their ketubot without the slightest change, even as it reads in our ketubah today[10]: הוי לי לאנתו כדת משה וישראל.

Further embellishments of the marriage declaration are given in the ketubah, to complete and to round out the marriage clause. The groom proposes, and his

[7] Jer. Kid. 59a: אני פב"פ לקחתי את פב"פ.

[8] הי אתתי ואנה בעלה מן יומא זנא ועד עלם. Note the proximity to the Biblical phraseology, Hosea 2, 4: הי לא אשתי ואנכי לא אישה.

[9] Tos. Ket. 4, 9; Jer. Jeb. 14a, Jer. Ket. 29a. That משה ויהודאי is to be preferred to משה וישראל is evident from Mishna Ket. 7, 7 (72b). B. M. 104a omits כדת משה וכו'. But the omission cannot be taken as significant. Cf. Freund, GES, p. 7, note 2. Aptowitzer (WZKM, Vol. 23, p. 396) judges by this omission that the phrase was used only in Alexandria.

[10] However, the Saadya ketubah, ed. Gaster, (MGWJ, Vol. 54) omits the phrase, "according to the law of Moses and Israel." The Karaites have substituted the formula by the following: היות לי לאשה . . כדת משה איש האלהים ודת **ישראל** הטהרים והקדישים.

proposal is put in the traditional marriage formula;[11] the bride accepts the proposal;[12] and the marriage is established.[13] Thus the marriage clause concludes with the words: וצביאת . . . . והות ליה לאנתו "And she was satisfied . . . . and became his wife."

The marriage clause is followed by the stipulation of the mohar. The mohar is so important an item in the ketubah that it is often designated by the term *Ikar ketubah,* the essence of the ketubah; or the word ketubah itself most often denotes mohar. It represents probably the oldest element in the Jewish marriage insitution.

Mohar means purchase price. It was paid in cash to the bride's father, later to the bride herself. With the enactment of Simeon b. Shetah, it was merely promised to the bride, and thus became a divorce price, rather than a marriage price. The conception of mohar has brought about a controversy among scholars as to the nature of the Jewish marriage. Some take it to be a matter of barter and sale;[14]

[11] In Papyrus G, the marriage formula does constitute part of the proposal, but is what we call here the establishment of the marriage.

[12] In Papyrus G this element is represented by the words: ומב לבבך. Our ketubot have the word וצביאת to establish the bride's consent. This word also implies *free consent* without compulsion. Some ketubot further elaborate the statement as to her free consent by the following: ואגיב לישאלו במלאת דעת וטיב לבב ורצון נפש (Samaritan ketubah. See also Karaitic ketubah). Likewise, some ketubot state that the husband acted as a free and responsible agent, by the following expression: מדעתיה וטיבותיה ומרעותיה בדלא אנים ולא משודל ולא רוי חמר. See, e. g., citations of Kaufmann, MGWJ, 1897.

[13] We use the phrase והות ליה לאנתו, a correct Aramaic translation of Ruth 4, 13: ותהי לו לאשה. The Samaritan ketubah has the exact Biblical quotation.

[14] Billauer, *Grundzuege d. babyl.-talmud. Eherechts.* Benziger, Nowack and Krauss in their Archaologies.

others hold it up to the level of romance and union.[15] The former find corroboration for their view in the halakah, the latter in the agadah. To steer clear of this controversy, let us understand the difference between form and content. The form of marriage is one thing, its content quite another. The Jewish marriage is in content all that romance and union imply. A wife is a God-given helpmate, flesh of her husband's flesh. But the form of the Jewish marriage is more concrete. It represents a transaction, a conveyance of rights. If marriage is romance in content, it is purchase in form. The ketubah is not a love-letter; it is a deed of conveyance. Dealing with the ketubah, therefore, we deal with the strictly legal, formal side of marriage, and from this angle, mohar is nothing more nor less than the purchase price.

The instititution of mohar is as old as human records go back, and is found among Jews and non-Jews in antiquity.[16] It began, like all commerce, before the medium of exchange was popularly used; hence a variety of kinds of mohar are recorded. Eliezer gives to Laban "precious things," Jacob gives seven years of

[15] Frankel, *Grundlinien d. mosaisch-talmud. Eherechts;* Duschak, *Das mosaisch-talmud. Eherecht*; Lichtenstein, *Die Ehe nach mosaisch-talmud. Auffassung; Neubauer,* BGE.

[16] The word מהר in Hebrew and Aramaic is equivalent to *Mahrun* in Arabic. Wellhausen (*Die Ehe b. d. Arabern*) points out that, like the Hebrew *Mohar,* the Arabic *Mahrun* was originally a cash payment to the bride's father. (Contra Michaelis, *Das Mosaische Recht,* II p. 126). The Arabic *Mahrun,* however, unlike the mohar, developed later to mean dowry, the equivalent to our *nedunya.* The root of the word is variously taken. Some derive it from מור exchange (Buchholtz, *Die Familie*; Friedmann, *Iggeret*), others connect it with מחר in the sense of the German *Morgengabe.* (Saalschutz, *Das mosaische Recht;* Neubauer, BGE). Cf. Freund GES, p. 20, notes 1, 2, 4, and p. 21, note 2.

service; Shechem offers any amount of mohar; Othniel offers valiant military service to Caleb; David offers to Saul a hundred foreskins of the Philistines; and Hosea buys himself a wife for barley. In the remote past, there probably was no standard at all, but in Biblical days we already note a minimum mohar. For seduction, the law prescribes a fine equal in sum to the mohar of virgins.[17] Now, what was that sum? The rabbis say rape and seduction are equal offenses, and if the Bible prescribes a fine of fifty shekels for rape,[18] then seduction must also be fined the same amount. In other words, the sum equal to the mohar of virgins is fifty shekels. The rabbis' logic is evident as it is compelling. Rape and seduction represent theft of virginity; mohar, the price of virginity. It is by the same logic, probably, that the Bible prescribes a fine of a hundred shekels, double the price of virginity, for the husband who falsely denies his bride's virginity,[19] as double penalty for a thief is not uncommon in the ancient law.[20] Our conclusion is, therefore, that the Bible knew of a minimum mohar of fifty shekels.

It is hardly possible that the rabbis ever doubted the Biblical origin of the mohar known to them, for their mohar of two hundred zuzim equals the Biblical fifty shekels. Yet the amoraim tell us that the tannaim before them had a discussion whether mohar is Biblical or rabbinical.[21] On examination of the

[17] Exod. 22, 15-16.

[18] Deut. 22, 29. See Mek. ad Exod. ibid., Ket. 10a, 29b, 30b, Jer. Ket. 27d.

[19] Deut. 22, 19.

[20] See Exod. 22, 3, 6, 8, Code Hammurabi, 9-12, 124-126. Cf. Freund, GES, p. 21.

[21] Ket. 10a, 110b; Jer. Ket. 36b. Here the Babylonian amoraim and the Palestinian amoraim cite diametrically opposed traditions. According to the Babli, all tannaim admit the

tannaitic sources, however, one fails to find any controversy on the subject among the tannaim. It is the amoraic construction upon the words of the tannaim that reveals this controversy.[22] If it be correct,

rabbinical character of mohar, except R. Simeon b. Gamaliel. The Palestinian Talmud completely reverses the report, namely, all adhere to the Biblical character of mohar, except R. Simeon b. Gamaliel. And what is stranger still, both Talmudim draw on the same tannaitic sources. *Hagahot Maimoniot*, Ishut 10, 7, notices the discrepancy, does not offer any solution, but chooses (with R. Simhah) to side with RSBG of the Jerushalmi and his opponents of the Babli, making mohar rabbinical. Mordecai (end of Ketubot) also notices the discrepancy, offers no solution, but chooses the opposite, RSBG of the Babli and his opponents of the Jerushalmi, mohar thus being adjudged Biblical.

[22] a) Mekilta ad Exod. 22, 16 and Mekilta d'R. Simeon b. Yohai ibid. assume definitely, and without a dissenting opinion, that mohar is Biblical. Mekilta ad Exod. 22, 15 taken together with Ket. 38a-b, cite R. Akiba and R. Jose of Galilee as of the opinion that mohar is Biblical. Their derivation of the amount of mohar is based on the parallelism between seduction and rape. That parallelism is expressed, according to R. Akiba in the use of אשר לא אורשה in both cases. According to R. Jose, כמהר הבתולות means "as the fine imposed for rape," thus pointing to rape directly.

b) Both the Babylonian and the Palestinian Talmudim cite a tannaitic text recording a controversy between RSBG and his colleagues, the former maintaining that mohar is rabbinical, the latter that it is Biblical (Ket. 10a, J. Ket. at the end). This text, however, is found in none of the tannaitic sources. Again, the Babylonian Talmud cites a tannaitic text in direct contradiction of this one, in which RSBG states that mohar is Biblical. Furthermore, altho this need not be taken very seriously, the Babylonian amoraim feel compelled to emend this text. The Palestinian and the Babylonian citations of this text do not agree, except in the words of RSBG. This makes the text wholly unreliable. If it is to be credited with genuineness, however, the Palestinian account of it must be the correct one, that RSBG maintains that mohar is rabbinincal, and the Babylonian emendation must be discarded. And as for the tannaitic text quoted in the Babli, in which RSBG says definitely that

though, that the tannaim did discuss this question, it must be understood that they did not doubt the historical origin of mohar in Bible days, but they simply sought to determine the legal status of mohar. For it is quite thinkable that the institution was known to the Bible as a fact, but was not commanded as an injunction. As an obligation it might be rabbinical, regardless of its history.[23]

mohar is Biblical, the probabilities are that it read simply: הואיל ותקנת חכמים הוא לא תגבה אלא מן הזבריות רשבגא' כתובת אשה בבינונית (Cf. Gittin 48b). The amoraim, assuming that RSBG's view is based on his considering mohar Biblical—else why give the woman such an advantage?—changed the text to read: רשבג' אומר כתובת אשה מן התורה.

c) The controversy between RSBG and his colleagues on this question is read by the amoraim into the last mishna of Ketubot. The mishna presents the case of a man who married in a foreign country and divorced his wife in Palestine, wherefore the ketubah is presented for collection in Palestine—and it asks in what currency must the husband pay the ketubah. RSBG says he pays in foreign coin; his colleagues would have him pay in Palestinian coin. The Babylonians, considering foreign coin advantageous to the wife, say that RSBG, contends for the Biblical nature of mohar, and his opponents for its rabbinical character. The Palestinians, on the other hand, considering Palestinian coin more advantageous to the woman, reverse the opinions of the contestants—RSBG maintains mohar is rabbinical and his opponents that it is Biblical. Evidently this is merely a controversy that arose in the minds of the amoraim. RSBG and his opponents argue the case on its own merits, that is, whether mohar must remain in its original Biblical form or whether it can be treated like an ordinary debt which the husband owes the wife from the moment of marriage. See also, Ket. 56b, Mordecai Ket. 135, and Asheri Ket. 19. See also *Melo hare'im*, Jacob Zebi Jolles, Warsau 1880, p. 97 f. Cf. note 28. Cf. also the last Tosifta of Ketubot, which seems to corroborate the Palestinian account that RSBG maintained mohar was rabbinical.

[23] I do not wish to press the point that the tannaim knew nothing of the controversy, though this is my feeling, because

Whatever the view of the tannaim, the amoraim among themselves differ as to whether mohar is Biblical or rabbinical. The Palestinian amoraim hold the view that it is Biblical;[24] the Babylonians maintain that it is rabbinical.[25] Their difference may be thus explained. Mohar has really gone through a vital change; from a marriage price, it became a divorce price. In Palestine, where the Biblical mohar was known, where the change from one mohar to another took place, where economic conditions presented a historical continuity, and where the system of currency continued from Bible days to amoraic times, the connection between the mohar of the amoraim and the mohar of the Bible could not be altogether over-

there is apparent unanimity between the Babli (Ket. 10a, without the correction given there) the Jerushalmi (end of Ket.) and Tosifta (by implication only, as given in previous note) that RSBG was of the opinion that mohar was rabbinical. If so, he would have to maintain that the hermeneutic method of derivation of הרי זה בא ללמד ונמצא למד yields only a rabbinical institution and not a Biblical one, for the very reason that it brings to light only a fact that existed in Biblical times, but not an injunction. The same rule seems to hold good for the tannaitic inference from כמשפט הבנות Exod. 21, 9. The Karaites hold mohar to be Biblical, but the amount to be post-Biblical. Cf. *Aderet Elijahu*, Nashim, 1. R. Nisim (end of Ket.) gives exactly this interpretation to RSBG.

[24] Jer. Jeb. 8a, 14d, Jer. Ket. 25b, 29b.

[25] Ket. 10a, 39a, 56a, 110a, B. B. 132a, Bekorot 52b, Jeb. 89a. An exception to this rule is found in B. K. 89b. The text, however, seems in itself corrupted, for if it really meant to indicate that mohar was Biblical, it could not set it at 25 zuzim. Rashi and Tosafot suggest reading "25 Sela'im" instead of zuzim. Mordecai Ket. 112 leaves out the entire phrase and cites a text which reads: דמשום פורתא לא מפסיד טובא. Evidently the text is not reliable. If the word דאוריתא does belong to it, it is merely a careless expression derived from the ketubah formula, "Biblically due thee," which is not fully in accordance with the halakah. See Tosafot ibid., s. v. לא.

shadowed. In Babylonia, on the other hand, the connection between the amoraic mohar and the Biblical mohar was easily severed by the many differences between them, emphasized by new conditions and new currency in a new world.

In post-Talmudic days, the Palestinian tradition—that mohar is Biblical—remained firm among the Palestinian authorities; while the Babylonian Gaonate was divided on the question. The Sura Gaonate, under the influence of Palestinian traditions, favored the view that mohar is Biblical. The Babylonian tradition that mohar is rabbinical was preserved by the Pumbedita gaonim.[26] Nor have the later rabbinic authorities given us a unanimous decision whether mohar is Biblical or rabbinical. There are representatives of either view among the leading teachers.[27]

[26] These views are recorded in *Hemdah Genuzah*, 66, *Hamakeri'ah*, 42, *Zedah Laderek* 3, 2, 2, *Sha'are Zedek*, 39. The tradition is reversed by error in *Orhot Hayim* and Solomon Lurie's *Hiluke Dinim* (Lewy's *Festschrift*, p. 225). Cf. Joel Mueller in *Hashahar* Vol. 7, 7, A. Buechler, *La ketubah chez les Juifs du nord de l'Afrique a l'epoque des guenim*, REJ Vol. 50. Cf. MGWJ Vol. 20, pp. 360f. See also Harkavey, *Responsa*, 73, and *Sha'are Zedek*, 22.

[27] On the side that mohar is rabbinical we have Alfasi (end of Ket.), Rashi (San. 8a: Rashi Commentary to Gen. 25, 6, would seem to indicate the contrary), Maimonides (Yad, Ishut 10, 7-8), R. Nisim (end of Ket.) and *Hagahot Maimoniot*, Ishut 10, 7, quoting *Halakot gedolot*, R. Hananel and R. Simhah. Some of the tosafists contend that even the view that mohar is Biblical (according to Babli, held by RSBG) also means that it is rabbinical, but that it has support in a Biblical verse. (Cf. Tosafot Sotah 27a, s. v. איש). On the side that mohar is Biblical we have Mordecai (Ket. 312) and perhaps also R. Jacob Tam, who is reported (Tosafot Ket. 10a) to have expressed himself in favor of the view that mohar is Biblical, but who is also reported to maintain that mohar is rabbinical (See *Ha-makeri'ah*, 42).

Upon the decision of this question depend many matters of law,[28] but its direct influence on the mohar clause in the ketubah is a two-fold one. If mohar is Biblical, the ketubah clause should read, "And I shall give thee the mohar of thy virginity . . . . Biblically due thee." If mohar is rabbinical, the clause should read, "And I shall give thee the mohar of thy virginity . . . . rabbinically due thee,"—or, at least, the reference to its Biblical origin should be omitted. Therefore we have legal decisions in favor of the one reading and the other, and we also have ketubot recording the mohar clause in the one manner or the other.[29] Yet

[28] The halakic points which the amoraim take as depending upon the question whether mohar is Biblical or rabbinical are the following:

a) Whether reduction of the mohar by common consent is permitted, as a violation of a rabbinical law, or not, as an undoing of a Biblical law (Ket. 54b).

b) In what currency shall the mohar be calculated, in Biblical currency or rabbinical currency? (Kid. 11a, Bekorot 50b, Jer. Ket. 25b).

c) Shall Palestinian coin be sufficient to pay a ketubah contracted for in a land of better currency? (Ket. 110a)

d) Shall the ketubah be paid of the worst of the husband's property, or not? (Gittin 48b, Ket. 10a)

e) Shall the ketubah have priority over other obligations that are rabbinical, or not? (Jer. Jeb. 8a, Jer. Ket. 29a-b)

f) Every disadvantage or advantage of the woman before the law in the matter of her mohar seems to depend upon the decision whether mohar is Biblical or rabbinical.

[29] The phrase "Biblically due thee" is generally used in ketubot as is also testified by Tosafot Ket. 10a and hosts of published and unpublished ketubot that one sees. The omission of that phrase or the substitution of it by the words "rabbinically due thee" is found in a ketubah ed. Israel Abrams (*Jews' College Jubilee Volume*, 1906, p. 105) Sephardic ketubot (one ed. Gaster, MGWJ, another ed. Grossberg, *Hebel Menashe*, London 1900) Saadya Ketubah, ed. Gaster, Italian ketubot, Maimonides ketubah, Yad, Yibbum, 4, 33 (according to MS reading: see

we are not in want of instances where the words "Biblically due thee" are inserted in ketubot, even though the halakic supposition is that mohar is rabbinical.[30] These instances, which ought to be the exceptions, are as numerous as the evidences of the rule itself, and furthermore, this is our general attitude to the question today: we take mohar to be rabbinical, and yet we persist in using the phrase, "Biblically due thee" in our ketubot.[31] This may serve as one of the illustrations of the persistence of an old form in defiance of the theoretical halakah.

The second point that hinges on the question whether mohar is Biblical or rabbinical is the question of the amount of mohar. The Biblical mohar, we have seen, was fifty shekels. In the earliest rabbinic times, even prior to R. Simeon b. Shetah, the mohar was counted in terms of zuzim instead of shekels, for the Tyrian zuz, a sterling silver coin of the value of a quarter of a shekel, was the popular coin in Jerusalem.[32] Thus, the mohar was two hundred zuzim. At the end of the tannaitic period, another zuz appeared on the market, the "current zuz," of a silver alloy and of the value of an eighth part of the Tyrian zuz; nevertheless, the mohar of the ketubah was still reckoned, in accordance with its historic background, by the Tyrian zuz. Throughout the entire tannaitic period, there was no deviation from this practice.[33]

MGWJ, Vol. 54, p. 576). In this connection, the legal material in note 26 may also be consulted.

[30] See Asheri Ket. 19, *Itur* ed. Warsau p. 30a, *Shitah mekubezet*, Ket. 10a, *Nahlat Shiv'ah* 12, 32.

[31] The Jerusalem ketubah ed. Berliner has כתובת תורת משה instead of our דחזי ליכי מדאוריתא. This expression is quoted in *Ha-makeri'ah* 42 as a Palestinian phrase.

[32] Cf. end of Tosefta Ket. and Jer. Ket. 25b.

[33] The interpretation which Tosafot (B. K. 36b, s. v. ושל) gives of the last mishna of Ketubot is perfectly correct, namely

There was evident need, however, to reduce the mohar, because two hundred Tyrian zuzim was an exhorbitant sum.[34] Some of the amoraim, therefore, manipulated the halakah towards that end. They began with the premise that, since the commercial coin is the "current zuz," any note, be it a ketubah or a note of indebtedness, has its face value in terms of the current zuz. Hence, the face value of the ketubah is two hundred current zuzim. And if the history of the mohar be invoked, their answer will be that face value is more important than historic implications.[35] Granted even that the husband owes his wife a mohar of two hundred Tyrian zuzim, so long as she has accepted in its place a note of the face value of two hundred current zuzim, this is all that he owes her.[36] This kind of argument seemed to them to be valid, even on the assumption that mohar is Biblical.

that RSBG and his opponents do not argue a reduction in mohar at all. Again an attempt is made by a Palestinian amora to prove by the omission of mohar in Mishna Bekorot 8, 5, that mohar was taken by the tanna to be payable in current coin. But the correct answer to it is made by R. Abin: Jer. Ket. 25b. The tannaitic sources offer no other suggestion that they consider reduction of mohar at all.

[34] How burdensome the amount of two hundred zuzim was to a Jewish husband in the past is pointed out by RIBSh (Responsa, 153) by the fact that the mishna (Peah, 8) teaches that a man who has fifty zuzim in circulation can not share in any of the prescribed offerings to the poor.

[35] If RSBG's statement in the last mishna of Ketubot does not yield the conclusion that mohar is rabbinical, at least it was the forerunner of the distinction drawn here between the face value and the historical value of the mohar clause in the ketubah, with emphasis on the former.

[36] This view of the matter is clearly expressed in Jer. Ket. 25b. According to this view, if she has no ketubah, she gets two hundred Tyrian zuzim, but with the presentation of the ketubah she gets only twenty-five.

If mohar is rabbinical, then the historical definition of the term "zuz" is altogether out of consideration, and what remains is only the face value of the ketubah, two hundred current zuzim. Furthermore, a tradition is cited in the name of Rab[37] that "all silver coin of the Bible is to be calculated in Tyrian coin; all coin of rabbinical enactments mean current coin." Consequently, the enactment of mohar and the face value of the ketubah call only for two hundred current zuzim, or twenty five Tyrian zuzim.

The direct connection between the question whether mohar is Biblical or rabbinical and the definition of the "zuz," it is true, is not given in Talmudic literature. The Palestinian amoraim discuss the term zuz of the ketubah, but their arguments in favor of the current zuz or the Tyrian zuz are valid even on the supposition that mohar is Biblical. The Babylonian amoraim are altogether silent on the question.[38] The direct connection between the issue whether mohar is Biblical or rabbinical and the definition of the zuz of the ketubah is a geonic creation. They base their opinion almost entirely on the principle uttered by Rab that Biblical zuzim are Tyrian and rabbinical zuzim are current. Hence, the Tyrian zuz is entered into the ketubah generally where the phrase "Biblically due thee" is employed.[39] Palestine, according to its tradition of the Biblical origin of mohar, demands two

[37] Bekorot 50b, Kid. 11a, etc.

[38] The Palestinian discussion is found in Jer. Ket. 25b, and without reference to the question whether mohar is Biblical or rabbinical, except by the commentators. The only Babylonian reference to the twenty-five zuz of the ketubah is in B. K. 89b where the text is wholly unreliable. See note 25, p. 63 above.

[39] See p. 65. The first to note that differences as to amount of mohar may be based on whether mohar is Biblical or rabbinical is R. Moses Gaon. *Chemdah genuzah,* 66.

hundred Tyrian zuzim. So does in general the Sura academy under Palestinian influence. Pumbedita, with its tradition of the rabbinical origin of mohar, permits a ketubah of only twenty five Tyrian Zuzim.[40] And, in this instance too, exceptions are not rare of the combination of twenty-five zuzim with the phrase, "Biblically due thee" [41] or the opposite combination of two hundred Tyrian zuzim with the phrase, "rabbinically due thee." [42]

The mohar of twenty-five zuzim became more popular in the Orient and finally was crystalized into a Sephardic custom,[43] while the two hundred Tyrian zuzim gradually became the mohar of the richer Occidental countries, Germany and France in particular, and is now almost synonomous with what may be called an Ashkenazic custom.[44] The mohar clause of Europ-

[40] See note 26 and 29 on pp. 64-65. See also Pinsker *Mazkir libenai Reshef*, 43, and MGWJ, Vol. 20, p. 360. The following ketubot support the general geographical divisions on the question: The Jerusalem ketubah ed. Berliner, having a mohar of 8 and 1/3 gold pieces, counting 24 zuzim to a gold piece. The Babylonian custom is represented by the ketubot edited in REJ 47, p. 301 and 48, p. 173, JQR 13, p. 220; etc.

[41] The explanation is partly given above that even on the basis of the conception that mohar is Biblical, there is still room for the argument that the face value of the ketubah is only two hundred current zuzim. A later theory, developed from an unknown source, is that the Bible itself indicates the number 25 in the כ of כמהר and the ה of הבתולות. Cf. *Ha-makeri'ah* 42, *Aderet Elijahu*, Nashim 1, 1.

[42] The explanation for this is that, though rabbinical, the mohar is given, at least as to amount, the dignity of a Biblical law. Cf. *Itur*, I, p. 30.

[43] It is so designated in *Itur*, ibid. Sephardic texts support this impression. See Yemenite and Sephardic ketubot, Yad, Yibbum, 33. Sefer *Ha-shetarot* has a mohar of twenty-five in his *Shetar Erusin* and two hundred in his ketubah.

[44] Cf. *Itur*, ibid. Tosafot B. K. 36b, s. v. וישל, *Mahzor Vitri, Nahlat Shiv'ah* and numerous other ketubah texts.

ean ketubot, therefore, reads: "And I shall give thee the mohar of thy virginity, two hundred silver zuzim Biblically due thee." ויהיבנא ליכי מהר בתוליכי כסף זוזי מאתן דחזי ליכי מדאוריתא.

Reducing the mohar by common agreement between bride and groom is a subject of discussion among the tannaim. According to one teacher it is wholly permitted; according to another it may be done only in this wise, that the full mohar be entered into the ketubah and the bride write a receipt for part of it; according to R. Meir, any reduction of mohar causes marriage to be fornication.[45] The halakah does not follow R. Meir,[46] yet, because of the force of his personality and the decisiveness of his utterance, Jews are scrupulous about giving the full standard mohar.

The important historical changes in the institution of mohar have already been given in connection with the tradition of the Simeon b. Shetah enactment.[47] Originally it was paid to the father of the bride, who kept it for himself; then it was given to the father as trustee for the bride; then it was kept by the husband as trustee for the bride; then the husband as trustee was permitted to use it for the purchase of household articles; and finally SBS permitted a note of indebtedness to be given to the bride instead of the cash mohar. With this enactment, the mohar became a divorce price instead of a marriage price.[47a] A substitute for the

[45] Ket. 54b, 56a-b.

[46] Because R. Meir's view, according to the amoraim, is based on his premise that mohar is Biblical, whereas the halakah teaches that mohar is rabbinical. See Yad, Ishut 12, 8 and *Magid* commentary.

[47] See above pp. 21-24.

[47a] In addition to the conception of divorce price which is expressed in the phrase שלא תהא קלה בעיניו להוציאה, the Talmud finds another cause served in the payment of mohar at

marriage price was found in the *kesef kiddushin* or the coin of the value of at least a peruta given to the bride at betrothal. This in turn has by usage been replaced with a ring. Therefore, historically, the marriage ring is the symbolical cash mohar. After the days of SBS, there is very little of real importance which the rabbis have done in the matter of mohar. The only far reaching change that the later rabbis have enacted is that of shifting the weight of marriage from betrothal to nuptials, and that had its effect on mohar also. The mohar was originally paid at betrothal. It stands to reason, therefore, that the mohar entered into the ketubah represented an obligation that had its inception with betrothal. Should the husband die before nuptials, the mohar still would have to be paid. This was the unanimous ruling of the tannaim.[48] But, as the writing of the ketubah together with most of its specifications was shifted to nuptials, the rabbis felt that mohar too should have its beginning with nuptials, not with betrothal. Should the husband die before nuptials, they felt, mohar was not to be paid. The amoraim reached no decision on the question; post-Talmudic authorities discuss the matter, but the final halakah seems to have decided that no mohar is due the betrothed unless the husband assumed this obligation voluntarily at betrothal.[49]

The standard mohar of two hundred zuzim is given as "the mohar of virgins." The virginity of the bride

the dissolution of the marriage, and terms it משום חינא, i. e. to give the woman some financial position so that she may remarry (R. Chananel), or to make the hazards of marriage less poignant to the woman (Rashi). Cf. Ket. 39b and Tosafot, ibid., Ket. 84a and Tosafot ibid., Ket. 97b, Gittin 49b, J. Gittin, 46d.

[48] Ket. 54b.

[49] Yad, Ishut, 10, 11.

had to be established or assumed in order that mohar was to be claimed at all. The non-virgin, in the spirit of Biblical legislation, was not entitled to any mohar.[50] Yet one can hardly doubt that even the non-virgin in antiquity had some kind of a mohar. The non-virgin did not have the market price of the virgin, but she must have had some market value. Therefore, we find Hosea paying mohar for a woman, "who had been beloved by a husband;" [51] and Papyrus G recording the mohar of Miphtahya, who had been previously married.[52] In rabbinic legislation, the non-virgin has a mohar of a hundred zuzim, half of the mohar of the virgin; and that mohar is accepted as a rabbinical institution.[53]

[50] This is evident from the simple statement of the Bible. Further, the three laws connected with mohar, rape, seduction, and evil report, apply only to the virgin. Cf. Sifre Deut. 22, 28.

[51] Hosea 3, 2.

[52] See Sayce and Cowley, Introduction to Papyrus G.

[53] The proportion of one half holds good, no matter what the standard mohar is. If the virgin's mohar is twenty-five zuzim, the widow or divorcee gets twelve and a half zuzim. Cf. *Sefer Hashetarot* p. 10 and note 1. If the virgin's mohar is two hundred Tyrian zuzim, the non-virgin gets a hundred, not current zuzim, but Tyrian zuzim. Cf. Tosafot B. K. 36b. The proportion of one half of the virgin's mohar for the non-virgin is expressed in Jer. Ket. 25b; Mordecai, Ket. 312. The proportion of one half is also maintained by the Samaritans, and the old usage reported of priestly marriages, as we shall see later.

That mohar for the non-virgin is rabbinical is apparently granted in the Talmud, but see Tosafot Ket. 10a. Many ketubah texts give for the ketubah of the non-virgin the formula דחזי ליכי מדרבנן. Some even object to the use of the word "mohar" for the non-virgin. Cf. *Nahlat Shiv'ah,* 12, 29. A reference is made in the Talmud to the Biblical character of the mohar of the non-virgin, in that the widow (אלמנה) is so called because her mohar is only (מנה) a hundred zuzim. Ket. 10b. But that need not be taken seriously.

The law recognizes two classes of non-virgins: the woman who is physically non-virgin through contact with a male,[54] and the woman who has the social status of a non-virgin.[55] To the first class belong the widow and divorcee who have had intercourse with their husbands. To the second class belong the widow and divorcee who, having entered the nuptial chamber, have had no contact with their husbands; the non-Jewish woman who has been proselytized; the captive who has been liberated; and the slave freed after the age of three years and a day.[56] The widow or divorcee who has been only betrothed, but not wedded, to her husband has the status of a virgin, except in Judea where license among betrothed pairs was rampant.[57]

A higher mohar was required by the priestly court[58] for marriages between priest and priestess, as

[54] Loss of virginity by accident is a subject of discussion between R. Meir and his colleagues. See Ket. 11a-b, Yad Ishut 11, 3.

[55] This is the exact definition that R. Meir gives to the status of the non-virgin in Jer. Ket. 25b. Not the actual physical fact so much as the girl's attractiveness from a social point of view is what determines her mohar value.

[56] Ket. 11a.

[57] Ket. 10b, 12a, Tos. Ket. 1, 4, Jer. Ket. 25c. That the Judean betrothed are of the status of the non-virgin and hence entitled to only one hundred zuzim as mohar is never set down as a law in the Talmud. Perhaps, despite the logic, the Judeans never permitted such a reflection against themselves and retained a mohar of two hundred zuzim for their girls who had been widowed or divorced after betrothal.

[58] *Shitah mekubczet*, Ket. 12a considers *Beth din shel kohanim* as a court of twenty-three judges holding sessions in priestly communities. This opinion is given geonic authority, and seems to be supported by Sifre Deut. ed. Friedmann, 144. Professor Ginzberg is of the opinion that it may refer to cities of priests that existed even after Temple days. The Sadducean element and the whole subject matter of family purity, however, put this tradition in Temple days. Cf. Geiger, *Urschrift*, pp. 114 f; Buechler, Schwartz's *Festschrift* pp. 133 f.

a token of aristocracy. It was to be four hundred zuzim, double the Israelitish mohar. It was limited to purely priestly marriages, so long as intermarriage between priest and Israelite was discouraged or prohibited.[59] This prohibition, however, broke down with the victory of the Pharisees over the Sadducees; and the higher mohar was thereafter applied to intermarriages between priestly and Israelitish families as well.[60] A century or so after the destruction of the Temple, the aristocracy of priesthood was replaced by the aristocracy of learning. Pure lineage was the inheritance of good families, not especially of priestly families. Hence any Israelitish family that wished to establish for itself a tradition of the priestly mohar of four hundred zuzim, to apply to its marriages, was given the authority of the court to do so. This is the condition we find at the beginning of the amoraic

[59] This represents the tradition of the mishna, Ket. 12a. The strictness in caste loyalty among priests is found in the Septuagint translation of מעמיו "of his own tribe." Philo understands the law to prohibit a priest marrying out of his tribe. Geiger in *Ha-haluz* 1860 supports this view. Professor Ginzberg in *Kebuzat maamarim* p. 405, is of the opinion that מעמיו means of his people. He admits, though, that it was contrary to custom, if not to law, to have intermarriages between priests and Israelites. The feeling against such marriages is echoed in the Jerushalmi expression: שיהא אדם מדבק בשבטו ובמשפחתו Jer. Ket. 25c.

[60] This is the Tosefta tradition, Tos. Ket. 1, 2, cited also Ket. 12b. I should prefer the reading: הנושא בכהונה והנותן בה תקנה שהתקינו ב"ד. The Palestinian amoraim understood the higher mohar for intermarriages between priest and non-priest to be a kind of fine for marrying out of one's tribe. *Shitah mekubezet* reads into it a willingness on the part of priests to give a higher mohar even for an Israelitish daughter, in order to escape the censure of being haughty. Babli gives the correct interpretation in the words: דאיכא צד כהונה which means, it represents an aristocratic marriage, as aristocracy was then defined.

period.[61] Subsequent to that, however, the increased mohar as a token of distinctiveness is altogether lost; all brides get a mohar of two hundred zuzim.

Contradictory tannaitic traditions are recorded in the Talmud as to the special priviliges that priests ordained for themselves in the matter of mohar. One records only four hundred zuzim for the priestly virgin, and is altogether silent on the question of the mohar of the priestly widow. Another records two hundred zuzim for the priestly widow, that is, double the Israelitish mohar for the non-virgin. A third reports only a mohar of one hundred zuzim for the priestly non-virgin, like the mohar of the Israelitish widow or divorcee. The redactor of the Talmud draws from these contradictory reports a systematic account of the history of the mohar of the priestly non-virgin, and his account is in all likelihood true to fact.[62] The court ruling of a double mohar for the priestess applied only to the virgin originally. The non-virgin priestess

[61] Ket. 12b. This tradition is delivered in the name of Samuel. It should be added to the entire subject of the mohar of priests, that the Samaritans still have a double mohar for a priest's daughter.

[62] Ket. 12a-b. The term 'widow of priestly families' is interpreted by Rashi to mean a priest's daughter and, by *Shita mekubezet,* a priest's widow. I take the former to be correct and, furthermore, it represents not only the widow but the non-virgin in general, except that the divorcee could not remarry a priest.

R. Ashi correctly takes the tradition of the mishna recording the double mohar for the priestly virgin and omitting any mention of the priestly non-virgin, to mean that the non-virgin of the priestly family was given no advantage at all. This represents the first tradition. This has also been perpetuated among the Samaritans, as will be seen later. The second tradition is that of the beraita, giving the widow also a double mohar. The third tradition is that which the mishna quotes at the beginning.

felt humiliated to remain at the level of mohar of her Israelitish sister—only one hundred zuzim—and the enactment was extended to include also the non-virgin, granting her a mohar of two hundred zuzim, double that of the Israelitish non-virgin. This high standard could be maintained as long as priesthood represented superior aristocracy. When that glory dimmed, men would say, rather than give two hundred zuzim for a non-virgin of the priestly family, we shall marry at the same price a virgin of an Israelitish family. The market value of the former fell, and she had to give herself in marriage for the mohar of a hundred zuzim only.

The position of the Karaites with reference to mohar is as follows: They accept mohar as a Biblical institution, but they contend that the amount of mohar is not standardized by the Bible. The amount depends, therefore, on the social position of the couple. Furthermore, the Bible knew of two kinds of mohar, one paid at betrothal, the other paid at divorce; one marriage price, the other divorce price; the former derived from Exodus 22, 16, the latter implied in Exodus 21, 11. The former is designated as *mohar mukdam*, early mohar, the latter is called *mohar m'uhar*, late mohar; the former is given to the bride in cash and remains her personal property, the latter is paid at divorce or at the husband's death, but is not paid to the wife's heirs in the event of her death prior to her husband.[63]

The Samaritans also take mohar to be Biblical, even as to the standard amount. The virgin gets 4900 Egyptian kritas and the non-virgin approximately half of that amount. The above sum corresponds approxi-

[63] Cf. *Gan 'eden*, Nashim 2, *Aderet Elijahu*, Nashim 1, Neubauer, *Aus d. Petersburger Bibliothek*, p. 25 and Karaitic ketubot.

mately to the fifty shekels of the Bible. The virgin of a priestly family gets a mohar of 6100 Egyptian kritas —as among the Jews, an increase over the mohar of the Israelite, yet not in the proportion of two to one but in the proportion of five to four approximately. The non-virgin of a priestly family gets no advantage over any other non-virgin, even as we have seen such a tradition among the Jews. The Samaritan mohar, like that of the Karaites, is also divided into two parts, the one half given in cash at the wedding, the other kept by the husband in trust for his wife and paid to her at the husband's death or at divorce.[64]

[64] See Gaster's article on the subject in MGWJ, Vol. 54. The payment of mohar at divorce is not known now to the Samaritans, for they have not had divorce for several centuries, on account of the decline of their population and, therefore, the small chances for remarriage.

CHAPTER V

MATTAN

Social usage in antiquity required the groom to give presents to his bride at betrothal, which were technically named *Mattan,* voluntary gifts. No Biblical legislation is connected with this, for it was not considered a legal obligation, though definitely recorded in the Bible. Eliezer gives Rebecca gifts when her family accepts his proposal on behalf of Isaac,[1] and Shechem offers for the hand of Dinah both mohar and mattan as may be required of him by Jacob.[2] It is evident in these instances that mattan comprised not merely the random engagement gifts, later known as *Siblonot,*[3] but was really institutionalized and had official recognition in the marriage ceremony. It did not affect the legality of a marriage, nor was a definite standard prescribed as to amount or kind of mattan.

Originally mohar and mattan were both paid in cash, yet were clearly distinct from each other. The former was given to the father, the latter to the bride; the former was legal and compulsory, the latter social and voluntary; the former expressed the commercial

[1] Gen. 24, 22. Jacob brought no gifts to Rachel, and thus placed in a tragic plight, he broke into tears on meeting her. See Gen. R. 70, 12.

[2] Gen. 34, 12. Gen. R. 80, 7 translates מתן by *Paraphernon* This term in Greek means dowry, but its rabbinic use may be due to the fact that mattan was often added to the dowry which the woman received from her father and included together under the *nedunya.* Cf. Freund GES, p. 36.

[3] Gen. 24, 22, 53 seem to place *Siblonot* and mattan side by side.

side of marriage, the latter the romantic. In the final stage, however, mohar and mattan became so closely allied as to make it difficult to distinguish between them. Mohar, as we have seen, became an obligation on the husband, to be paid to his wife at divorce or death; and this point of development was also finally reached by mattan. The commercial nature of the one and the romantic character of the other were lost, but the practical consideration, to provide the woman against untoward conditions, became the motive for both. Neither affects the validity of the marriage in any way; they are nevertheless legal and compulsory obligations. Finally, allowing only for a certain amount of legal shading, both prescribe a standard sum. Hence, in rabbinic terminology, mohar and mattan are grouped together under the term ketubah, and when distinguished from each other are called *Ikar ketubah* and *Tosafot ketubah* respectively, taking the mattan as an addition to the mohar.

The mattan is entered into the ketubah in a special clause. It appears first in Papyrus G, following the mohar clause but in no way indicating the relation between them. The mattan clause found in rabbinic records appears to have followed the mohar clause, and designated the mattan as an addition to mohar—thus reading, "I have voluntarily added . . . . to the two hundred (of mohar)."[4] In some such manner is the mattan recorded also in post-Talmudic ketubot.[5]

[4] Ket. 43b.

[5] As in the case, for instance, of Ginzberg, Geonica, II, p. 78, mattan clause following that of mohar and containing the formula: ואוסיף על כתובתה so also Ketubah, ed. Schechter (JQR, 13, p. 220), that of REJ, 48, p. 173, Saadya Ketubah ed. Gaster (MGWJ, 54), Rashi, Ket. 47a, s. v. לימא, *Mahzor vitri*, *Magid*, Ishut 10, 8 quoting RSBA, and Yad, Yibbum 4, 32. Ketubah Jerushalmit, ed. Berliner, has הוסיף לה על קידושיה instead of the formula given above.

A slight deviation from this practice, however, is often found, in recording the mattan after the dowry clause, and in indicating the relation of mattan to mohar, as to character, and its relation to dowry, as to sum,[6] wherein the mattan clause reads in this wise: "and the groom has voluntarily given her in addition (to mohar), out of his own, a hundred zuzim, corresponding to these (articles of dowry):"[7] וצבי חתן דנן והוסיף לה מדיליה עוד מאה זקוקים כסף צרוף אחרים כנגדן. This has remained the usage among present-day European Jews. Theoretically, the mattan need not have a separate clause for itself, but may be included in the mohar clause as increased mohar;[8] yet, not a single ketubah is found where the scribe has availed himself of this permissible abbreviation.

The historical development of mattan is in many respects similar to the development of mohar, traced in the previous chapter. It began as a cash payment and, like mohar, turned into a promise inserted into the ketubah, maturing at the husband's death or at divorce. This change came about not through the enactment of Simeon b. Shetah, who is responsible for the corresponding change in the mohar. Remembering that mohar was a legal obligation but mattan only a voluntary social formality, one can easily see why the pressure for reducing the mohar did not apply to mattan. Mattan was not necessary for marriage, and

[6] *Sefer Hashetarot*, pp. 30, 55-56.

[7] The articles of dowry are estimated as of the value of a hundred zuzim, hence the meaning of this word כנגדן. In some ketubot, however, the word is omitted.

[8] So decided by Nachmanides, R. Nisim (Ket. 54b) RIBSh (Responsa, 68); Cf. *Magid*, Ishut 10, 7, Isserlis, EH 66, 7. Some authorities, however, prohibit mixing mohar and mattan in one clause. Cf. Tosafot Ket. 12b, s. v. בד' and Mordecai ibid. But, see *Helkat mehokek* EH 66, 30.

when required, the amount was not prescribed. And, if a certain social vanity was satisfied by the giving of large sums of mattan, the court did not seem quite interested in legislating on behalf of vanity.

No records going back to Temple days indicate in any way that mattan was promised and not given in cash. A cash payment of mattan is apparently reported by R. Jonathan b. Zakkai in the case of the marriage of the daughter of Nakdimon b. Gorion.[9] It is, therefore, to be assumed that during Temple days, mattan was still paid in cash. One generation later,

[9] According to the reading of Ket. 66b, the ketubah contained a million gold dinnars as dowry "besides her husband's gifts." Sifre, ed. Friedmann, p. 130a and Aboth d'R. Nathan, ed. Schechter, p. 33a read "a million gold dinnars from her father-in-law's possessions." According to either reading, mattan is here recorded in the ketubah. The circumstance in which the ketubah is cited is what leads me to the conclusion that the mattan was paid in cash. R. Johanan b. Zakkai finds the bride in poverty, and he wonders first where her personal money has gone, that which she brought from her father's house, her dowry (של בית אביך); secondly, where the mattan has disappeared. Should the assumption be that the bride at that time had already been widowed and the Rabbi expected her to obtain her mattan from her husband's estate, then של בית חמיך would not be the right technical term but נכסי הבעל; and then, again, there would be no point in making separate mention of dowry and mattan when both are due from the estate, and when in fact neither mohar nor mattan would be necessary, since all she asked was the maintenance due her by a special ketubah clause. And, besides, why should we introduce a circumstance which the tanna himself does not mention? All I can see is that R. Johanan b. Zakkai expected her to have money, either her personal property or her mattan.

If mattan in those early days was paid in cash, we shall understand the difference between the addition to the mohar introduced by the priests and the addition to the mohar represented by the mattan, the former credit, the latter cash. Hence, we need not resort to the forced explanation of Tosafot Ket. 12b, s. v. 'בד.

tannaim are found dealing with the case of a widow who seeks the payment of her mattan out of her husband's estate.[10] Evidently, the change in the case of mattan from a cash payment to a promise took place at about the fall of the Second Commonwealth. No court enactment is mentioned in connection with this change, and in all probability it came about through no official act whatever. At the basis of it was social pressure on the groom to keep up a high standard of mattan, which he could not afford to pay in cash, and which, therefore, following the example of mohar, he inscribed in the ketubah as a debt and secured by a lien on his property. Probably this method was resorted to at first only by individuals, who in conditions of poverty had to keep up an appearance of opulence; but with the fall of the commonwealth the practice became general because the generally impoverished Jew could not live up to the standards that he had been accustomed to.

The amount of mattan was not fixed, but varied according to the social position of the couple. As might naturally be expected, a sense of social distinction developed in connection with high and extravagant mattans. The humbler classes may have felt the sting of oppression under the extravagant standards of the rich, but in Talmudic days the rabbis made no attempt to establish a moderate standard of mattan.[11] Thus we have the mattan recorded in the Talmud ranging from a million dinars to a hundred zuzim.[12] The geonim recognized family standards, but in no way made these

[10] Ket. 54b. The date of this mishna is indicated by the citation of R. Elazar b. 'Azaria, of the first century of the common era.

[11] Ket. 54b.

[12] See Ket. 66b, 43a-44b. See also B. B. 40b.

standards compulsory on every marriage within those families.[13] In their time also local standards of mattan came to be known. An African standard, for instance, is reported of a mattan of 375 zuzim, to be added to the mohar of 25 zuzim, making a total of 400 zuzim.[14] Various sums of mattan are recorded in mediaeval ketubot, some representing individual cases, others local standards.[15] Standardization of mattan at a moderate level may be noticed, however, to have been the tendency since Talmudic days, culminating in the Sephardic and Ashkenazic standards. The former inscribe in their ketubot twelve hundred pieces Fuirtes, half of which is denominated an addition to the mohar, the other half a counter gift as against the dowry; the latter record in their ketubot a mattan of a hundred zuzim, which bears the double character of an addition to the mohar and a counter offer to the dowry.

In the standardization of mattan a few things should be noticed. First, the standard represented only the minimum, but in no way excluded the possibility of a higher mattan if the groom wished to give it. Secondly, the standard was not legally binding and might be reduced if the bride consented to it. Thirdly, the standard expressed itself in round figures, or raised the combined sum of mohar and mattan to four hund-

[13] Cf. Harkavey, *Responsa*, 210; *Responsa* of R. Meir Rothenberg, ed. Prague, 852.

[14] Harkavey, ibid. See also *Itur*, p. 58b.

[15] REJ, Vol. 48, p. 173, JQR, Vol. 13, p. 220. Tosafot Ket. 54b records a mattan of a hundred litters which is probably equal to the combination of 50 for mattan and fifty for dowry referred to by *Mahzor Vitri*. *Magid*, Ishut 10, 8 quotes a standard in the name of RSBA of a mattan of two hundred zuzim. *Itur* records a mattan of four hundred zuzim, of which only a third is ever paid. In Algiers, a court enactment required mattan for the virgin to be equal to half of the value of the dowry. Cf. *Responsa*, Duran (TShBZ), 2, 292, 1.

red zuzim—which is the mohar of priests—or established a certain proportion between the mattan and both mohar and dowry.[16] Therefore, although there is no source for it in the Talmud or the earlier codes, the mattan of the widow or divorcee has been standardized at half of the mattan of the virgin, to correspond to the same reduction in the mohar.[17]

Between the original stage of giving a cash mattan outright and the final stage of merely promising the mattan to be paid at the dissolution of the marriage, there was a middle stage of paying part in cash and leaving the balance a debt upon the husband. This usage is not found in the Talmud and is entirely lost in the modern Sephardic and Ashkenazic ketubot, but is found recorded in mediaeval documents, continuing to the present day in the Yemenite ketubah.[18] The cash mattan was termed *kiddushin* or "early mattan," or

[16] Illustrations of mattan in round figures are our own Ashkenazic ketubah, also Tosafot Ket. 54b. Mattan sometimes adds to the ketubah to make the total a round number. Thus *Itur* has a mattan which, added to the ketubah, makes the total a thousand. Illustrations of cases where mohar and mattan combined formed four hundred zuzim are found in *Responsa* Harkavey ibid. and our present Ashkenazic ketubah, where, however, the dowry is also included in the total sum.

Illustrations of the establishment of certain proportions between the mattan and either the mohar or dowry are found in Songs R. 4, 25: כדרך חתן להיות כופל כתובה של כלה, the Ashkenanazic and the Sephardic ketubot, *Mahzor Vitri*, Itur, and *Sefer hashetarot*, 56b (though, in this instance the zuzim of mohar become dinnarin in mattan).

[17] This represents our present practice. A similar reduction is made in the estimated value of the non-virgin's dowry. Cf. *Nahlat Shiv'ah*, 12, 47. R. Raphael Meldola, *Hupat hatanim*, ed. Lublin 1872, p. 31 states that the non-virgin gets no mattan at all.

[18] Cf. REJ, 48, p. 173, MGWJ, 54, *shetar erusin* ed. Gaster, Harkavey, *Responsa*, ibid. and a number of unpublished Genizah ketubot.

"early mohar;" the unpaid mattan was called "later mattan" or "later mohar." The early mattan, when received by the bride, became part of her dowry. It went back to the husband together with the gifts from the bride's father, and was entered into the ketubah under the heading of *nedunya*. Thus, the early mattan conferred double dignity on the couple, the dignity of the mattan itself and the dignity of a costlier dowry. If the husband wished the early mattan to remain the private possession of his wife and fully in her control, he would write a special deed, called *shetar mattanah lehud*, conveying that mattan to his wife under such terms as would annul his statutory dower right in it.[19]

The Samaritans and the Karaites have no mattan at all, but they divide their mohar in the same manner as the Rabbinites divide their mattan. We can trace no historic connection between them that would sufficiently account for their agreement in this respect. It is not improbable that the three sects independently followed the general non-Jewish custom of the day, which required the giving of certain moneys or property to the bride at the time of the marriage and to provide for certain payments in the event of the dissolution of the marriage. On the basis of inner Jewish life, we can venture an explanation of a sociological nature. Back of the development of mohar and mattan and nedunya is evident the operation of a conflict of two opposing forces. On the one hand, social aspirations tended to raise them to ever higher sums; on the other, economic conditions forced them down to lower levels. For the Rabbinites mohar was out of this conflict with the enactment of Simeon b. Shetah; but mattan fell under its sway. For the Samaritans and Karaites, to whom the enactment of Simeon b. Shetah

[19] *Sefer ha-shetarot*, pp. 56-57.

did not exist, mohar remained an object of conflict. The compromise between these opposing tendencies is represented by a part payment and an unpaid balance, remaining as a debt of the husband to his wife. This took the place of the Simeon b. Shetah enactment among the Samaritans and the Karaites, and became their established law and custom. That compromise which applied to the mohar of the Samaritans and Karaites applied also to the mattan of the Rabbinites. For the Rabbinites, however, this did not prove to be the final solution, for it was only a compromise and not a stable condition. The only stable condition they could create was to establish a standard mattan. Wherefore, the more widely the standard was recognized, the less general became the practice of giving the early and the late mattans.

Mattan, like mohar, was originally given to the bride at betrothal. Later, when mattan became a ketubah obligation instead of a cash payment, it was still considered as becoming effective from the moment of betrothal. R. Elazar b. 'Azariah is the first to declare that the obligation of mattan is effective only on the condition that nuptials take place. Should the marriage be dissolved prior to nuptials, therefore, mattan need not be paid.[20] The view of this tanna prevailed in the amoraic halakah, but the amoraim stressed the fact that not the nuptial ceremony but actual intercourse was necessary before the mattan obligation became effective.[21] In our final halakah we have the decision that mattan is not paid unless copulation had already taken place.

The dependence of mattan upon intercourse is responsible for a suspicion that has come to light that

[20] Ket. 54b.

[21] Ket. 55a-56a. See also Alfasi a. l.

mattan is in its origin a gift to the bride in reward for the enjoyment of the *nox prima,* what the Germans call *Morgengabe,* and that its illegitimate counterpart is the *Etnan,* the gain of a harlot.[22] Whether such an institution existed in antiquity in the Orient at all, in connection with legitimate marriage, is doubtful; in what form it existed or what relation it had to the marriage ceremonies, is unknown. The whole matter is, therefore, mere speculation. The mattan known to us from Biblical and rabbinical records in no way answers the description of *Morgengabe.* Mattan is offered by Shechem not in connection with cohabitation, which he obtained by violence. Rape and seduction appear to be theft of mohar, but not of mattan. The opponents of R. Elazar b. 'Azaria would obligate the husband to pay the mattan even if nuptials never took place. Their view is apparently the older one, for in all ancient ketubot mattan was entered, even though they were written at betrothal. The dependence of mattan upon copulation is merely one phase of the general process of shifting the husband's responsibilities from the moment of betrothal to that of nuptials. So far, we account for the view of R. Elazar b. 'Azariah. The next step, that of the amoraim and later rabbinic authorities, to limit the meaning of nuptials in this case to actual copulation, is prompted by their general principle to be as lenient as possible with the husband in matters of the ketubah, particularly in a voluntary obligation assumed by him.

Mattan appears more to be part of a systematic arrangement to provide for the couple after marriage.

[22] Cf. Freund, GES, pp. 36 f. He is also of the opinion that the term נדה of Ezekiel 16, 33, and *nudunu* of CH, 171-172 are synonymous with the *tosafot ketubah* of later terminology. He suggests that mattan may have originally been termed *nedunya.* Cf. B. M. 74b and Taanit 24a. See note 2, p. 78 above.

Mohar was the price and went to the bride's father. When the bargain was struck and the couple were on the threshold of becoming husband and wife, then the parents on both sides settled on the couple certain valuables or moneys to help them in their common life. That which the bride's father gave was dowry and that which came from the groom's father was mattan.[23] For the best interests of the couple, it was deemed advisable that the wife have the right of title and the husband the right of usufruct in these gifts. But each father gave his child, besides these presents, special gifts which were to remain the private possessions of the bride and the groom respectively. In the light of this scheme alone does mattan appear through the earlier records. The later records emphasize the need of providing for the bride against the eventuality of being widowed or divorced. It takes actual cash or valuables to provide the wherewithal to start home life, but a promissory note is sufficient guarantee for the woman against mishap in the marriage career. The latter idea wholly superceded the former, and hence mattan no longer provided for the marriage union but for the marriage dissolution.

[23] See Kid. 9b, B. B. 98b.

CHAPTER VI

Dowry

The records of antiquity often refer to the custom of the bride's father giving dowry to his daughter at her marriage. Early Babylonian records call it *Seriqtum;* the later Babylonian writers denominate it by the term *Nudunu,* a term that has gone over into the rabbinic writings, where it is called *Nedunya.*[1] Instances of dowry are not uncommon in the Bible. Sarah has a slave, Hagar; Rachel and Leah have Bilha and Zilpa as their slaves, given to them as part of the dowry.[2] Caleb gives his daughter a field and springs of water as *Berakah,* blessing, that is, a marriage gift with parental blessing, or rather, with parental care for her future comfort.[3] Pharao gives his daughter, the wife of Solomon, the city of Gezer as a wedding gift, which he calls *Shiluhim,* a "send off."[4] Papyrus G devotes a special clause to the enumeration of the dowry; the Book of Tobit speaks of a very liberal dowry, half of the father-in-law's possessions; and Sirach denounces men who marry for the lust of a large dowry.[5]

[1] Cf. note 22, p. 87 above. Cf. Freund GES, p. 38. That the term *nedunya* meant at one time the gifts of the husband to the wife and later denoted dowry is an indication that at one time the husband's gifts were of greater significance in the marriage, while at a later time the dowry was more important. The term remained, but its content changed. The terms *pherne, parapherna* and *ketubah* went through similar changes.

[2] See Gen. R. 45, 1: הגר שפחת מלוג היתה.

[3] Joshua 15, 18-19.

[4] I Kings, 9, 16.

[5] Ecclesiasticus 25, 20.

Among ancient peoples, dowry is commonly conceived as a daughter's share of inheritance in her father's possession. The sons succeed their father; the daughters leave him. In lieu of succession, therefore, the daughters on leaving receive their share of inheritance.[6] This is probably the conception of *Shiluhim*, sending the girl away from the parental estate, a settlement on her in lieu of inheritance. There must have been lingering in Jewish law at least a shadow of the teaching of Hammurabi, that the unmarried daughter gets a share in the estate of her father at his death because she has not received any dowry[7]—for Philo reports this to be the Jewish usage;[8] and later halakah corroborates Philo, not to the extent of giving the daughter's claims on her father's estate the status of succession, but to the extent of giving the unmarried daughter a statutory claim on the estate for maintenance prior to and dowry at marriage, as a practical substitute for succession. Throughout the halakah it is evident that the rabbis, fully aware that the daughter cannot have the status of an heir, feel that in some other legal form, one that most suits her needs, she is entitled to share the family fortune with her broth-

[6] Cf. Freund, GES, p. 41.

[7] CH 180.

[8] Tischendorf, *Philonea*, p. 41; Ritter, *Philo u. d. Halacha*, p. 96. In this light we may conjecture that the Mosaic legislation in connection with the daughters of Zelaphchad applied only to unmarried daughters, for married ones are out of their father's family and have their inheritance in the form of dowry. If this were not assumed by the Bible, the Bible would leave us in doubt as to the case of a man who died without sons, but who left daughters who prior to his death had married out of their tribe. Cf. Nachmanide's Commentary, Num. 36. See also B. B. 143b: ההוא דשדר פסקי דשיראי.

ers. Dowry is in that sense a substitute for succession.[9]

Next to the idea of succession and in the course of time superceding it, is the thought that dowry is a parental obligation in the interest of attracting suitors to the girls. The amoraim believe that this duty upon the father is Biblical.[10] One may seriously doubt, however, whether this particular conception of dowry is not altogether post-Biblical, for in Biblical days the position of the Jewish woman was such that bribes and baits were not offered to suitors but taken from them. The conception of dowry as an inducement to marriage is post-Biblical, and the duty upon the father to give dowry in that interest is one imposed on him by late tannaitic legislation.[11]

By the term dowry we understand the gifts which the bride's parents give to the couple at the wedding as a marriage portion, and it is distinct from the property or money received and owned by the bride, over which she exercises full and independent control. In Jewish terminology, dowry is called *zon-barzel*,[12]

[9] See Ket. 52b. Cf. Ket. 69a: בת יורשת הויא.

[10] Ket. 52b, based on Jer. 29, 6, but see also Ket. 53a on top, where it is termed a rabbinical enactment.

[11] The Talmud, Ket. 68a-69b, raises the question whether dowry is due the daughter by a special rabbinic statute or by the terms of the ketubah between father and mother. Of tannaitic sources some give the impression that dowry is a separate statute (Mishna Ket. 67a, the discussion between R. Hiya and Rabbi p. 68a above), others seem to indicate that it is part of the ketubah terms (Tos. Ket. 6, 1-3 and tannaitic texts cited Ket. 67b on top). If the latter teaching is correct, then it dates back to early tannaitic times. Cf. Freund, GES, p. 43 and notes.

[12] This term has a parallel in Roman law, *pecus ferreum*, and in Old German law, *Eisenvieh*, and represents not only a specific property arrangement between husband and wife, but every form of conveyance of property on a basis of tenancy

literally, iron-sheep, or *nedunya*[13] or *ketubah*[14] *or shum*;[15] while the private possessions of the bride are termed *mulug*[16] or *parapherna*.[17] The former is conveyed

and possession. A zon-barzel conveyance is legally superior to tenancy and inferior to title, but represents title to the property to the extent of the value of its fruit and insofar as the productivity is part of its capital value. The term according to Freund, GES, p. 40, note 4, is not derived from the Roman, but reflects a highly developed commerce in live cattle, whence this figurative term arose to denote 'iron security.' Cf. Jeb. 66a and Rashi on top, Bekorot 16b, B. M. 70b.

[13] This term is employed mainly by post-Talmudic writers. The tannaim never use it, and the amoraim use it only in three instances in the Talmud. It denotes to them mainly the trousseau. Taanit 24a, B. M. 74b, Ket. 54a. Cf. note 1, p. 89 above

[14] As dowry became important in marriage, the ketubah was looked upon as most prominently the record of the dowry. Hence the identification of ketubah and dowry. It is not very frequently employed in the Talmud, but see Sab. 130a, Jeb. 66b below, Derek Erez Zuta 10: והנושא אשה לשם כתובה, but the oldest use of the term ketubah in a sense distinctly inclusive of dowry is that of the *Ketubat b'nin dikrin* clause, Ket. 52b.

[15] *Shum* literally means that which is appraised, and designates a dowry of valuables, not cash, appraised at a certain value. Cf. Tos. Ket. 4, 13 and 6, 5-6, Jeb. 66b.

[16] Derived either from the Babylonian *Mulugu* or from the Greek *amelgo* or from the Latin *mulgeo* to milk. The rabbis themselves seek its origin (Jer. Jeb. 8a, Gen. R. 45, 1) but refer us to a standard phrase כמה דתימר מלוג מלוג which does not enlighten us. *Aruk* defines mulug as plucking, akin to the Latin sense of the word. It describes property of which the husband plucks the fruit without carrying any responsibility for the safety of the principal. Cf. Freund, GES, p. 45, note 2, Delitzsch, *Handwoerterbuch*, p. 412, *Fick, Assyrisches und Talmudisches*, Berlin 1903, p. 24. This term is used in tannaitic sources and in the writings of the Babylonian amoraim.

[17] The Palestinian amoraim employ this term, adopted from the Greek, but sometimes it means to them mattan. See Gen. R. 80, 7, and note 2 of p. 78 above. It is rendered in Hebrew characters: פרה פרנון or פראפרנון. Cf. Jer. Ket. 30b, 31c, Jer. B. B. 17d, Jer. Gittin, 47b, Jer. Nazir 54a. Although in Greece

under terms of tenancy to the groom, the latter is given outright to the bride; the former is entered into the marriage deed, the latter is not.[18]

Such a disitinction was known to the Babylonians in the time of Hammurabi;[19] and as far back as the fourth dynasty of the Babylonian monarchy, legal technical names were assigned to each of the two kinds of marriage portions.[20] But we have no record of any

the *parapherna* was also entered into the ketubah (Freund GES, p. 45), it was because Greek law gave the husband the right of possesion of all his wife's property, regardless of kind (Mitteis, Reichsrecht, p. 267).

[18] In Jewish law also the Greek term *pherne* rendered in Hebrew פרנא is employed for *zon-barzel*, but it is used in a variety of meanings more akin to the term *ketubah*. Septuagint translates כמהר הבתולות and מהר ימהרנו and Onkolos translates הרבו עלי מאד מהר by the term *pherne*, exactly as Mekilta remarks ואין מהר אלא כתובה. The deed of the ketubah itself is sometimes called *parna*. So are the terms of the contract including dowry, or specifically dowry, designated by that term. Cf. Jer. Ket. 29 b, 31c, 33a, 43b, Jer. Sotah 19a, Jer. B. B. 17a, Gen. R. 60, 13; 80, 7, Sab. 130a, Ket. 67a. A sociological explanation for the use of this term in so many senses is given by Freund, GES, p. 11, note 3. Frankel suggests that פרן comes from the Greek *antipherne* which represents an archaic use of the root, *pherne*, for in classical Greek, he insists, *pherne* can mean nothing else but dowry. Cf. Frankel in MGWJ, 1861.

[19] CH 147 indicates that women were permitted independent control of their property. As against that, CH 137, 138 gives the husband the possession of his wife's dowry either as tenant or guardian. Evidently the woman was in possession of her own private property, and the husband held her dowry as trustee.

[20] The woman's private property was termed *Mulugu* in a document of the fourth dynasty. See *Keilenschriftliche Bibliothek*, Vol. 4, p. 78. When it consisted of money, it was called *Kupu*. Peiser, *Babylonische Vortraege*, Nos. 10, 26, 88. The Talmudic קופה a fund of money, appears to be very close to it, but their philologic connection is rather unwarranted. For dowry the Babylonians use *seriqtum* and *nudunu*.

such order of things among Jews prior to the appearance of the ketubah. The Biblical dowry seems to represent parental gifts to the bride at the wedding, remaining her private possession, without even usufruct privilege for the husband.[21] The entire conception of *zon-barzel*, a kind of tenancy, is missing in the Bible. Dowry in Bible days, as was said above, savored of the conception of inheritance, not of a bait to men; therefore, it was not given to the groom at all. It was the bride's private possession.

Dowry as a wedding gift to the groom under terms of tenancy, and distinct from the bride's private property, is first recognized in the Assuan papyri.[22] It is termed "the property which she brought with her." Title to it rests with the bride; possession of it is given to the groom. He receives it under stipulated value, receipts it in the ketubah, manages it as tenant, uses it for his needs, guarantees its return to the bride at the dissolution of the marriage, and is liable for its loss or destruction to the amount of its stipulated value. He cannot sell it because title to it is held by the wife; she cannot sell it because of the husband's right of tenancy in it.

No doubt the social conditions that forced the enactment of Simeon b. Shetah to permit the husband to appropriate his wife's mohar under special guarantees exerted a like influence on the dowry. There was

[21] See Gen. 16, 1-6; 30 3-9; Jud. 17, 2-4; II Kings 8, 3-6 Cf. Freund GES, p. 45. The rabbis also are of the opinion that the husband's right of ususfruct in his wife's mulug is post-Biblical. Cf. Ket. 47b, 80a, Jer. Ket. 28d, etc. Cf. Benzinger, *Archaologie*.

[22] This is pointed out by Freund, GES, pp. 45-6, that כל זי הנעלת בידה represents property of one category and נכסיה וקנינה represents property of another category. He further points out that papyri C, D, E, F, K, speak of property belonging to Miphtahya outside of the dowry enumerated in papyrus G.

constant pressure in the direction of giving the husband greater privileges in his wife's dowry under the security of the lien clause. While there is no evidence that Simeon b. Shetah had anything to do with reforms concerning dowry, his lien clause helped to turn the husband's tenancy of his wife's marriage portion into practical ownership. The cash money of the dowry was immediately turned over to the husband with full title to it, for, in money, tenancy and ownership are very close to each other.[23] Greater freedom was also extended to the husband in the use of his wife's dowry articles, so that the wife's hold on these was gradually thinned down to being only a claim for payment of their stipulated value. The husband's tenancy, therefore, came to be conceived as an ownership of the wife's dowry for the enjoyment of his tenancy privileges. When, therefore, the Hillelites say, "The ketubah is held by the husband; the property that comes and goes with her is held by the wife," [24] we should in-

[23] It may be noted that the SBS formula of the lien clause is given in Tos. Ket. 12, 1 as: כל נכסי אחראין וערבאין לכסף כתובתיך while the other texts omit the word לכסף. May this not be due to the fact that the earlier authorities applied the lien clause only to cash money, but later authorities included in it also the articles of dowry, and therefore omitted the word לכסף?

We may also note that men were particularly interested in cash money as dowry. Thus a litigation between groom and father-in-law is cited in Ket. 108b over cash dowry—הפוסק מעות לחתנו; Abot d'R. Nathan, ed. Schechter, p. 33a, employs the phrase "money of thy father's house" to describe dowry; Kid. 9b describes to the negotiations between the groom's and the bride's fathers by the expression, "How much do you give your daughter?"

[24] In order to clear up the text itself on which we base our conclusions, we must first disentangle it from the maze into which the commentators involved it. The mishna reads: (I) "A woman awaiting levirate marriage who came into possession of property, according to the Shamaites and Hillelites,

clude under the first term mohar, mattan, and dowry, and under the second term the wife's private property. Save for some commentators, this interpretation of

may sell it and give it away, and the conveyance is valid." (II) "If she dies, what becomes of her ketubah and the property that comes and goes with her? The Shamaites say the husband's heirs and the father's heirs divide equally. The Hillelites say the property retains its former status; the ketubah is held by the husband's heirs; the property that comes and goes with her is accounted as held by the father's heirs." (Ket. 80b, Jeb. 38a).

a) This mishna is contorted by the amoraim (Jed. ibid.) because they see a contradiction between case I and case II. In one, even the Shamaites declare the mulug as definitely in the wife's *hazakah,* while in two they consider it as of doubtful *hazakah.* To this my answer is, it is not the doubtfulness of the *hazakah* that accounts for the Shamaitic view in case two, but the ineffectiveness of *hazakah* to settle a doubtful claim. Thus the *hazakah* of the ketubah is definite, yet even that is to be divided according to the Shamaites. Similarly, mishna B. B. 157a gives a case of a positive *hazakah* where the Shamaites order a division because the claim is a matter of doubt. The whole amoraic discussion is therefore superfluous. One thing becomes evident, however, from their discussion, that "the property that comes and goes with her" is understood by them to mean *mulug.*

b) Rashi and Tosafot (Ket. l. c.) and Maimonides (Mishna Commentary Jeb. l. c.) are committed to the reading וכתובה instead of כתובה in the Mishna. According to this reading the mishna has three terms, *nikasim* which means dowry, *ketubah* or mohar and mattan, and "the property that comes and goes with her," which refers to mulug. This reading must be rejected, even as it is by RID and R. Nissim and others, because the mishna refers to only two terms in the question: מה יעשו בכתובתה ובנכסים הנכסין ויוצאין עמה. *Nikasim,* therefore, must be taken as a general term including both *ketubah* and "the property that comes and goes with her."

The source of the eroneous reading is mishna B. B. 158a: "A house fell on the husband and wife together. His heirs say the wife died first and the husband next; her heirs say the husband died first and the wife next. The Shamaites say, they divide; the Hillelites say the property (*nikasim*) retains its former status; the ketubah is accounted as held by

the view of the Hillelites is true to tradition and yields the inference that already in Temple days was title of a kind granted to the husband in his wife's dowry.

the husband's heirs; the property that comes and goes with her is accounted as held by the heirs of the (wife's) father." In comment upon this mishna the amoraim ask: בחזקת מי R. Johanan says the *hazakah* is that of the husband's heirs; R. Elazar says the *hazakah* is that of the wife's heirs; R. Simeon b. Lakish says they divide equally, quoting a beraita of Bar Kapara to that effect. Now, what may this amoraic discussion mean, the commentators ask themselves. Hence they conclude that נכסים בחזקתן is a separate term, referring to dowry, which remains unexplained in the Hillelitic statement. The parallelism between this mishna and the one in Ket. and Jeb. is evident. Therefore, if the reading וכתובה is impossible there, it is also impossible here. Furthermore, that נכסים בחזקתן according to R. Simeon b. Lakish, should mean they shall divide equally is evidently far fetched, and represents in fact a concession on the part of the Hillelites to the Shamaites. Again, one might ask why the amoraic discussion of B. B. is omitted in Ket. and Jeb? See *Shita Mekubezet* ad B. B. l. c. Tosafot ibid. and Ket. l. c. and *Sefer Hajashar* of R. Tam, 6, 57.

The truth is that the words כתובה בחזקת יורשי הבעל נכסים הנכנסין ויוצאין עמה בחזקת יורשי האב do not belong to the mishna in B. B. at all, but have been taken over from Ket. and Jeb. by a scribe after the days of the amoraim. My arguments are the following: (a) This mishna is one of a series of three with the formula נכסים בחזקתן, summarizing the view of the Hillelites, without further additions. (b) The talmudic question בחזקת מי appears to follow the simple statement נכסים בחזקתן, else the question itself is indefinite. (c) The words כתובה בחזקת יורשי הבעל נכסים הנכנסין ויוצאין עמה בחזקת וכו' are a direct answer to the question of מה יעשו בכתובתה ובנכסים הנכנסין ויוצאין עמה which question occurs in Ket. and Jeb. but not in this mishna. (d) The words בחזקת יורשי האב do not fit properly into the context of this mishna, for the litigants are יורשי הבעל and יורשי האשה. Hence my conclusion that the mishna here simply cited in the name of the Hillelites נכסים בחזקתן. Now, to the amoraim its exact application was a problem. It was evident that the *hazakah* of the ketubah was definitely the husband's, and possibly this was all that the Hillelites meant to teach, but how apply this principle to the private property

At about the beginning of the second century Jewish law adopted the term *zon-barzel,* to describe any tenancy which implied a capital ownership of the ob-

of the wife, in which title belonged to the woman but possession was enjoyed by the husband? The mishna in Ket. and Jeb. which lays down the rule . . . כתובה בחזקת יורשי הבעל נכסים בחזקת יורשי האב could not be applied here, for in the case of the levirate woman, her full possession of her mulug is definite —witness the fact that she can sell her mulug—but the mulug of a married woman has quite a different status. The amoraim could be guided only by their own logic, and so to R. Johanan it appeared that mulug was of the husband's *hazakah;* to R. Elazar it seemed that the title should be the determining factor; while R. Simeon b. Lakish feels that the *hazakah* of a married woman's mulug in the case of litigation cannot be determined.

c) We are, therefore, now left with a simple text which declares in the name of the Hillelites that the husband has the *hazakah* of the keutbah, and the wife has the *hazakah* of the "property that comes and goes with her." The question remains as to where the dowry belongs—to ketubah or to "the property that comes and goes with her?" In this I follow the traditional interpretation of the amoraim that "the property that comes and goes with her" describes only mulug, and that dowry is counted under "ketubah." The term ketubah is used to designate also dowry in the *Ketubat benin dikrin* (Cf. Ket. 52b) formula. Here the context even suggests that dowry is included in the term ketubah, for, the situation being that the levir is a doubtful heir, the Hillelites teach that no claim is honored because the burden of proof is on the claimant. Now, dowry represents a ketubah claim, for were the ketubah not recognized, there would be no record of dowry. Regardless of the status of dowry, until her ketubah is ordered paid, she does not get actual possession of her dowry but has only a ketubah record of her title to or lien on her dowry. Hence, even in respect to the legal principle, the dowry falls under the category of "ketubah." It must be admitted, though, that the other interpretation, namely, putting dowry in the category of "the property that comes and goes with her" is not impossible. But it sounds unnatural to me and, at least, it has nothing in its favor to permit us to reject the traditional view. It sounds unnaural for this reason: the dowry would have to be divided between the two terms, for surely cash money would belong under the term "ketubah."

ject of the tenancy.[25] This term was adopted together with the principle that the tenant is the owner for all legal purposes. From this time on the law is perfectly definite that the husband and not the wife is the owner of the dowry during the time of the marriage. If, therefore, the husband be a priest, the zon-barzel slaves may eat of the heave offering, even if the wife herself is denied that right.[26] According to Biblical law, the loss of a tooth or an eye caused by the master to his slave gives him his freedom. The master in the case of zon-barzel slaves, it is declared by the rabbis, is the husband, not the wife.[27]

With title to dowry thus vested with the husband, the wife's sale of her dowry is naturally void. All she can sell is her claim to her dowry, which is of no value unless she be divorced or survive her husband.[28] Yet the fact that genetically and historically the dowry is really hers is not altogether ignored by the law. The

[25] The first mention of the term *zon-barzel* is found in Mishna Jeb. 66a where the term is defined as also the term mulug. In the *takanat Usha* (Ket. 50a, B. K. 88b) the term mulug is used as of certain meaning without need of definition. Hence the mishna referred to must be somewhat prior to the *takanat Usha*, or about the beginning of the second century. The term *zon-barzel* as a general name for that special kind of tenancy, is found in mishna Bekor. 16a and B. M. 70b. Cf. the amoraic discussion in both of these instances as to the legal ownership of *zon-barzel*.

[26] Jeb. 66a, Tos. Jeb. 9, 1.

[27] Jeb. 66b. Jer. Jeb. 8a quotes a tradition that neither zon-barzel nor mulug slave is freed by the loss of a tooth or an eye caused either by the husband or the wife (part of that tradition is quoted in B. K. 89b). Evidently this tradition leaves out of account the question of ownership, and renders its decision on the basis of a view expressed by R. Elazar that this Biblical legislation excludes any case where title is divided between two or more people. Cf. B. K. 90a.

[28] Tos. Jeb. 9, 1, B. K. 89a.

husband is not permitted to sell any of her dowry articles[29] and his sale of dowry realty is void unless there is positive proof of her consent to the sale.[30] At divorce, she can demand the return of her dowry, as much of it as is left, even if the husband would rather give her its cash value.[31] In Talmudic days this law operated entirely to her advantage, for she was paid for depreciation even as she had to pay her husband for appreciation. But a geonic enactment declared that the husband need not pay for depreciation of dowry if he returns the original dowry article, so long as they retain some of their original usefulness.[32]

The early halakah prescribed no standard amount of dowry, and in practical life the lack of any standard is but too evident in all ketubah records. Fathers gave according to their generosity and means. In the Talmud, dowries range from zero[33] through four hundred zuzim,[34] a thousand dinarim,[35] a million gold dina-

[29] Cf. mishna Gittin 5, 6, Jer. Ket. 30d, B. K. 102b, Yad, Mekirah 30, 5. Whether his sale of *zon-barzel* personalty is valid is a matter of discussion between Maimonides and RSBA. Cf. Yad, Mekirah, 30, 4 and Magid thereto.

[30] Jeb. 66b, Gittin 55b, B. B. 49b. According to some commentators, his sale without her consent is valid at least for the time being until the wife claims her ketubah (RSBM, B. B. 49b and Tosafot ibid. 50a). According to Rashi, the sale is valid but she can annul it (Rashi Jeb. 66b). According to R. Hananel (Tosafot Jeb. 66b), the sale is altogether void. This opinion is corroborated by Jer. Jeb. 8a. Cf. Alfasi Gittin 41a and Jeb. 66b, Yad, Mekirah 30, 4-5, Malveh 18, 4, *Eben Haezer* 90, 13.

[31] Jeb. 66a-b. An amoraic opinion is expressed that the choice is left with the husband whether to give the wife the dowry articles or their value in cash, but the law decides against this amora.

[32] Cited by Alfasi Jeb. 66a-b. See Yad, Ishut 22, 35.

[33] Mishna Ket. 67a.

[34] Ket. 54a-b, B. M. 104b.

[35] Ket. 66a, Jeb. 67a.

rim,[36] up to the very last zuz of the father-in-law's possession.[37] Nor is any standard to be noticed in the mass of Genizah ketubot.[38]

The tannaim, and later the amoraim, however, did not leave us altogether without guidance as to the standard of dowry. They make it compulsory on every father to give his daughter at least a dowry of fifty zuzim, an amount sufficient to buy a woman's wardrobe for a year. To the tannaim it meant fifty zuzim of pure silver, to the amoraim, fifty current zuzim, an eighth of the value of pure silver.[39] In the same manner, a dowry of fifty zuzim must be provided for the orphaned girl out of her father's estate.[40] Where the estate is insufficient or the father too poor to give the minimum dowry, the charity fund supplies it.[41]

An upper limit was not known to the tannaim. Only

[36] Ket. 66b.

[37] Ket. 53a. Cf. Ket. 54a-b, and 66a-b.

[38] A ketubah dated Egypt, 1030, contains a dowry of fifty gold dinarim (REJ 48, p. 173); another of the same place and approximately the same date records a thousand gold dinarim as dowry (JQR 13, p. 220). No principle of uniformity nor any similarity can be traced in the other genizah ketubot.

[39] See Ket. 64b, 65b, 67a, Tos. Ket. 6, 4.

[40] The portion of the estate that is set aside as dowry for the unmarried daughter is technically termed *Parnasah.* It differs legally from ordinary dowry, which the father gives while alive, in that the latter represents only a moral obligation on the father while the former—according to certain authorities—represents an obligation contracted for by the father under the ketubah clause, which specifies that the daughters will be supported out of the estate. The necessary supplies for marriage is included in support. See Ket. 68b, 69a. Brockelman, *Syrische Grammatik,* derives the term *Parnasah* from the Greek *pronoös.* Frankel, MGWJ 1861 connects it with *pherne.* It came more especially to mean clothes, which always formed the most prominent item in the dowry. See Ket. 68a.

[41] Ket. 67a.

where the dowry had to be drawn from the father's estate was the dowry definitely fixed by the tannaim, either on the basis of an estimate of what the father might have given, had he been alive,[42] or on the mathematical basis employed by R. Judah Ha-nasi—namely ten percent of the estate.[43] The father himself had no restrictions. To the amoraim, however, it appeared that excessive dowries deprive the sons of their rightful inheritance[44] and, therefore, they ruled that the father himself be not permitted to give his daughter a dowry exceeding ten percent of his possessions.[45]

Local usages, however, have developed prescribing standards of dowry, which standards were probably followed in most marriages in the respective localities, but were never legally binding on every couple. The first instances of a standard dowry are that of *Mahzor Vitri,* a French legal work of the twelfth century[46] and *Sefer Ha-shetarot,* a Spanish work of the same date.[47] These two are probably the fore-runners of the Sephardic and Ashkenazic standards of dowry in vogue today, which have at least one thing in common—that the dowry is equal in sum to the mattan.[48] So long as

[42] Ket. 68a.

[43] Ibid. and Tos. Ket. 6, 3.

[44] Ket. 53a. See Asheri Ket. 24, Mordecai Ket. 162.

[45] Ket. 52b. The halakah is stated in the name of Raba and Abaya.

[46] P. 791. The dowry is fifty littres, probably identical with the dowry referred to by Tosafot Ket. 54b, totalling 100 littres for dowry and mattan combined.

[47] P. 56. A thousand dinarim is given as the dowry. Its correspondence with the mattan which is found in our Sephardic ketubah is not yet given in *Sefer Hashetarot.*

[48] The Askenazic ketubah has a mattan and nedunya of 100 zuzim each, the Sephardic has standardized each at 600 pieces Fuirtes. In our ketubah the word כנגדן added at the end of

a standard dowry was not in vogue, the ketubah actually enumerated every article of dowry and appraised it at its market value, but with the introduction of the standard, the listing of articles in the ketubah was done away with, and in its stead came a formal statement that the bride brought with her—whether she actually did or did not—the usual household and personal objects; and that the groom accepted them at the value of the amount standardized by custom. Thus every Ashkenazic ketubah gives the dowry clause in the following form:

"And this is the dowry which she brought him from her father's house, consisting of silver, gold, jewelry, wearing apparel, household utensils, and bedding, all of which he accepted at the value of one hundred zuzim."

It is interesting to note a few of the earlier local customs in connection with dowry, prior to the time of its standardization, customs aiming in most cases to give the marriage an appearance of aristocracy and wealth. R. Jose of Galilee reports a custom of the bride's father offering, instead of real dowry, a note of indebtedness as his daughter's marriage portion.[49]

the mattan clause conveys the idea that the mattan was given in return for the nedunya, hence the equation between them. Sometimes the nedunya clause precedes and sometimes follows the mattan clause. Of the former kind are Ginzberg, *Geonica* II, p. 78, Rashi Ket. 47a and B. M. 104b, Tosafot B. B. 94b, R. Hananel ibid., *Mahzor Vitri* and the present day Sephardic and Ashkenazic ketubot. To the latter group belong JQR 13, p. 220, Saadya ketubah, MGWJ 54, and Yad, Yibbum 4.

[49] Tos. Ket. 4, 13. B. M. 104b. The interpretation here given of the text is that of Rashi. Another interpretation is possible, namely that it represents a note of indebtedness issued by the husband as security for the dowry. If this were the case it would correspond to כתובת אשה שזקפן במלוה (Gittin 18a) which is treated not as a local custom but as a general practice.

That was not altogether unfair, since the groom gave nothing more than a note for his mohar and mattan, and it served the purpose of enabling poor people to make a rich appearance. This custom was not more than local in Talmudic times, but it seems that it was more generally accepted in post-Talmudic days, for we hear too often of litigations between groom and father-in-law about the unpaid dowry. The same tanna reports another local custom, that of appraising the dowry at double its value, honoring the dowry clause in the ketubah, therefore, when presented for collection, at half its face value.[50] The gain in this custom was merely the fact that the dowry clause in the ketubah sounded rich to the wedding guests. This practice persisted even through the amoraic period, and yielded in geonic times to the general practice of overvaluating the dowry—resulting in much litigation, where the woman demanded the face value of the ketubah and the husband claimed a reduction for over-valuation. A gaon denounces this practice as "robbery and extortion" and stresses the need for truthful appraising of the dowry at its market value.[51] Hence, the geonic ketubah often has the following statement in connection with the dowry: "and this dowry was delivered into the hand of the groom, and we (witnesses) saw that it was worth the amount stated above."[52] From tannaitic times we also hear of a custom of augmenting the dowry by adding to it the mattan which the bride received from the groom. In other words, the mattan received by the bride was returned

[50] Tos. Ket. 4, 13; B. M. 104. Cf. also Tos. Ket. 4, 6 and an elucidation of it in Jer. Ket. 30d.

[51] Ginzberg's *Geonica* II, pp. 77-78; Yad, Ishut 23, 11. *Lehem Mishna* feels some difficulty in Yad believing that it was based on Ket. 66a instead of this geonic utterance.

[52] *Geonica* ibid. See Ketubah Jerushalmit, ed. Berliner.

to the groom as dowry.[53] This custom too continued through geonic times, but the gaonim disapproved of it, for it made the same objects mattan and dowry at the same time and confused time honored institutions.[54]

Another local custom originating in tannaitic days and lasting through geonic times is that of recording in the ketubah an addition of fifty percent to the cash money brought by the bride as dowry and a reduction of twenty percent from the market value of the dowry articles. For, it is estimated that the groom would be willing to add fifty percent for the use of cash throughout his married life, and equally, the wife would be glad to reduce twenty percent of the value of her dowry articles for the security which the husband offers for these articles.[55] While in tannaitic days this custom appears to have been only local, later rabbinic literature has given it more general recognition, applying this standard of calculation to all ketubot, unless the contrary was the specific local custom or the specific provision of the ketubah. Some post-Talmudic ketubot definitely record the overvaluation of the cash money of the dowry.[56] Our present day ketubot leave out any mention of it, but according to certain authorities, the hundred zuzim of mattan is calculated to pay the fifty percent addition to the cash money of the dowry.[57]

Referring back to a conclusion reached in a previous chapter, namely, that the ketubah was originally written at betrothal, we add the further inference that the dowry was originally transferred to the groom's

[53] Jeb. 66b; Yad, Ishut 23, 11.

[54] *Geonica* ibid.

[55] Ket. 66a-b; Tos. Ket. 6, 5-6; Jer. Ket. 30c-d.

[56] Cf. *Itur*, ed. Lemberg, pp. 42b-43a, *Bet-Hadash ad Tur Eben Haezer*, 66, *Bet-Shemuel*, ad *Eben Haezer* 66, 23, *Noda' Biyehudah* 100.

[57] Cf. *Nahlat Shiv'ah*, 12, 50.

keeping at betrothal and from that moment on his rights in it were established. If this were not so, then a ketubah written at betrothal would be impossible, for the date of the ketubah would antedate the actual conveyance of the dowry, secured by a lien—which constitutes in Jewish law a falsification and invalidates the deed. To be sure, there are sufficient reminiscences in the Talmud of the older practice of conveying the dowry to the groom at betrothal. The mishna justifies the groom who refuses to enter into nuptials with his betrothed on the ground that the father-in-law did not deliver the promised dowry.[58] A late beraita declares that the agreement for dowry between the parties, followed by betrothal, constitutes a legal conveyance.[59] Another beraita cites a case of a bride whose ketubah contained a dowry of fruit, clothes, and vessels, and who died prior to her nuptials. In the question as to who gets the dowry, R. Nathan (of the second century) rules that it goes to the husband, against his colleagues who grant it to the father.[60] Another beraita distinctly suggests that it is possible that the dowry be in the groom's possession or in the father's hands prior to the nuptials.[61]

[58] Ket. 109a.

[59] Kid. 9b. The words הנקנין and קנו mean legally a conveyance concluded, although transfer has not been made.

[60] Ket. 47a. The logical interpretation of this text is that of Rashi, which I follow here. Nahmanides in *Milhamot* adds geonic authority to this interpretation. The interpretation of R. Tam, RID, and *Hamaor* differs.

[61] Tos. Ket. 4,4 and Ket. 48b. This beraita belongs either to the time of the *mishna aharona* because of its similarity to mishna Ket. 48b; or it is somewhat later, because its restrictions in the matter of the bride's eating of the heave offering are serverer than those of the *mishna aharona*—for *traditio puellae* is not considered sufficient. The doubt in this matter consists mainly in the question whether the words במה דברים אמורים in the beraita are original or a later addition.

CHAPTER VII

MULUG

Mulug is the term employed in rabbinic literature to designate the wife's private estate. The term is of foreign origin[1] and was adopted in Jewish legal terminology about the beginning of the second century.[2] In Biblical times, mulug and dowry are not distinguished from each other. Biblical dowry corresponds in legal status to later mulug. A distinction may have existed between such mulug as the woman may have come bv from any other source, and mulug which was her father's wedding gift. The legal distinction between mulug and dowry, as was said above, was noted first in the Assuan papyri, where mulug is described as "her property and possession." In the earlier tannaitic sources it is denominated "the property that comes and goes with her." [3]

In the earlier records mulug is in the fullest sense the wife's private property, to which the husband is a total stranger. Whatsoever privileges he may seek in his wife's mulug, he can obtain only with the wife's free consent.[4] The law gave him none. The wife had full freedom to dispose of her own property and to deal with it wholly independently of her husband.[5] This

[1] See note 16, p. 92 above. See also note 20, p. 93.

[2] See p. 99 above and note 25 thereto.

[3] See note 22, p. 94 and note 24c, p. 98.

[4] This is evident in the Biblical records of the patriarchs treating their wives' slaves as their wives' private property. See also note 21, p. 115.

[5] Papyri E and F of the Assuan papyri give dealings of the woman independently of her husband. See also note 19, p. 93.

applied to mulug which the wife received as a wedding gift, as well as to any other private property she may have come by prior to betrothal, after betrothal, or after marriage. At the end of the Second Commonwealth, the first restriction was introduced. The schools agreed that "as to the property acquired by the wife after nuptials, if she sold it, the husband can claim it back from the purchaser." The reason for this legislation was that the husband is a part owner of the property, since the wife acquired it at a time when she herself was owned by the husband. Rabban Gamaliel found this legislation already established; he calls it *Hadashim,* a new institution, but disapproves of it.[6] The Hillelites who represented the newer tend-

[6] Mishna Ket. 78a. Amoraic and post-Talmudic authorities have complicated the issues involved in this mishna. As I read it on the basis of its apparent content, I find three cases cited by the Shamaites and Hillelites. (1) Mulug acquired prior to betrothal, in which both agree that no restrictions are made against the woman's exclusive rights. This represents also the mulug gotten by the bride as a wedding gift from her father. (2) Mulug acquired during the period of betrothal; the Shamaites permit its sale, the Hillelites prohibit it; both, however, agree that legally the sale is valid. (3) Mulug acquired after nuptials, where both agree that the wife has no legal power to sell. The question involved is how far is the husband's right over his wife's acquisitions to be driven. Shall he get only her earnings, or the things she may find, or even the things given to her personally or inherited by her from a relative? The time when the sale is made by the wife does not matter; what matters is the time when the acquisition was made by the wife. In support of this interpretation, I have the evidence of the *Gemara* itself in the expression בזכותו נפלו (ibid.) or (Jer. Ket. 32a) משנתארסה לזכתו ולזכתה נפלו. Hence, Rashi's inference that case (1) implies that the woman sold it during the period of betrothal is not quite correct, and is really in itself difficult—as RSBA points out clearly (in Tosafot Ket. ibid.). Hence also the amoraic question לימא תנינא לתקנת אושא

ency sought further to restrict the woman's liberty with her property. They taught that the property which she acquired after betrothal she may not sell, although legally the sale would be valid. Rabban Gamaliel opposed this restriction. He went even further. Property acquired by her after betrothal may be sold by her, he taught, even after the nuptials.[7] He was

is fully answered, for this mishna refers to the special condition of the mulug being acquired after nuptials. Otherwise, the amoraic answer to their own question cannot hold water, for if the Shamaites and Hillelites have made the sale of mulug impossible what need was there for the Takanat Usha, whatever their special object may have been? Rashi's comment on מתניתן בחייה ולפירות is altogether forced, in view of such expressions as מכרה בטל. See also Tosafot Ket. 78b s. v. לימא.

The academy of Rabban Gamaliel wished to restrict case (2) further, namely to declare the husband a part owner in the mulug acquired by the wife during the period of betrothal, for to them it seemed that there should be little difference between betrothal and nuptials as regards the husband's rights over his wife. Rabban Gamaliel did not permit that restriction, for he argues that the "new reform"—granting the husband part ownership in mulug acquired after nuptials—is in itself unjust, and you cannot build further reforms of the "old" on top of it. Then, the academy sought to introduce the additional question, not touched upon so far by the Shamaites and the Hillelites, namely the time of the sale. They argued, therefore, that in case (2)—mulug acquired during the period of betrothal—even if the woman has the legal right to sell it prior to the nuptials, she should not be able to sell it after nuptials. Raban Gamaliel did not concede even that much, for to him as to the Shamaites and Hillelites, the time of sale did not matter. Cf. Jer. Ket. 32a אילו הן חדשים משנישאת which forms the source for the different interpretations of the terms *Hadashim* and *Yeshanim*. Significant for my interpretation of these terms is the expression in Jer. ibid אלא שאתם מגלגלין חדשים על הישנים. Cf. Freund GES, p. 49, note 1.

[7] Whether Rabban Gamaliel permitted her to sell or, while prohibiting her to do so, declared the sale legally valid, depends upon two readings in the texts of Mishna Ket. 78a and Tos.

alone in his insistence on the woman's freedom to do with her property as she chose, for his disciples opposed him, declaring that she had no freedom in any of her mulug save that which was given to her prior to betrothal. Rabban Gamaliel's view seemed to prevail, and so for a considerable period after temple days the woman's freedom in her mulug wedding gifts was not at all challenged; her freedom in mulug which she acquired after betrothal was legally upheld; and the law restricted her freedom only with mulug which she acquired after nuptials. This last restriction was evidently due to the new conception that the husband, by the ownership of his wife, is a party to the acquisitions made by her after nuptials.

Two considerations were introduced after Rabban Gamaliel's day further to limit the wife's exclusive rights in her property. In the first place, the husband is heir to his wife. How can she be permitted to disregard his right of succession altogether? Therefore the academy at Usha, about the time of the Bar Kochba

Ket. 8, 1. That both these texts have different readings of the same tradition is known to the amoraim. The Palestinian Talmud does not seek to change either text, but records the mishna reading מוכרת ונותנת and the Tosiphta reading מכרה ונתנה. The Babli seeks to change one of the texts to agree with the other. Just how the change is to be made is a matter on which commentators differ. See Tosafot Ket. 78b s. v. תני and the Arabic text of Alfasi, printed in the Wilna 1912 edition of the Talmud. As a matter of conjecture, the original statement of Rabban Gamaliel was probably מוכרת ונותנת and the change to מכרה ונתנה was prompted in amoraic days by the feeling that Rabban Gamaliel would not side with the Shamaites against the Hillelites. This feeling, however, is unfounded, for in his entire position in this question Rabban Gamaliel is evidently on the side of the Shamaites and even more conservative than they in preserving the old freedom for the wife in her mulug.

rebellion, ruled that after the wife had sold any mulug, if she died first, the husband could reclaim it from the purchaser.[8] In the second place, the husband has a right to expect certain privileges in his wife's private property and the law has really granted him the right of usufruct. What becomes of all this, if the wife is permitted to sell her mulug? Therefore, R. Simeon b. Yohai, of the same period, rules that the woman is never permitted to sell her mulug—yet the sale is valid only if the husband had no knowledge of that mulug nor even had reason to expect it.[9]

[8] Ket. 78b. The amoraim comment upon this Usha *takanah* that it gives the husband a legal right to his wife's mulug, which is *sui generis*, not based on any known legal principle. The husband is better than an heir to his wife's mulug, for were he only an heir, he would lose his right by the wife's selling her mulug during her lifetime. He is better than a tenant or a mortgagee. He is apparently given the status of a purchaser—although, he has only the right of usufruct and no capital right—for the law considers him as if he had from the moment of the marriage bought the mulug for the yield of its fruit. He is even a degree better than that, for, even those who maintain קנין פירות לאו כקנין הגוף דמי, "the purchase of something for the yield of its fruit does not constitute ownership of the capital," admit that the husband's claim upon the mulug does constitute ownership of the capital of the mulug. Cf. B. B. 139a-b. B. K. 88b-90a, B. M. 35a and 96b. According to *Takanat Usha*, it is taken by the codifiers, the sale is valid for the lifetime of the wife, but the husband's rights supercede those of the purchaser at the wife's death. Cf. Yad, Ishut 22, 7.

[9] Ket. 78a. The definition of what is "known and expected" and what is "unknown and unexpected" is in itself a matter of legal import. According to some, all realty belongs to the former, all personalty belongs to the latter; according to others no property is considered unexpected unless it be an estate of a relative residing beyond the seas left to the wife. Cf. Ket. ibid., Jer. records this last opinion in the following way—"an inheritance which she came by while her husband was away beyond the seas." Cf. Yad, Ishut, 22, 8. Later halakah rules

The concluding and complete restriction of the woman's right and freedom in her own mulug came with the legislation of R. Judah Nesiah in Palestine, and Rab and Samuel in Babylonia at the beginning of the amoraic period—that a married woman has no legal power to sell any of her mulug whether acquired before betrothal or after nuptials.[10]

So systematic and complete were the restrictions and the curtailment of the woman's right in her own property that the richest woman was for all practical purposes penniless. Therefore, a mishna sums up the pitiful poverty of a married woman in the following words: "A woman and a slave are bad opponents: whoever injures them is liable for damage, but they are not liable for injury to others" [11]—since they have nothing to pay with. Often the Talmud asks: "How can a woman have anything; whatever is hers belongs

that the sale of unknown property can be valid only prior to the husband's getting knowledge of it. Cf. Asheri Ket. 79b, *Eben Ha'ezer*, Ket. 90, 12. It appears that the amoraim knew of no such restriction, else a definition for the terms known and unknown would not be necessary.

[10] This agreement between R. Judah Nesi'ah and Rab and Samuel (Ket. 78b) is not conceded in Tos. Ket. 8, 1 and Jer. Ket. 32a, for they report that Rabbi Judah (רבותינו) refers to the specific case of property acquired during betrothal and sold by the wife after nuptials. It is strange that the codifiers do not concede that the enactment of *Rabbotenu* or Rab and Samuel restricted the woman even above that of *Takanat Usha.* The further restriction, as I understand it, consists in the fact that according to *Takanat Usha* the sale is valid until the husband becomes heir; while according to Rab and Samuel the sale is altogether invalid, for they extend the ruling of the mishna to apply also to property acquired at any time, and in the mishna הבעל מוציא מיד הלקוחות is definitely synonymous with מכרה בטל. Probably the codifiers rely on the *Gemara* statement מתני׳ בחייה ולפירות and apply this also to Rab and Samuel. Cf. Yad, Ishut 22, 7.

[11] B. K. 87a.

to her husband?"[12] What is his is his and what is hers is also his. Her mohar and mattan are his, her zon-barzel and mulug are his, her earnings and what she may find in the street are also his. The household articles, even the crumbs of bread on the table, are his. Should she invite a guest to the house and feed him, she would be stealing from her husband.[13] If she works in her husband's store, he can at any time summon her before the court to testify under oath that she has not stolen anything of the earnings or the stock of the store.[14] She has only one chance left to her. Should the husband die first, she would regain her dowry, her mohar and mattan, and her mulug. That chance she may sell, if she can get a buyer. For all practical purposes, therefore, the woman gives up all she owns in this world at the moment of her marriage. Jewish law, it must be supposed, assumed such complete responsibility for the protection of the wife during her married life that it felt free to deprive her of all property rights (which would be useless to her as a married woman) and to extend the husband's rights and privileges to encourage his attempt to make an honest living for his family.

Throughout the entire period of legislation, however, the husband has never been recognized as having independent capital ownership in his wife's mulug. His sale of the wife's mulug, therefore, without the latter's consent, is void.[15] He may sell only his right

[12] San. 71a, Nazir 24 b.

[13] Gittin 62a, at head.

[14] Ket. 86b.

[15] B. B. 50a, B. K. 89a, etc. Asheri (B. B. ibid.) infers from Babli that where the husband sold his wife's mulug, though the sale is void, the right of succession is nevertheless thereby conveyed to the purchaser. He cites an opposing view expressed in

of succession, on the chance that he may survive his wife, or he can sell his right of usufruct, provided the money derived from the sale is employed for the comfort of the family.[16] If both agreed on the sale of the mulug, according to a certain amoraic opinion, the sale would be invalid, because neither has the legal power of conveyance,[17] but according to the final halakah the sale is valid, without regard as to which made the offer to sell, the husband or the wife.[18] In fact, if the mulug does not yield a sufficient return, so that the husband is deprived of the due usufruct privilege, and if the woman does not claim special family sentiments to be connected with her mulug, the court will order the mulug to be sold and more productive property to be bought for the money.[19]

The usufruct privilege is the outstanding claim of the husband on the wife's mulug, in rabbinic law. It is conceded by the rabbis that "the right of fruit," as they call it, is a rabbinical institution and has no support in Biblical law.[20] We agree fully in this view, for there is no record of the husband's usufruct privilege in the Bible; and, furthermore, in the Assuan papyri we find a contract between the husband and the wife, granting the former the usufruct of the latter's property in exchange for certain improvements he proposes

the Jerushalmi. Maimonides takes the sale of a wife's mulug to be equal to a son's sale of his inheritance prior to the father's death. Cf. Yad, Mekirah, 30, 4. See also B. B. 137a, B. K. 88b.

[16] Ket. 80a-b and Asheri B. B. ibid.

[17] B. K. 90a.

[18] B. B. 50a-b, Yad, Ishut, 22, 16.

[19] Ket. 79b. Old slaves and old fruit trees are cited as examples.

[20] Mishna Ket. 46b, beraita ibid. 47b, Jer. Ket. 28d.

to make,[21] thus yielding the conclusion that the husband had no usufruct by statute, but was given it by contract for a specified consideration.

The right of usufruct is granted the husband by other ancient peoples,[22] and was instituted in Jewish law towards the end of the Second Commonwealth.[23] This privilege is not recorded in the ketubah, for more than one reason. In the first place, the ketubah deals mainly with guarantees for the wife; in the second place, mulug is not entered into the ketubah and, therefore, provisions concerning it are also left out. Usufruct is a statutory provision in Talmudic law, and gives the husband the right to the yield of his wife's mulug whether by his effort and expense or without either.[24] The reason for granting the right

[21] Papyrus C. specifies that the husband be permitted to build on a field given to his wife Miphtahya by her father. If he do so, she cannot leave him without forfeiting her field to him and after his death to his heirs. If she take it away from him—conveying it to another—she forfeits half of it. This is the reading given by J. N. Epstein in *Jahrbuch d. jued-lit. Gesellschaft*, Vol. VI, p. 360. Sayce and Cowley render the second clause as follows: If he divorce her, she shall take half.

[22] See Freund, GES, p. 41.

[23] Freund, GES, p. 47, argues that the right of usufruct was recognized in Jewish law after the destruction, for to him the Babylonian tradition that fruit is in exchange for ransom reflects days of unrest. I believe the institution is older and had its beginning in Temple days. The Babylonian tradition is unsound and cannot yield historic proof. Furthermore, ransom is a ketubah clause of Temple days. Surely the amoraim believed that usufruct was an institution of Temple days, for they believe the law concerning the wife's right to sell her mulug (Mishna Ket. 78a), which was formulated before the days of Rabban Gamaliel, had reference to usufruct. Cf. מתניתן בחייה ולפירות Ket. 78b. Usufruct is also referred to in mishna Ket. 46b, which is a very old mishna. See Appendix A.

[24] Mishna Ket. 80b.

of usufruct to the husband, according to the Palestinian tradition, is out of consideration of the care that the husband gives his wife's property.[25] The Babylonian tradition teaches that the husband is given usufruct in exchange for the ransom which the law imposes upon him in the event his wife is made captive.[26] Between the two traditions, we feel compelled to accept the Palestinian. For one reason, usufruct in exchange for care of the property is logical, and makes the rabbinical enactment a direct historical outgrowth of the contractual usufruct recorded in the Assuan papyri;[27] while the connection between usufruct and ransom is artificial. For another reason, the Babylonian tradition is based on unreliable sources.[28]

The husband's right of usufruct places upon him the obligation of caring for her mulug, expense of upkeep of inanimate objects and food for animate objects.[29] No calculations, however, are made as to the ratio between income and expenditures; loss and gain are both his.[30] If he derived no profits at all, according

[25] Jer. Ket. Chapter 4, sec. 6.

[26] Ket. 47b.

[27] Notice Papyrus C, line 10: חלף עבידתא זי אנת עבדת and line 11: חלף בנויא זי אנת בנית בביתא זך.

[28] The Babylonian amoraim have no tannaitic text expressly giving the reason for usufruct. They emend a text (Ket. 47b), but their emendation is not convincing. It is based only on a comparison between the mishna (Ket. 46b) and the beraita cited by them. The former has three terms, sustenance, ransom and burial, whereas the beraita has only sustenance and burial. Hence they add ransom to the beraita and arrive at the conclusion that ransom belongs in juxtaposition to fruit.

[29] Jeb. 66a, Ket. 79b.

[30] Ket. ibid. An exception to this rule is made in the case of a marriage to a minor orphaned girl (Ket. 80a, B. M. 39a), and in the case of the insubordinate woman (Yad, Ishut, 23 10).

to tannaitic law, he is reimbursed for his expenses; but according to amoraic ruling, he is reimbursed only to the extent of the improvement of the capital value of the mulug.[31]

The right of usufruct is not the husband's private right, but as head of the family. He can, therefore, use the fruit only for the household benefit, not to increase his personal wealth. If the yield is greater than the family can use, the surplus is sold and the money applied in other ways to make the family more comfortable.[32] Yet this principle was often loosely interpreted. The following case is a striking illustration: A woman brought with her two mulug female slaves. The husband married a second wife and gave her one of the slaves as a present. The first wife, the owner of the slave, brought suit to regain her slave. But the court sustained the husband's action, for by giving the slave to his second wife, he put her service at the disposal of a family member, thus employing his right of usufruct for the family benefit.[33]

What consitutes fruit and what capital is often hard to decide, and the law is put to the task of defining the terms. The standard case is that of a field which yields fruit. If the mulug consists of money, a fruit yielding field is bought for it; likewise, if it consists of a non-productive field, it is exchanged for a productive one.[34] If it consists of a field already laden with fruit, according to R. Meir, both field and fruit are capital; according to his opponents, the field alone is capital.[35] The older halakah considers the offspring

[31] Ket. 80a.

[32] Ket. 80a-b, Yad, Ishut 12, 15.

[33] Ibid.

[34] Ket. 79a.

[35] Ket. 79a-b. However, since the husband takes the fruit which she brought, she can also take the fruit on the field left

of mulug cattle as fruit but the offspring of mulug slaves as capital, because the offspring of slaves are calculated to replace the parent slave when he grows old or dies. Later halakah, however, also declared the offspring of slaves as fruit.[36] Products of a mine are fruit, if the mine does not become exhausted. If it does, R. Meir would declare the products capital; his opponents, fruit.[37] The wearing of a garment, even to the point of becoming worthless, is given to the husband as usufruct.[38] If the woman's mulug consists in "right of fruit," as for instance the right of milking someone's goat or picking the fruit of someone's orchard, the husband takes over the entire right, leaving the woman no capital at all.[39]

In tannaitic halakah, the husband's right of fruit includes also the "fruit of fruit," [40] but the amoraim have denied the husband the right to the fruit of fruit.[41] The application of this amoraic legislation is found in the instance where the offspring of a mulug cattle was stolen, the thief found and made to pay double its value according to Biblical prescription. In that case, though the offspring itself is the husband's, the fine paid by the thief is the wife's, because it is fruit of fruit.[42] Or, if the woman sold her ketubah to another, the husband

in it by the husband at the time she leaves him, at divorce or at his death. Husbands are therefore cautioned to pick off all the fruit of the mulug orchards before divorcing their wives. Tos. Ket. 8, 2; Jer. Ket. 29a.

[36] Ket. 79b; Jer. Jeb. 8a. At divorce, however, she may take them with her on payment of their market value.

[37] Ibid.

[38] Ibid.

[39] Ibid.

[40] Tos. Ket. 9, 2; Ket. 83a.

[41] Ket. ibid. Tosafot seeks in vain to make the amoraic view agree with the tannaitic. See Ket. 79b s. v. פירא.

[42] Ket. 79b.

cannot claim the use of the money, for the ketubah itself is not payable; the purchase price is only a yield of the ketubah, or fruit. The use of the purchase price would, therefore, be fruit of fruit.[43]

Exceptions to the husband's right of usufruct are the following. If the woman receives a gift from her father[44] or a stranger[45] with the expressed stipulation that the husband shall have no claim to it, he has no right of usufruct. If the husband himself gave his wife a gift, or even if he sold her something, the implication is that he waived the right of usufruct.[46] R. Johanan is the author of this legislation, and the "leading scholars" agree with him, but Rab accepts his ruling only in the case of a gift—not in the case of a sale from husband to wife. If the woman receives money as a settlement for an injury inflicted on her, whether from a stranger or her own husband, Talmudic law would grant the husband the right of usufruct in it.[47] But, Maimonides cites a geonic ruling that if it is received from the husband himself, he forfeits the usufruct.[48] Jewish law knows also of an instrument that is effective in depriving the husband of his usufruct in his wife's mulug. The woman makes out a fictitious deed of conveyance of her mulug prior to her marriage.[49] Because the witnesses who testify to the deed

[43] B. K. 89a.

[44] Nedarim 88a.

[45] Nazir 24b, San. 71a.

[46] B. B. 51b, Jer. Ket. 32d. Cf. Asheri, Ket. 19a. The Talmud, however, rules that the sale of property to one's wife is not binding, because the husband can claim that he proposed the sale only for the purpose of finding out how much money his wife had of her own. See Yad, Ishut 20, 29.

[47] Tos. B. K. 9, 14.

[48] Yad, Hobel u-Mazik 4, 16. R. Nisim, Ket. 65b.

[49] Tos. Ket. 9, 2.

know it to be fictitious, the conveyance is without effect,[50] and because the husband is faced with an apparently valid deed of conveyance, its effect is to annul his right of usufruct.[51]

According to the tannaim, the husband can waive the right of usufruct, and he expresses his waiver in the formula: "I lay no claim or suit to thy property, its fruit, or the fruit of its fruit for ever," [52] oral or written. The amoraim, however, declare a waiver of fruit ineffective, for usufruct is not all of the nature of a privilege. It involves also responsibility, as caring for the property or paying ransom for the wife.[53]

[50] R. Simeon B. Gamaliel, however, would consider the deed binding unless it read, "it be a gift to thee from me at this moment to be effective at such time as I may choose!" Should the wife leave some of her mulug not included in this fictitious deed, then it might operate as evidence that the deed was not meant to be fictitious. In such event, the amoraim counsel that the above formula shall be used.

[51] The reason is this. When the husband is so deceived, the mulug gets the status of mulug acquired by the wife while unknown and unexpected by the husband (Ket. 79a). The fictitious contract, however, does not deprive the husband of the right of succession, for a real deed would not do so either since the *Takanat Usha.*

[52] Ket. 56a-b, 83a, Tos. Ket. 9, 2, Jer. Ket. 32d. The expression דין ודברים reminds us of the לא דין ולא דבב of the papyri, apparently a technical term.

[53] Cf. Jer. Ket. 28d. Cf. RSBM, B. B. 49b, challenging this law. See also Gittin 77a, s. v. וכדרב and Ket. 47b s. v. זמנין and B. B. 49b s. v. יכולה. It is granted, of course, that the wife cannot waive the privilege of ransom for the freedom to keep her own fruit.

CHAPTER VIII

SUCCESSION

Succession in Jewish law is based historically on the conception of tribal ownership of land; wherefore, a person's heirs are those who take his place in the tribe. Sons are, therefore, heirs of the first order. Daughters have no tribal personality. They are owned —before marriage, by the father; after marriage, by the husband. Hence the ancient law gave them no right of succession at all. Later Biblical legislation, however, recognized them as possessing tribal personality, but capable of changing their tribal connections through marriage. Therefore Moses rules that daughters who remain in their father's tribe are heirs of the second order, succeeding their father, if no sons remain.[1] A father succeeds his son only as heir of the

[1] Numb. 36, 3. Sifre Numb. 27, 8 understands from this verse that a daughter causes the transfer of property from one tribe to another by the fact that after her death she is succeeded by her husband and children. Perhaps this was not altogether the feeling recorded in the Bible. The transfer, from the Biblical point of view, is caused by the fact that the woman herself, at marriage, becomes a member of another tribe. Nachamanides, in comment upon this verse, raises the question —supposing the daughter was already married out of her tribe, does she or does she not succeed her father? He concludes that she does. Historically that was impossible. In the first place, that would mean direct conveyance of property from one tribe to another; in the second place, the married daughter, in Biblical days, had not the status of an heir at all, for she received her dowry in lieu of inheritance.

The Bible gives us no instructions as to a daughter's share in the estate of her mother. Is she excluded altogether, or is she equal heir with her brothers? From Code Hammurabi, one

third order, that is, if neither son nor daughter remain. Mother and wife are no heirs at all.[2]

gets the impression that male and female children are treated equally in the succession to their mother's estate, for, with reference to succession to the mother, it speaks of "children" (162, 163, 173, 174, etc.) while succession to the father is given to "sons" (166, 167, etc.). The reason for the distinction is evident. The mother's property has not the tribal ties which the father's has, and while the father's estate is partly given to the daughter in the form of dowry, the mother's estate is not touched for that purpose. Perhaps this was also Jewish law in Bible days. At the end of the Second Commonwealth, R. Zechariah b. Ha-kaceb holds this exact view, that "son and daughter are equal heirs of their mother's estate" (B. B. 111a). A tradition is given that Rab supported this view, but another tradition denies it. The amoraim, however, conclude that the daughter is heir of the second order also to her mother's estate, succeeding to it only if there are no sons.

It is curious to notice that the daughter's right of succession in Jewish law is in many striking points parallel to that of Babylonian law, even in this later enactment of declaring the daughter an heir of the second order, which is also a point of development in the later Babylonian law. Cf. Kohler-Peiser *Hammurabi's Gesetz*, I, p. 125.

Still later Jewish law removed even the restriction ordained by the Bible that the daughter who succeeds her father must marry within the tribe. The Talmud takes this abrogation to be Biblical. Cf. B. B. 120a, Ta'anit 30b. This view is not wholly correct, for even in the Book of Tobit (7, 14) we have yet a reminiscence of the Biblical restriction. The restriction faded with the fading of tribal distinctions and tribal loyalties.

[2] B. B. 108a, 111b-113a. Samuel cites a law, though, that "if the husband wills his wife a share in his estate, she is treated as one of the heirs" (B. B. 128b). Later amoraim interpret this halakah of Samuel to mean that the husband gives the wife a gift not to exceed the value of an heir's share in the estate. She is therefore at a great disadvantage in the eyes of the law; if more heirs are discovered her share is reduced; if the property has risen in value she does not share the increase. Samuel is the authority for another law, however, which says that "if the husband willed his wife his entire property, she is no more than administratrix" (Gittin 14a, B. B. 131b, 144a).

Under conditions of polygamy or in successive marriages, where there are children born of different mothers, the same rule applies, for all children are equal in relation to their father. Children of a concubine are considered in Babylonian law little better than slaves, and, therefore, not the legal successors of their father. In Jewish law, however, even in Biblical times, the children of a concubine are the equals of their brothers by a legitimate wife.[3]

This ruling is declared by later amoraim "a law without reason," yet the social reason—if not the legal basis—is evident. It is a check on the husband against being unjust to his offspring on account of a too strong affection for his wife.

[3] Polygamy is Biblically and rabbinically permissible, but an aversion to it is already felt in the Bible. The wives are called *Zarot,* enemies of one another (Lev. 18, 18) and Laban forces a promise from Jacob not to marry more wives (Gen. 31, 50). See Nowack, *Lehrbuch d. heb. Archaologie,* pp. 158 ff. and 349f. In the Talmud (Jeb. 65a) an opinion is expressed, though not halakacally accepted, that marrying a second wife constitutes a cause for divorce for the first wife. Many ketubah clauses are found in post-Talmudic times stipulating that the husband shall not marry another wife. RITBA (Jeb. ibid) rules that monogamy is an implied condition of every marriage, unless the contrary is definitely stipulated. Under all circumstances, however, no one may marry more than four wives. Cf. Jeb. 44a, Yad, Ishut 14, 3. Regardless of law, the Talmud records (Ket. 64a) that it was difficult for men in those days to get a wife under polygamous conditions. The end of polygamy among European Jews came with the enactment of R. Gershon Me'or Ha-golah in the tenth century. Cf. Jewish Encyclopedia, s. v. Polygamy.

Concubinage is frequently met with in the Bible. Josephus makes no mention of concubinage as part of the social complex of his day. The tannaim discuss the status of the concubine with apparently no practical view in mind except as a matter of Biblical exegesis. Cf. Jer. Ket. 29d. However, Jews had concubines even in post-Talmudic times. Thus Nachmanides, in correspondence with R. Jonah Girundi, permits concubinage, and this decision is cited in *Zedah Laderek* III, 1, 2, p. 122b as guid-

The statutory order of succession, both in Babylonian and ancient Jewish law, does not limit a person's testamentary privileges. To every man is left the right to order the manner of succession to his estate, even though contrary to statute. It is this right of the head of the family that is invoked in the case of Ishmael against Isaac, of Esau against Jacob, and of Adonijah against Solomon. Deuteronomic law, however, deprives the testator of the freedom to order succession to his estate contrary to statute, and in this rabbinic law fully concurs.[4]

When, therefore, upon this background of Jewish law we find in Papyrus G a clause such as this one: "I shall have no power to say I have another wife than Miphtahya and other children than the children which Miphtahya shall bear to me," we must conclude that the clause, in the main, was prompted by Baby-

ance to people "because there are many in this country who take concubines." (See Halberstamm *Kebuzat maamarim 'al debar sefer hamoreh*). That no distinction is made between the children of a legitimate wife and those of a concubine is evident from the equality of all the sons of Jacob. Cf. Edward Gans, *Erbrecht* . . . in Zunz *Zeitschrift*, p. 425, Nowack *Archaologie* I, p. 349, Benzinger *Archaologie* I, p. 135. Freund GES p. 5 opposes this view. His proofs from Gen. 36, 11-12, Jud. 8, 30-31, and I Chron. 3, 9 are not conclusive. I cannot see how Amalek, for instance, is discriminated against among the sons of Esau (Gen. 36, 12, 15) or Abimelech among the sons of Gideon (Jud. 9). That children of a concubine are named separately may be a matter of convenient classification. Talmudic law recognizes no distinction between children of a wife and those of a concubine. The law excludes from succession only children of a female slave who was not made a concubine, whose children, therefore, are slaves and the property of their master, not his successors. Cf. Jeb. 22a-b and Yad, Nahlot 1, 7.

[4] See Deut. 21, 17. Significant is the phrase לא יוכל לבכר which means he has not the legal power. The rabbinic law in this matter is given in the mishna, B. B. 126b.

lonian, not Jewish law. This clause prohibits polygamy but permits concubinage. In so far it may be Jewish as well as Babylonian. But its main aim is to hold the children of the concubine down to a position below the level of an heir and to prevent the father from raising them to such a level. Now Jewish law does not consider the children of the concubine as being inferior in right to those of a wife, and, after the Deuteronomic legislation, does not recognize the father's power to change or alter the manner of succession. This clause, therefore, has reference to Babylonian law[5] and hence it was never, as far as we know, repeated in Jewish marriage contracts, and no trace of it is to be found in the halakah.

It is rather with the husband's right of succession to his wife that the rabbinic ketubah concerns itself. A number of ketubah clauses deal with it and foremost among them is the *Ketubat benin dikrin* clause. But in order to understand fully the implications of these clauses and the legislative enactments in the matter of the husband's right of succession, we must view them against the background of their historical development. The traditional view is that since Mosaic days the husband was recognized as first heir to his wife's estate—preceding every blood relative. On the basis of this view rests the traditional interpretation of every ketubah clause in connection with succession. But a critical examination of the sources reveals a history of the law of succession which the rabbis did not suspect and a new interpretation of the ketubah clauses of succession, more especially of the *ketubat benin dikrin* clause, may be thus set forth.

The husband as successor to his wife has made his way to the foremost position by a series of legal

[5] See Code Hammurabi 170.

changes. In Babylonian law he is never given the right of succession to his wife. He is only the keeper of his wife's marriage portion as long as he lives.[6] This was probably the original Jewish law also.

Then the law elevated the husband to the position of heir of the third order, preceding the father but following the daughter and the son.[7] This reform—even if we differ with the rabbis as to its Biblical origin—is certainly a very ancient legislation.[8] Then

[6] See Code Hammurabi 162, 163, 167, 173, 174. See also note 10 on p. 129.

[7] It seems that there never was a time when the husband was heir of the fourth order—preceded by father but prior to every other relative. This would be impossible in Jewish law where the principle is (pharasaic) that one's right of succession continues in his own heirs after his death. If the father is prior to the husband, then the father's descendants, after his death, are also prior to him. It would mean that the husband would never be admitted to succession.

[8] The tannaitic inference from the Bible as to the husband's right of succession lends itself to one of two interpretations. Either they inferred that the husband was heir, as against the possibility of his being denied the right of succession altogether; or they sought to prove that the husband was heir of the first order. Logically, Num. 27, 11 can prove only the first point, not the other alternative, for it specifies—according to their reading of it—the order of succession to be: sons, daughters, brothers, uncles, and *she'ero* i. e. he to whom she is wife. See B. B. 109b, 111b. One suspects, however, that even in R. Akiba's days the husband was the first heir to his wife's property (See note 12, p. 133), and that the Tannaim aimed by their inference from the Bible to reach that conclusion.

The tannaim did not succeed in establishing proof from the Bible that the husband succeeds his wife. R. Akiba bases himself on וירש אותה and translates it, the husband shall succeed his wife, while in reality it means, "he shall inherit it,"—that is, the nearest of kin shall inherit the estate. R. Ishmael finds a number of instances in the Bible (Numb. 36, 7-8-9, Josh. 24, 33, I Chron. 2, 22) where a son is spoken of as in possession of property not given to him by his father. He infers, therefore,

the husband was moved up one step further; he became heir of the second order, ahead of the father and daughter but still preceded by the son. It was the task of the final halakah to declare the husband the first heir, prior even to son. On top of the original status of the husband, the law has seen three reforms, first giving the husband the status of heir of the third order, secondly, as heir of the second order, and finally as heir of the first order.

In Papyrus G we find a ketubah clause which reflects the first reform of the law, declaring the husband heir of the third order. It reads: "If tomorrow or any other day Miphtahya shall die having no issue whether male or female by As-hor her husband, As-hor shall be heir to her goods and her chattels." The following deductions can be made from this clause. There was yet a lingering reminiscence in that Egyptian Jewish colony of the ancient law putting the father ahead of the husband in priority of succession. Hence, the term of the contract, giving the husband priority to the father. Or, it was not a reminiscence of the old Jewish usage, but a general guardedness on the part of the Jewish community against the Babylonian law of that day, giving the husband no right of succession to his wife. I believe the latter is the case, and the contract simply binds the couple to the mode of succession pre-

that he got that property by inheritance from his wife. The weakness of his evidence is apparent. As against these tannaitic opinions giving the husband's right of succession Biblical origin, the amoraim infer that R. Eliezer (Mishna Bekor. 52b) and Rab. (Ket. 83b-84a) hold the view that the husband's right of succession is a rabbinical enactment. The decision of Maimonides is that it is rabbinical. See *Mishna Commentary* Ket. 83a. The Karaites repudiate the law which declares the husband heir to his wife; they find no proof for it in the Bible. See *Eshkol Hakofer*, AB-259.

scribed by Jewish law as against Babylonian law. Again, the implication of the clause is that if children, male or female, did remain behind, they would be the heirs, and not the husband. In other words, this clause gives us the instance of the first step in the elevation of the husband to the position of heir; he is prior to the father but not to the son or the daughter.

In the next stage of development of the law of succession, the husband was raised to the level of heir prior not only to father but also to daughter, though not to son. This stage of the law is also reflected in a ketubah clause cited in the mishna and designated in rabbinic literature as *ketubat bnin dikrin* (KBD). It reads: "The male children which thou shalt beget by me shall inherit thy ketubah above their share among their brothers."[9] This ketubah clause reflects a law in Code Hammurabi which reads: "If a man marries a woman and she bore him sons, and this woman dies a natural death, and thereafter he marries another woman and she bore him sons—after the father dies, the sons shall not divide according to their mothers.

[9] Ket. 52b; Tos. Ket. 6, 6; B. B. 131a. For variants in text, see Fischer, *Urkunden*, p. 91 and notes. This clause prescribes that at the death of the mother, if she is survived by her husband, her ketubah, i. e. mohar, mattan, and nedunya, remains with the husband. After the latter's death, however, it goes back to her children, without any share in it for the children which the husband may have of another wife. And it does not matter whether the other children are born of a polygamous marriage or of successive marriages. Nor does it matter whether the other wife survives her husband or not. If she survives him, she gets her own ketubah and the first wife's children get their mother's ketubah; if she died before him, then the two sets of children get the ketubot of their respective mothers and divide the estate of their common father. See Ket. 90a and *Geonim Kadmonim* 152.

Their mothers' dowry shall they take and shall divide equally the possessions of their father's house."[10] The motive of the ketubah clause and the latter half of the Code Hammurabi provision is simple. The heirs to the mother's possession are her sons, not her husband. The husband, however, does not need to return the dowry as long as he lives. At his death, therefore, should he have children by another wife, they are not permitted to take any part of that dowry. It must go to her own sons only. In other words, the return of the mother's dowry to her sons is not due to their special privilege as heirs of the father—as the Talmud understands it—but to the fact that sons are prior

[10] Code Hammurabi, 167. The intention of this section of the law is a twofold one. In the first place, it instructs that the father's estate shall be divided according to the number of children he has, not according to the wives. Else, we might believe that the children of one mother represent one unit and the children of another represent another unit. In the second place, it teaches that the mother's dowry does not go into the general estate. It goes to the mother's heirs, not to the father's. When, therefore, the mother has died and is survived by her husband, he holds the dowry until his death, and after his death it is given to her children. In view of CH 162 which gives a woman's estate to her children, not her husband, one may wonder—why does the husband hold her dowry until his death? Why is it not given to the children immediately upon her death? The explanation lies in the fact that the ancient law, Babylonian as well as Jewish, gave the husband a tenancy over the dowry which does not terminate until his death, unless he undoes the marriage contract by divorcing her. This is the meaning of לא נתנה כתובה לגבות מחיים which is a popular legal dictum of some antiquity, and whose real intention and force was no longer known to the later rabbis. To them it had no general meaning, for to them the husband was, after his wife's death, first heir, no more tenant. The later rabbis found its application valid only in the case of a levirate marriage, as will be shown later.

to the husband in succession to the woman. If there are no sons, the husband is the rightful heir to his wife, prior to daughter and father.[11] This old tannaitic

[11] In my interpretation of the KBD clause, I differ from the rabbinic interpretation mainly in this respect. I take the husband, from the time of the wife's death to his own death, to be a tenant with respect to his wife's ketubah; the rabbis, according to their view of ירושת הבעל take him to be heir. We agree on the motive of the clause as expressed by R. Simeon b. Yohai (Ket. 52b—Jer. gives it in the name of R. Ami, Jer. Ket. 28b and 29a) "in order that a man may be encouraged to give as liberally to his daughter as he would give to his son." Should it be possible for the wife's property, if she was survived by the husband, to go to another woman's children, the woman's father would not be liberal with the giving of dowry to her. This reason is sufficient both for the rabbinic interpretation and my interpretation of the KBD clause. I feel, though, that it applies more directly to my interpretation than it does to the rabbinic interpretation. According to my view, the husband's right of succession has been limited, not to supercede the sons, else the dowry would at the moment of marriage go over completely to the husband and his heirs—unless the assumption were that the husband would die first or the pair would be divorced. According to the rabbinic view, the husband's right as heir remains untouched, but the woman's children are especially privileged heirs of their father with respect to their mother's dowry. This form of reasoning, while not faulty, it seems to me, is going round about the objective instead of directly to it. Many difficulties beset the rabbinic interpretation of the KBD clause. The R. Simeon b. Yohai explanation suffices for nedunya, but why are the mohar and the mattan included under the terms of the clause? The rabbis answer that difficulty, but in an artificial manner. They say, the father will be liberal with giving of dowry only if the husband shows equal liberality by permitting the mohar and mattan which he gave to his daughter to be funded with the dowry and given to her children. The R. Simeon b. Yohai explanation raises the question, why should not the clause provide also that the daughters shall inherit their mother's ketubah in the event she has left no sons? To this the rabbis say—supposing sons have remained of another wife, then giving the daughters of this wife any kind of succession would be contrary to Biblical pre-

ketubah clause, therefore, gives us a record of the second stage of development of the husband's right of succession to his wife, namely his being ahead of father and daughter but not of son.

scription, and if there are only daughters against daughters, it was not worth while for the court to make a special enactment to privilege this woman's daughters in succession to their mother's ketubah. Another difficulty which the rabbis overlooked is this one. What becomes of the wife's mulug? The term "ketubah" includes mohar, mattan, and dowry, but definitely not mulug. Therefore, according to the law, the mulug belongs to the husband without restrictions, and after his death to his heirs by any wife. The absurd situation arises, therefore, that the mattan which is the husband's goes to her children, the mulug which is the wife's goes to his children. The mulug is evidently more the private property of the wife than the dowry; if the children succeed their mother in the latter, they surely should succeed her in the former. The rabbinic explanation of the KBD clause encounters a few more difficulties. According to them, the children's right of succession to their father is modified by the KBD agreement. But, then is it not an invalid agreement because it is contrary to Biblical prescription, they ask. See B. B. 130a, 131, Ket. 33a. If it represents a gift made by the husband at the time of the marriage—when the clause is written—to his children that will be gotten by her, it violates the principle of אין אדם מקנה דבר שלא בא לעולם "a man cannot convey anything prior to his acquisition of it"—and surely not to children who are not yet born. B. B. 131a. Furthermore, if the children in taking their mother's ketubah are merely privileged heirs of the father, then if the father sold it after the mother's death, the children would have no claim, for it is not any more part of the father's estate. Or, if he sold or gave away any part of his property during his lifetime on which was a lien for the payment of the ketubah, the mother herself could collect her keutbah from the purchaser, but the children do not—according to the rabbinic interpretation—represent their mother, but are heirs of the father—so what claim can they have? Of what value then is the KBD clause, if the father can deprive the children of that privilege in so many ways? Rabbi reports that in his day the heirs of the KBD had valid claim even on property sold by the

The final victory came for the husband when the law declared him the first heir of his wife's property, superceding every other heir. How early this law was

father (B. B. 131a) and he seems to have incorporated, as the amoraim point out, this decision in the Mishna (Ket. 10, 1). But he also records the fact that the opposite practice, or legal opinion, was not unknown, namely to cancel the KBD claim against any property that was sold by the father. Both practices are reported as having existed in Babylonia. In Pumbedita, the claim was not honored against property that was sold; while in Mehasia it was honored (Ket. 55a). These two halakic practices, in the view of the rabbis, correspond to two readings in the KBD clause; one would read יירתון; the other would read יסבון. The former reading would be impossible, if the clause is honored against property that was sold by the father. For, how can an heir have any claim against property sold by the testator during his lifetime? Hence the emendation *yisbun*, "they shall take," meaning that the ketubah was a gift made by the father at the time of the marriage to the children who were yet unborn. (See B. B. ibid.; Ket. 55a; Jer. Ket. 29a; Jer. B. B. 16b. The Palestinian emendation is יטלון.) Now, the emendation is utterly incorrect, for no text gives anything but *yartun* in the KBD clause. R. Elazar b. 'Azaria (Ket. 49a) bases a halakah on the reading. The entire idea of מותר דינר (Ket. 91a) is illogical on any reading but *yartun*. So does Admon, an authority of Temple days, argue against an old halakah which quotes the KBD with the reading of *yartun* (Ket. 108b). The emendation is apparently untrue, but forced by the fact that the later rabbis sought to interpret the KBD clause in terms of the law they had, namely that the husband was first heir. Hence, they could understand by the term *yartun* only "they shall inherit their father." Hence the difficulties.

All these difficulties vanish when the KBD clause is understood in the light of an earlier law of succession, making the husband heir to his wife, next in order to the son and prior to the daughter. For, let it be remembered, the clause is a very old one. Evidence for it is the fact that Admon argues against a law which was formulated prior to his day, in which the KBD clause is quoted in part. Furthermore, Rabbi discusses the reading of the mishna, (יירתון תנן) but not the reading of the ketubah text, evidently because the clause was not so popularly used in ketubot in his day. It was in his day already

recognized cannot be told with certainty, but the author of the Mishna found it already definitely accepted,[12]

antiquated as a mere clause. It had become a statute. If the parallelism between the KBD and the Code Hammurabi does not indicate antiquity, it proves at least one thing, that the KBD need not necessarily imply the husband's right as first heir to his wife, for CH definitely denies the husband such a right. If we base ourselves on the assumption that in the KBD clause the order of succession implied is: Son, Husband, Daughter, and Father, then our interpretation of יירתון will be "they shall inherit their mother," and it provides that at the woman's death, her mulug goes directly to her sons, but her ketubah, i. e. dowry, mohar and mattan, remains with the husband, not as heir but as tenant until his death; and that after his death it goes to the original heirs of the mother, her sons. Now we understand why mohar and mattan and nedunya are included in the KBD clause, but not mulug. We also understand why the KBD specifies privileges for sons and not for daughters, because the husband is prior to the daughters. Again, the KBD does not modify succession to the father; it records the law of succession to the mother. As heirs of the mother, the children can lay claim to any part of the dowry sold by the father or to any of his property which bore a lien for the payment of the mother's ketubah. Honoring the KBD clause against property that was sold by the father does not, therefore, necessitate deleting the word *yartun*. On the contrary, because "they shall inherit their mother," they force payment of the ketubah in the same manner as the mother would have done, had she survived her husband. The practice recorded not to honor the KBD against property that was sold is due either to an independent legislation to curtail the force of the KBD or is a result of the misinterpretation of the clause.

[12] B. B. 109b, 111b, B. K. 42b, Ket. 83b, Bek. 52b, Sife Numb. 27-28. As was said above (note 8, p. 126), the inference from the Bible may only be directed to the conclusion that the husband is one of the heirs but not necessarily the first heir. There is enough evidence, however, to support our suspicion that the tannaim already had the final stage of the law of the husband's succession to his wife. Mishna Ket. 91a, quoting R. Simeon b. Yohai, Mishna Ket. 83a quoting R. Simeon b. Gamaliel and the *takanat Usha* are based on the husband's prior right of succession.

and this is the final Jewish law.[13] Naturally, this newer halakah did not leave the *ketubat bnin dikrin* clause in its original force and implication, but reinterpreted it in terms of the new law. It ruled that the KBD clause is not honored against property that was sold by the father, that any of the father's indebtedness is paid out of his estate before the KBD is honored,[14] for the heirs of the KBD are regarded only as privileged heirs of the father, whose claim, therefore, rests only on the estate left after all creditors have been paid. According to this new halakah, it was also found necessary that at least a dinnar's worth of property remain in the estate (מותר דינר) after the payment of the KBD, else the other heirs would have nothing and the clause would thereby undo the Biblical law of succession.[15] Should the woman sell her ketubah in her lifetime, according to the older law, there would be no KBD privilege left to her children, for as heirs to their mother, they cannot inherit what she has sold; but the newer law recognized the KBD clause even in such a case, for since the husband survived her, her sale of her ketubah is void, and since the husband now has in his possession the ketubah of his

[13] See Yad, Ishut, 22, 1.

[14] Ket. 90b. Jer. Ket. 33d.

[15] Ket. 52b, 91a. The Talmud rules that if that dinnar's worth of property is subject to a lien for the payment of a debt, it still does validate the KBD clause. Although there will be no actual inheritance, the payment of the debt is itself a form of succession. If, however, that dinnar's worth of property is encumbered by the lien of widow and minor orphaned girls for their maintenance, it does not count, for inheritance begins to count after these obligations are met. That dinnar's worth of property must consist of realty, not of personalty, according to certain tannaitic views, but the halakah decides against this view. Ket. 50b, 52b, 91a. Cf. Asheri Ket. 91a, *Tur Eben Haezer* 111, and *Beth Joseph* ibid.

wife, her children still remain privileged heirs of their father—entitled to their mother's property above their share in the rest of the father's estate.[16] Yet contrary to the logic of the KBD clause as interpreted by the later rabbis, because of the fact that this privileged succession to the father is termed "ketubah," it is payable, like the ketubah, only out of realty, not out of personalty.[17] And when later the geonim legislated that the ketubah be paid also out of personalty,[18] the *ketubat bnin dikrin*, according to the prevailing halakic view, still remained under its former limitation, to be paid only out of realty.[19]

The *ketubat bnin dikrin* clause is a condition assumed in every marriage, even though not specified in the marriage deed. But the woman may waive that clause by written or oral statement or even by indication of some act of hers.[20] With the woman's forfeiture of her ketubah, as in the case of prohibited marriages or unfaithfulness or unbecoming conduct, the KBD clause is also cancelled,[21] and succession to the woman's property reverts back to the final statute—the husband as first heir, and after him his heirs without distinction as to their mothers.

In geonic times, a number of authorities ventured to abolish the whole KBD provision, for, they say, its aim is to make fathers as liberal to their daughters as

[16] Ket. 53a. Cf. Yad, Ishut, 17, 19.

[17] Ket. 50b, 52b. Cf. Rashi (50b) s. v. דילמא. Jer. Ket. 33d infers this law from R. Simeon's statement in mishna Ket. 91a.

[18] Yad, Ishut, 16, 7-8. The reason given for this legislation is that people had ceased to be land owners.

[19] Asheri Ket. 52b and 91a, Mordecai Ket. 162, Yad, Ishut ibid, *Tur Ebem Haezer* and *Beth Joseph* 111, and *Perisha* thereto, sec. 32.

[20] Ket. 53a, B. K. 89b.

[21] Jeb. 91a, Yad, Ishut, 24.

to their sons, but people are becoming too liberal with their dowries to their daughters, even to the point of depriving the sons of their rightful inheritance.[22] R. Hai Gaon opposes this abrogation, which causes later authorities to consider the matter as undecided. As a statute, the geonic discussion has brought the KBD to a doubtful culmination, but as a ketubah formula, it comes to us mainly from the times of the very oldest mishnayot. Since then, we have almost no examples of marriage deeds where this clause occurs. The Talmud cites none; post Talmudic halakic writings cite none; and of the ketubah collections of the Genizah there is none of Babylonian or Egyptian origin containing the KBD clause. There are only three known to us containing the clause, all apparently coming from Palestine or from sections directly under Palestinian influence.[23] The clause is altogether lost from the present day ketubah, because of the geonic abrogation of it, because of the prevalance of monogamy, and because of the different *takanot* that have been formulated to govern the husband's right of succession to his wife.

The full and first right of succession which the husband got at the hands of the law to the possessions of his wife, of necessity had to call forth a counter tendency of the law to prescribe and limit his right. Very significant in this process was the shifting of the

[22] The first authority is R. Matathias of the ninth century, cited in R. Jeruham; *Itur, Ketubah demirkasa,* and Mordecai Ket. 162 cite R. Dosa; *Shaare Zedek,* 4, 4, 17 and Asheri Ket. 52b cite R. Judah. See Asaf in *Hazofeh* Vol. 10, 1926, pp. 18-30.

[23] *Ketubah Jerushalmit,* ed. Berliner and a Genizah fragment in the Cambridge University Library, marked T-S 12.659, quoted in Appendix A, and ketubah edited by Asaf in *Hazofeh* ibid, p. 28.

husband's right of succession from betrothal to nuptials. Originally, whatever right of succession the husband had, he came by from the moment of betrothal. Possibly this condition continued to the latter part of the tannaitic period. But with the gradual shifting of the marriage focus from betrothal to nuptials, the husband's right of succession was recognized by the law to begin with nuptials only.[24] His right of succession was also narrowly defined to apply only to the property actually in the possession of the wife at the time of her death, not the property which she acquired, either by increase or addition, after her death.[25] Nor

[24] Mishna Ket. 80b and Jeb. 38a definitely establish that the שומרת יבם is not so much under the ownership of the *levir* as the betrothed is under her husband. Yet, the mishna implies that the *levir* is heir to the *yebamah*. The inference is, therefore, clear that the *arus* is heir to the *arusah*. Therefore, the beraita (Ket. 78b) which records Rabban Gamaliel's argument to show that the betrothed is less subject to her husband than the wedded wife, points to מציאתה מעשי ידיה וכו' but does not point to ירושה which would be most pertinent in the question of the right of the betrothed to sell her mulug. The difference between the *arusah* and the *nesu'ah* in the matter of succession applies only, according to the Hillelites, in the case of the marriage of a minor orphaned girl. (Jeb. 89b). The earliest mention of the law that the *arus* is not heir to his betrothed is given as a tannaitic tradition submitted by Rab Hiya (Ket. 53a) and quoted again by R. Hiya bar Ami in the name of Ula (San. 28b) and quoted in שמחות as an anonymous statement (4, 3). The tradition's tannaitic origin is very doubtful. A late tannaitic statement, later in time than the *Mishna Aharona* (if the addition במה דברים אמורים belongs to the original text), gives the *arus* the right of succession from the moment the groom's agents have received the bride under their care, even prior to nuptials. On these evidences, we base our conclusion that the older halakah recognized the husband as heir from the moment of betrothal.

[25] Tos. Bek. 6, 19, B. B. 113a, 125a, B. K. 42b. This legal maxim אין הבעל נוטל בראוי כבמוחזק is quoted in the name of R. Joshua b. Karha.

does the right of succession survive the husband, as it does every other heir. With his death, his right of succession comes to an end.[26] The law permits the wife's natural heirs to buy from the husband at its market price any property which he inherited from his wife with which there are connections of family sentiment, but the amoraim apply this law only to a family cemetery.[27]

The counter tendency to the husband's right of succession expressed itself also in contractual agreements specified in ketubah clauses. Thus R. Jose reports a Palestinian custom of inserting in the ketubah the clause: "If she dies without issue, her possessions shall return to her father's house." [28] The object of this clause is just the opposite of that of Papyrus G. In the one case, we have a Jewish attempt to increase the husband's right against the non-Jewish usage of denying it to him; in the other case, it is an attempt to establish a non-Jewish usage[29] above the Jewish law.

[26] B. B. 114b. See Tosafot B. B. ibid, s. v. מה. This legal maxim is expressed in the words אין הבעל יורש את אשתו בקבר. It may be noted that RSBM (B. B. ibid.) takes this legal maxim and the former one to be synonymous.

[27] Bekor. 52b, Tos. Bekor. 6, 19. Tosifta reads the statement of R. Johanan b. Berokah as an independent statement; the mishna reads it in connection with the law of the return of property on the jubilee year. The Talmud already doubts the correctness of the word אף in the statement of R. Johanan. From the amoraic discussion it cannot be said with certainty what their reading was.

[28] Jer. Ket. 33a, Jer. B. B. 16b. Variants are given by Alfasi, RABD notes and Asheri ad Ket. 83b and *Hagahot Maimonyot*, Ishut 23, 5.

[29] The origin of this usage should be sought in the Roman law. Cf. Shom's *Institutes*, English translation, Oxford 1901, pp. 480-83, Aptovitzer, *Beitrage zur Reception* . . . . . Wien, 1907, pp. 39f, Freund, *Zur Geschichte der Eheguterrechts bei Aufloesung der Ehe*, WZKM, Vol. 30, p. 163.

This Palestinian custom gained in popularity, and even under the influence of the Babylonian gaonate, it was not uncommon to insert that clause or a similar clause in the ketubah.[30]

The appeal of this clause was irresistible. Already among the Talmudic authorities it was said: "The verse, 'And your strength shall be spent in vain,' applies to the man who married off his daughter and gave her a large dowry and, before the seven days of festivity were over, his daughter died; thus, he buries his daughter and loses his wealth." [31] To prevent such a double tragedy, the Palestinian clause, with some additional provisions, was gradually incorporated in the body of Jewish law as statute, making the insertion of the clause in the ketubah unnecessary. This legislation came about in two successive steps. It began

[30] An unpublished fragment of the Genizah in the Cambridge University Library, (J-3-Y) dated Egypt, 1089, also T-S 12.659, *Yahrbuch,* Hebrew section, p. 62–בשר ע'ג גחלים—provide in the event of childlessness that all of the dowry be returned to the wife's natural heirs. Other documents record an arrangement that only half shall be given to the woman's heirs. Cf. ketubah ed. Schechter, JQR 13, 220, *Ketubah Jerushalmit,* ed. Berliner, Genizah fragment cited in Mann's *The Jews in Egypt and Palestine Under the Fatimids,* Vol. 2, p. 259, note 7, and an unpublished fragment in Cambridge University Library marked J-3-Y, dated 1116. Schechter takes the Palestinian custom to be the forerunner of the *takanot shum.* I should rather believe it to be the parent of the Toledo enactment, first because these ketubot, continuing the Palestinian usage (and referring to it by the words (כמנהגא רבני ארץ ישראל) are of the Sephardic territory where the Toledo enactment later prevailed; secondly, the provisions do not take into account the time when the woman dies, which is the earmark of the Toledo enactment; thirdly, the provisions are referred to in the above documents as a minhag, or *kahal* enactment, which is the character of the later Toledo enactment, but the Shum enactment is based on legislation of rabbinic origin.

[31] *Yalkut Shimeoni* 674 in comment on Lev. 26, 20.

with a *takanah,* an enactment of R. Jacob Tam, the famous French tosafist of the twelfth century, and was supplemented by a set of takanot of the communities of Speyer, Worms, and Mayence, designated as *Takanot Shum.* The Tam enactment provides that:

1. Unpaid dowry cannot be collected after the wife's death, whether issue remains or not.[32]

2. If the wife dies childless during the first year of her marriage, her property reverts to her father or his heirs.[33]

The Shum enactment has added:

3. If she dies childless during the second year, half of her property is returned to her father or his heirs.[34]

4. Equally, the husband's heirs shall take all gifts

[32] According to Tosafot Ket. 47a s. v. כתב Mordecai, and the codifiers, this provision is not part of the takanah, but a talmudic law, in view of R. Tam's interpretation of beraita Ket. 47a, below. However in REJ, 17, pp. 71-72 and in Responsa of R. Meir Rothenberg, ed. Bloch, Prague, No. 1022, this provision is counted among the takanot of R. Tam.

[33] Tosafot Ket. 47a omits by mistake the necessary condition that the wife die childless. According to Asheri (Responsa, 54) only dowry is to be returned but not mulug. The statement that R. Tam later rescinded his enactment is corroborated by REJ ibid. Iserliss in his notes to *Eben Haezer,* end of 53, designates this as the Tam enactment, R. Meir Rothenberg, ibid., designates it as part of the Shum enactment. Cf. Mordecai Ket. 155, TShBZ, ed. Amsterdam, Vol. 2, 292, and *Yam Shel Shlomo,* Jeb. 4, 18-20.

[34] REJ and Rothenberg cite this together with the other provisions. Mordecai cites it as a special provision. Later halakah has more definitely designated this clause as *takanot shum.* By some anxiety on the part of a scribe to abbreviate the report of the takanah, the text in Mordecai conveys the impression that if the husband dies childless, *his own* property is divided between his wife and his heirs. Of course, it is an incorrect statement of clause five of the takanah. Cf. *Eben Haezer,* end of 53, *Nahlat Shiv'ah* 9, 15-16.

which he had given to his wife, if he died childless during the first year of his marriage.[35]

5. If he dies childless during the second year of his marriage, his wife shall return to his heirs half of the gifts she had received from him.

The takanot of R. Tam and Shum are the basis of the ashkenazic practice. The Ashkenazic ketubah has as a rule no reference to it, but the *tena'im* or the engagement contract specifies that: "because of the possibility of death and litigation, it was agreed by them prior to the marriage that the enactment of Shum shall apply . . . . and after the second year, the law again remain as of Sinai." [36]

The Sephardic practice in the matter of succession is based upon the Toledo enactment, instead of *takanot shum,* which provides that:

1. If issue remains, the woman's dowry, after her death, is divided between the husband and the children.

2. Whether issue has remained or not, any parcel of the dowry which the woman received from her mother is divided, after her death, between her mother and her husband.

3. If no issue is left, the husband and the heirs divide her dowry.

[35] This clause of the takanah has its root in a very frequently occurring evil of the brothers extorting her last penny from the wife of a deceased brother who died childless, on the threat of not freeing her by *Halizah.* This takanah forbids taking any of the woman's possessions and granting her even half of the gifts which she had received from her husband. Mordecai reports that this was included in the *takanot shum,* under the general scheme of returning to the natural heirs all of the property if death occurred during the first year of marriage, and half if it occurred during the second year. Isaac Adrabi in *Dibre Ribot,* responsum 50, dated 1561, includes under the *takanot shum* all of the four foregoing items. See *Eben Haezer* 53, and *Beth Shemuel* notes and *Nahlat Shiv'ah* 9 and 10.

[36] *Nahlat Shiv'ah,* 9, 1.

4. At the husband's death, with or without issue, the wife gets her dowry and above that, in settlement of the other ketubah obligations, no more than the value of half of the estate.[37]

Variations in practice on the matter of succession is reported in some other localities. In one instance, we hear of the practice of giving the husband no succession and the wife no right to her gifts from him, if either died childless during the first year; allowing him half succession and her half of the gifts if either died during the second year of their marriage; and allowing him two thirds of her estate, and equally allowing her two thirds of his gifts if either died during the third year.[38] Some localities rule that all property be returned to the natural heirs if death occurred during the first three years, and that half be returned if death occurred during the fourth or fifth year after the marriage.[39]

The halakah recognizes the power of the Jewish court to modify the order of succession—hence these enactments. But, whether any agreements can be made between husband and wife in the matter of succession contrary to statute is a subject of discussion among

[37] *Tur Eben Haezer*, 118, *Dibre Ribot*, 219, 296; in Algiers, according to the testimony of R. Simeon Duram, clause 3 read that a third of the dowry be given to the wife's heirs and two thirds to the husband, while for the fourth clause of the enactment, they ruled that the wife gets none of the mattan. Cf. TSh-BZ II, 292, 4, 5.

[38] *Eben Haezer* 118, 19.

[39] Cf. *Pithe Teshubah, Eben Haezer*, 53, 14. The press announces the appearance of a monograph by S. Asaf on "*The Various Enactments and Usages in the Matter of the Succession of the Husband to his Wife*," (Hebrew) Jerusalem, 1926. I have not yet seen that work, but no doubt the author has collected and systematized the large mass of details in this matter, which I have omitted for fear that they would overburden this work.

the tannaim. A waiver of succession by the husband is declared by R. Simeon b. Gamaliel void; his opponents declare it valid. Although sentiment is expressed in favor of the view of R. Simeon b. Gamaliel,[40] the halakah, nevertheless, decides that the waiver is valid, because in the first place the husband's right of succession is not conceded to be a Biblical law, and therefore subject to contractual modifications; and in the second place, because it represents a deviation from statute only in matters of money, which would be permissible even were it granted that the husband's right of succession to his wife is a Biblical ordinance.[41]

[40] Ket. 83a, Tos. Ket. 9, 2, Ket. 83b-84a, Jer. Ket. 32d. R. Hai Gaon renders a legal decision that the view of R. Simeon b. Gamaliel prevails—*Teshubot Geone Mizrah u-Ma'arab*, 228.

[41] Cf. Kid. 19b, Jer. Ket. ibid, Alfasi, Asheri, Mordecai, and *Milhamot* of Nahmanides ad Ket. 83b, Yad, Ishut, 23, 5-7.

CHAPTER IX

BED AND BOARD

The elemental obligation implied in marriage is sexual contact between husband and wife. Without specific statute, therefore, or without any provision in any contract, husband and wife owe each other the duty of living together in conjugal union.

Because Jewish law permits polygamy and does not permit polyandry, the duty of conjugal contact is considered a duty upon the husband, who, under the circumstances holds the position of advantage. The wife is considered as holding certain rights of sexual attention from her husband. From Bible days we know that these rights were sometimes conveyed from one wife to another[1] and were respected even in the case of a wife-slave.[2] The Biblical injunction in the case of the wife-slave is applied by the rabbis also to the free-born wife, and on this they base their conclusion that the right to marital satisfaction is Biblically granted to every Jewish wife.[3] A mutual agreement between husband and wife to forego conjugal union is void, therefore, because contrary to Biblical prescription.[4]

The frequency of intercourse, as prescribed by the rabbis, depends upon the husband's vocation, ranging

[1] Gen. 30, 15-16.

[2] Exod. 21, 10.

[3] Mekilta ad loc.; see also Ket. 47b. R. Elazar b. Jacob also admits that the obligation of intercourse is Biblical. See *She'eltot,* 60

[4] Kid. 19b.

from daily contact to once in six months.[5] The husband's absence from home deprives his wife of her due attention, and therefore, without the wife's consent, laborers may be absent only for one full week, students for one month. Later halakah permitted students to be away from their wives for two and three years at a time.[6] Since the average husband gives his wife sexual satisfaction once a week, the rabbis advise that even under polygamy, no one shall marry more than four wives, so that he can be with every wife at least once a month.[7] Inability to fulfill the sexual obligation constitutes a ground for divorce;[8] his wilful neglect of that obligation constitutes "rebellion" (מורד), and is punishable by a fine of three dinnarim — according to another view, three trepekin — per week, which is added to the wife's ketubah.[9]

The wife's refusal to have conjugal union with her husband is also "rebellion" (מורדת), punishable by a severer fine[10] of seven dinnarim — according to another view, seven trepekin — per week, deducted from her ketubah until the ketubah is cancelled;[11] and then she

[5] Ket. 61b.

[6] Mishna Ket. 61b. and Gemara 62b.

[7] Jeb. 44a.

[8] Jeb. 65a-b.

[9] Ket. 63a ff. It seems that the treatment of the rebellious husband was not changed since the days of that mishna. Cf. Yad, Ishut 14, 15.

[10] The severer fine for a woman rebel is to be understood by the fact that it is a greater infringement upon social conventions for the woman to defy them, but the Talmud gives the reason that denial of sexual intercourse is harder on a man than on a woman — witness the fact that men pay harlots — therefore the woman's rebellion is more serious. See Ket, 64b, Jer., Ket. 30b.

[11] There is a view in the Mishna that the deduction is continued even to the extent of infringing upon her private mulug.

is divorced. This was the older practice. Later tannaim instituted the following procedure. For a period of four weeks, announcement in the synagogue is made on every Sabbath[12] of her rebellion against her husband, and at the end of that period[13] a court messenger warns her that if she does not yield she will be divorced and forfeit her ketubah. If she persists, she is given a year's separation from her husband without support,[14] and thereafter she is divorced with the total loss of her ketubah, taking with her of her dowry only what she can get possession of.[15] The gaonim of the

The divorce following is either a matter of choice with the husband or a ruling of the rourt, depending upon the interpretation of the Talmudic procedure. See Yad, Ishut 14, 10 and *Magid* at end of 14, 9.

[12] Tos. Ket. 5, 7, Ket. 63b. The reading of Tos. shows that the announcement was made once a week, not necessarily on the Sabbath day nor in the synagogue. Maimonides, Yad, Ishut, 14, 9, believes that the announcement was made every day.

[13] According to the amoraim, two warnings are sent, once before that period and once after it. See Ket. 63b. I have followed the interpretation of R. Nisim, Ket. 63b, that the warning states that she will lose the ketubah. Rashi believes that she is told that she will lose seven dinnarim per week. RABD believes she is told that she will lose either the whole ketubah at the end of the four weeks or seven dinnarim per week, the choice being left with her.

[14] This is saboraic. Maimonides and others take this procedure to apply to rebellion out of malice. According to Rashi, this soboraic enactment applies only to the case of rebellion out of revulsion. See *Shita Mekubezet*, Ket. 64a.

[15] Because there is no decision reached whether she can even take with her what is left of her dowry, only that is hers which she can make herself possessor of(תפסה לא מפקינן מינה). Ket. 64a. I have followed Maimonides in this and the previous matter. His decision is based on the belief that the case of R. Zebid's daughter-in-law (Ket. 63b) illustrates rebellion out of malice. Were it rebellion out of revulsion, there would be no forfeiture of the dowry in any form. Rashi, Nahmonides, Adret, and others believe that it illustrates the case of rebellion out

seventh century[16] modified the procedure, out of fear that the woman might institute proceedings in a Gentile court. They did away with the year's separation, and ordered her to be divorced immediately with the forfeiture of her mohar and mattan. Her zon-barzel was returned to her at the value entered into the ketubah, and her mulug went back to her in the condition in which it was at the time of the divorce.[17]

The rebellious woman, according to the dominant conception, is the one who refuses to cohabit with her husband out of malice toward him, or the betrothed who out of malice to her spouse refuses to enter into nuptials, or the levirate woman who in like spirit refuses to accept her *levir.*[18] But the wife who does not

of revulsion. According to them, the woman who rebels out of malice loses her dowry and ketubah completely, taking only what is left of her mulug. Should she make herself possessor of her dowry, the court would order her to return it. See *Magid,* Ishut, 14, 8-9, *Beth Sh'muel, Eben Haezer,* 77, 7.

[16] The authority for this enactment is R. Hunai of Sura. The takanah is reported in Alfasi, Ket. 64a, *Itur,* p. 68d, *Hagahot Maimon.* ad Yad, Ishut 14, 13, Tosafot RID ad Ket. ibid. *Responsen d. Geonim,* Harkavey, 230, *Hemda Genuzah* 89 and 140, *Shaare Zedek,* 15, p. 56, *Teshubot Geonim Kadmonim* 91. See JQR N. S., Vol. 10, p. 121 and Aptovitzer *Beitrage zur mosaisch. Rezeption in armenisch. Recht,* SKAW, Phil.-hist. Klasse, Vol. 157, pp. 9f. Mann, in JQR l. c. maintains that the geonic enactment was never more than of local influence.

[17] The geonic Takanah was not wholly clear even to early authorities. See Joel Mueller, *Einleitung in die Responsen der babyl. Geonim,* pp. 63 and 115. *Itur* believes that the geonic enactment dealt wholly with the case of rebellion out of revulsion, but did not alter in the least the Talmudic procedure in the case of rebellion out of malice. Her loss of both mohar and mattan according to the geonic enactment is reported in *Shaare Zedek,* 15. Other sources report that her mohar is given her.

[18] Cf. Ket. 64a, *Teshubot Geonim Kadmonim* 91, Yad, Ishut, 14, 12.

live with her husband out of an honest revulsion to him is a lesser offender.[19] The Talmudic method of dealing with her is variously understood. According to one view, she is of the same status as the real rebel, and is divorced after a year's separation without maintenance at the total forfeiture of her ketubah, save what she can take possession of out of her dowry.[20] According to another view, out of respect to her feelings she is granted a divorce upon application, but she forfeits mohar and mattan, taking along her dowry in the condition she finds it.[21] According to the third view she is compelled to wait a year, not as a punitive measure but as an attempt to effect a reconciliation; the attempt having proven futile, she is divorced only at her husband's pleasure, but without any loss of her ketubah.[22] However, the geonic enactment, superseding Talmudic law, provided for the same treatment of "rebellion" of any kind, whether out of malice or out of revulsion.[23]

The geonic enactment was but too short lived. Alfasi still finds it in vogue, but Maimonides finds it repudiated in his day. It was too lenient a measure for rebellion. Post-geonic law, therefore, returned to Talmudic legislation in the treatment of "rebellion."

There is no record through the entire Talmudic

[19] (מאים עלי). The distinction is amoraic.

[20] The opinion of Rashi, who interprets the whole amoraic legislation, including the story of R. Zebid's daughter-in-law, as referring to the rebel out of revulsion. See note 15 above. According to him, the rebel out of malice has no claim upon dowry at all.

[21] Maimonides, Yad, Ishut, 14, 8.

[22] The teaching of R. Nisim and Tosafot RID, Ket. 64a.

[23] This seems to be the consensus of the geonic reports with the exception of *Itur* cited in note 17 above.

period of a ketubah clause specifying the sexual obligation. Two reasons may account for this. For one, the obligation is so elemental that its specification in the ketubah was deemed unnecessary; for another, as long as the ketubah was not definitely the instrument of nuptials, an agreement for intercourse would have sounded indelicate. In post-Talmudic days, however, the clause of conjugal contact made its appearance in the ketubah, reading, "and I will go in unto thee according to the manner of the world." [24]

The husband's duty to support his wife arises from the conception that he owns her as he owns his slave.[25] There can be no doubt that this obligation upon the husband is coeval with the institution of marriage, but no definite injunction in this matter is found in the Bible. The Bible has a reference to it in the following verses, "If he assign her (the Jewish female-slave) to his son, then shall he do unto her after the right of the daughters.. . . .her food, her raiment, and her duty of marriage shall not be diminished." [26] To the tannaim, these verses teach us that the duties of a master to a slave-wife are the same as those to a free-born wife, namely, food, raiment, and marital union. This is also the interpretation of the *Targumim*. On the basis of these verses, the tannaim declare the alimentation obligation to be Biblical.[27] A tannaitic text very unreliably transmitted, however, speaks of alimentation as a rab-

[24] It reads ומיעל עליכי כאורח כל ארעא. This phrase is taken from the *Targum* of Gen. 19, 31. Later ketubot read ומיעל לותיכי either by error or because of the greater delicacy of the expression.

[25] Ket. 47b, Jeb. 66a. Gitin 11b-12b.

[26] Exod. 21, 10.

[27] Ket. 47b-48a and Mek. ed. Friedmann, p. 78b and note 28. RSBM (Tosafot Ket. 48a s. v. רבי) points out that R. Elazar

binical obligation,[28] due to the fact, probably that the Bible does not give a direct injunction to support the

b. Jacob (Ket.) and equally R. Jonathan (Mek.) do not deny the Biblical character of the alimentation obligation. It is evident also from the fact that they admit that clothing is a Biblical obligation that they could not have maintained that food would not be Biblical. The amoraic interpretation of these tannaim does not force them to assume otherwise. That R. Elazar b. Jacob maintains that the alimentation obligation is rabbinical is first taught by *She'eltot* 60, ed. Dierenfurt 1785, pp. 19b-c, and thereafter followed by Nahmanides (*Bible Commentary*, Exod. 21, 10), R. Nisim (Ket. 47b.) *Magid* (Yad, Ishut 12, 2) and others. Cf. *Hinuk*, 46. Maimonides (Yad ibid.) and Adret (*Tur Eben Haezer* 69) decide halakically that alimentation is Biblical. See the learned article in *She'elat Shalom* in comment on *She'eltot* l. c. A number of tannaitic sources assume the Biblical character of alimentation. Sifra, Lev. 25, Mishna Ket. 5, 2, Mek. p. 76 dealing with the woman's right to eat of heave offering, or Tos. Ket. 4, 7, Ket. 56a, Kid. 19b dealing with the right of waiving the alimentation obligation by mutual agreement.

[28] Ket. 47b, which the amoraim correct (ibid. and 58b) in an unnatural manner. The amoraim, both Babylonian and Palestinian, follow this tannaitic text and teach that alimentation is rabbinical. Maimonides, who admits that the alimentation obligation is Biblical, says this by way of explanation for the amoraim: Since the arrangement is to give the husband the right over the wife's earnings in exchange for her support, the whole matter is termed a rabbinical enactment, even though alimentation in itself is a Biblical obligation. The Babylonian amoraic view is recorded in Ket. 58b, 83a, Jeb. 89a, etc. The Palestinian amoraim seek evidence from tannaitic sources, but without much success. They cite (Jer. Ma'asrot 50b.) the mishna of Ma'asrot 3, 1 on the subject of the woman's right to eat of the grain belonging to her husband before it was tithed. They also cite Tos. Shevi'it 5, 22 concerning the woman's right to eat of the products of her husband's field in the Sabbatical year. They infer from these cases that the Bible does not recognize the husband's duty — according to the tannaim — to support his wife. The matter is otherwise to be understood. The use of grain before tithing or in the Sabbatical year is per-

free-born wife but refers to it as an accepted practice.[29]

The amount of maintenance which a husband owes his wife is determined, in general, by the husband's means, provided she gets her necessities according to the standards to which she is accustomed.[30] In the most modest circumstances, he must give her a weekly ration of two *kabin* of wheat or four of barley, half a *kab* of peas or beans, half a *loeg* of oil, a *kab* of dates or figs or other fruit of corresponding portion, wine for cooking and an extra portion of it for the nursing mother.[31] This ration provides fifteen to sixteen meals for the week, two meals a day for herself and two extra meals for company. A third meal for the Sabbath is not in-

mitted; the sale of it is prohibited. When used by the woman in a separate domicile, according to the tannaim, it looks as if a debt is paid by it or it is put to some such commercial use. They also cite (Jer. Ket. 31b) mishna Ket. 6, 7, which teaches that the husband's vow depriving his wife of the enjoyment of any of his property is valid. On this basis they say that the Bible does not recognize the alimentation obligation. But, the fact is that it is not a question as to how much right he has over his property, in view of the lien on it for the support of his wife. It is based on the husband's right over his wife's person, for he can also impose a vow on her not to enjoy her own property.

[29] The inference from the Bible is based on the words כמשפט הבנות which imply that the Bible found this practice in existence, namely, husbands being required to support their free-born wives. The hermeneutic principle of this Biblical derivation is formulated as הרי זה בא ללמד ונמצא למד, the same as was employed to derive mohar from the words כמהר הבתלות (See note 23, p. 62 above), and evidently this principle of deduction, according to certain views, yields only a rabbinical institution.

[30] Ket. 48a, 61a. "The wife ascends with her husband, but does not descend with him" is a legal maxim, giving the woman the advantages of her own standards as well as the husband's.

[31] Ket. 64b-65b, Jer. Ket. 30b, Ekah Rabba, ed. Buber, p. 86.

cluded in the budget, because she eats the first Sabbath meal at his table, regardless of what provision he has made for her for the weekdays.[32] In richer families, the wife is also provided with wine for beverage purposes, provided the husband is in a position to watch her conduct, for wine encourages levity.[33]

The obligation on the husband to give his wife raiment may be treated as part of his alimentation obligation,[34] but the Bible mentions it specifically and, therefore, it is accounted by the rabbis as a distinct Biblical obligation.[35] Her clothing included a head cover, a girdle, a pair of shoes at the approach of every holiday season, and fifty zuzim worth of dresses — the kind that will become her age and stature — at the beginning of the winter season.[36] If his wealth or her station warrant greater demands, he must meet either of these standards, even to the point of buying her silks and perfumes.[37] In certain localities, the husband was expected to spend on his wife's perfume ten dinnars for every *maneh* of dowry that he received.[38] Of household articles, he must give her a rug or a mat, a bed and mattress — in richer families, even a pillow — a cup, a jar, a pot, a flask, a candle, and a wick lamp.[39] And, in addition to all these luxuries, he must

[32] Ibid.

[33] Ket. 65a, Tos. Ket. 5, 8, Jer. Ket. 30b.

[34] It is so understood by R. Nisim ad Ket. 47b.

[35] There is no amoraic opinion contesting this view. However, Nahmanides in his *Bible Commentary* and R. Nisim, ibid. maintain that clothing is a rabbinical obligation.

[36] Ket. 48a, 64a.

[37] Ket. 65a, 66b.

[38] Ket. 66b. It is uncertain whether it means ten dinnars per week, per year, every year, or only the first year.

[39] Tos. Ket. 5, 8, Jer. Ket. 30b, Ket. 65a.

give her in cash a silver *maneh* per week for spending money.[40]

In the remote past, the husband's obligation to support and clothe his wife probably commenced with the betrothal, and even later it was not unusual for the groom to support and clothe his betrothed.[41] But later halakah decides that these obligations commence with nuptials. If the nuptial ceremony has been delayed beyond the customary date on account of the groom's neglect, he must pay for her support and clothing during the period of delay.[42] The obligation terminates at divorce, only if the divorce permits her to marry another. If it is of doubtful validity, so long as she cannot marry another, the alimentation duty continues.[43] In a levirate marriage, the *levir* takes over the deceased husband's alimentation obligation, but assumes that obligation on his own account from the moment his nuptials with the levirate woman are solemnized.[44]

As the husband's alimentation obligation is based upon the conception of his ownership of the wife, so, similarly, is his right to her earnings. In fact, his right to her earnings appears to be a more fundamental manifestation of that conception.[45] But as the idea of ownership was gradually replaced by the finer idea of marriage contract, the law discovered a correspondence

[40] Ket. 64b. Cf. Yad, Ishut 12, 10.

[41] Cf. Appendix A. Ket. 67a, Jer. Nedar. 42a, Jer. Ket. 34b.

[42] Ket. 57a. See Ket. 2a-b, Jer. Ket. 29d.

[43] Gittin 74b, Ket. 97b, Jer. Gittin 49b.

[44] Tos. Ket. 5, 2.

[45] It was a valid question that arose in the minds of the amoraim (Ket. 58b) whether מזוני עיקר or מעשי ידיה עיקר. Our view favors the choice of the latter, namely, that the conveyance of the girl's labor is more fundamental in the conception of marriage than the obligation of supporting her. Cf. Nowack, *Archaologie*, p. 152.

between support and earnings, the one in exchange for the other. For the duty of supporting his wife, the law gives the husband the right to her earnings.[46] In toto, this exchange is simple enough, but the halakah treats the matter in greater detail. It divides support into three categories, necessary food and clothing, the increment above the line of necessity (מותר מזונות and מותר בלאות), and the further addition of spending money (מעה כסף).

Likewise, the woman's earning has a triple division:— normal labor under normal effort, standardized as five *selaim's* worth of woof work in Judea,[47] the increment of earnings above the normal standard(העדפה); and extra earning through unusual effort and skill (העדפה שע'י הדחק). The correspondence between these items appears simple, yet it is a subject of much discussion among the amoraim, how every item of support is in exchange for a corresponding item of earning.[48] The conclusion, however, is that the husband is entitled to all items of his wife's earnings, but the wife is not permitted to pocket anything left above her needs from her allowance for maintenance, except the partly worn clothing which, it is deemed, may be of use to her on some inauspicious occasion.[49]

What a woman finds, without the exertion of any labor, is also the husband's as part of the marriage bargain. It goes to the husband even as part of her

[46] Ket. 47b.

[47] Ket. 64b.

[48] See Ket. 59a, 66a. The prevalent view seems to be that the basic support pays for the normal labor, while the spending money pays for the earnings above that margin. He need not pay for extra earnings through unusual skill and effort, for this is treated as a "find" (מציאה) which also belongs to the husband.

[49] Tos. Ket. 5, 9, Ket. 65b.

earnings.[50] This is the legal position; historically, the husband's right to the things found by his wife cannot be derived from his right to her earnings. There is a tradition in the name of R. Akiba that what the woman finds belongs to herself,[51] but later halakah was not overawed by this eminent authority and decided that the husband is the rightful owner. For one reason, peace in the family required such a concession to the husband, and for another reason, that without this grant to the husband the wife would have every chance to steal from him and protect her booty by the claim that she found it.[52]

The schedule of a woman's work in the house comprises grinding flour, baking, washing, cooking, wool knitting, nursing the infant, making her husband's bed, mixing his drinks, washing his face, hands and feet.[53] The husband may not compel her to do these labors for others nor to do any work that is unbecoming, unpleasant, or harmful to her physical charms.[54] She is not to be expected to earn a living for the family, and there is no blessing in a home supported by the wife.[55] The woman may delegate some of her labors to her slaves, but not the personal care she owes her husband, such as washing his face, hands, and feet, or making his bed.[56] In no case is she permitted to throw off so much of her work as to make her idle, for "idleness leads to distraction."

[50] Ket. 65b.

[51] Ibid. But the tradition is very unreliable.

[52] Jeb. 90b (משום איבה), Jer. B. B. 8a, Jer. Ket. 30c (משום קטטה).

[53] Ket. 59b, 61a.

[54] Ket. 61b.

[55] Pesah. 50b.

[56] Ket. 61a.

The woman is always given the choice of keeping her own earnings and of supporting herself,[57] provided she performs the duties of personal attention she owes her husband. If she is supported by her husband and refuses to do her work, and more especially if she refuses to render the private services which devolve upon her, she is treated, according to a certain amoraic view, as a *moredet,* a rebel, and is fined in accordance with the law as given above.[58] The final halakah, however, does not support that view. It does not consider a woman's refusal to work as a case of rebellion. If the husband is not resourceful enough to cope with the problem himself, the court permits him to break her stubbornness either by the threat of the lash or by the more dignified method of starving her.[59]

[57] Ket. 58b.

[58] The view of R. Jose b. Hanina, Ket. 63a. Her fine should be seven dinnarim or trepekin per week for failing to perform the seven kinds of labor which the mishna imposes on her. See Jer. Ket. 30b and Tosafot Ket. 63a, s. v. פוחתין. Tosafot (ibid) seeks to make this view of R. Jose compatible with the view that the wife may choose to keep her own earnings if she demands no support, which view would imply that the wife can never be a rebel for not working for her husband. These views are here adjusted by us in either of two ways. Though the wife can refuse to labor for her husband, she cannot do so if she takes his support, without being termed a rebel; again, under no circumstances can she free herself from the duty of performing the private services for her husband. She can then be declared a rebel if she refuses to do that specific work. See Tosafot ibid. and R. Nisim ad Ket. 63a. The latter explanation is not wholly acceptable to me, because the Jerushalmi prescribes a punishment of seven dinnarim for the seven kinds of labor — apparently rebellion is applied to all the labors which a woman should do but fails to perform.

[59] Though R. Hai Gaon accepts the view of R. Jose b. Hanina, the final halakah opposes him. See *Itur,* p. 68, Alfasi and R. Nisim ad Ket. 63a. Since the rule of *moredet* does not apply

If the husband is guilty of voluntary non-support of his wife, according to Rab he is compelled to divorce her and pay her the ketubah; according to Samuel the court employs such methods as it may choose to compel him to support her; while a later amora believes that he is to be dealt with in accordance with the disciplinary methods prescribed for the rebellious husband.[60] If he fails of his alimentation obligation because of poverty, the court may, in the opinion of a tosafist, compel him to hire himself out for labor in order to earn a livelihood, for thus he asserts in the ketubah: "And I shall work . .. and shall support thee."[61] But the prevalent opinion gives the woman no redress in such an instance except to get her divorce and a judgment on her husband for the payment of the ketubah.[62] In the event the husband is admittedly incapable of making a living, the law evidently has no choice but to grant the wife a divorce and a judgment on her husband for the payment of her ketubah.[63]

The court supports the wife out of the husband's estate in the event that he becomes insane[64] or if he has

RABD and Maimonides discuss whether the husband shall discipline his wife, for refusal to do her work, by the lash or by starvation. See Yad, Ishut 21, 10 and RABD thereto.

[60] Tos. Ket. 13, 1, Ket. 77a and Ket. 63a. The last view here mentioned is taken by the Talmud as in no way contradicting the first view, for even if the wife is treated as a rebel the final step in the treatment is divorce. The halakah seems to favor the view — that of Samuel — that the husband be compelled to support the wife. See Yad, Ishut 12, 11.

[61] See Tosafot Ket. 63a s. v. באומר and *Hagahot Maimoniyot*, 8 ad Yad ibid.

[62] Tosafot Ket. ibid. arguing against the interpretation of אפלח of R. Elijah. See Responsa of RDBZ, Vol. III, 566.

[63] Yad. ibid.

imposed a vow on her restraining her from the enjoyment of his property.[65] In the case of desertion, by a ruling of Rab and Samuel, the court does not act on her petition for alimony until three months have elapsed after the husband's departure, for it is assumed that no household is ever short of a three months' supply of necessaries.[66] After that period the court sells of the husband's estate as much as is necessary for the wife's alimony. Without court action, however, the wife may sell on her own account four or five dinnarim's worth of her husband's property for the purpose of buying herself a headdress.[67] Should she sell a greater amount than that for her support without a court order, in spite of the fact that her action is not authorized, the sale is valid, if the goods brought the standard market price.[68] If in her husband's absence she has been supported by a private person, that individual "has put his money on a deer's horn"— he has no action against the husband or his estate.[69] If she has borrowed from a private person for her support, that debt must be paid by the husband or his estate.[70]

Whenever the husband fails of his alimentation ob-

[64] Tos. Ket. 13, 1, Ket. 48a, 107a.

[65] Tos. Ket. 7, 1, Ket. 70a. Since the wife may not get her support directly from her husband because of the vow, a guardian is appointed by the court to support her and draw his funds from the husband's estate.

[66] Ket. 107a. Samuel would apply the three months' limit only to permanent alimony; for temporary alimony, that is, if there is no ground for suspicion that the husband died, he would extend the time limit. The halakah is against him.

[67] B.K. 119a.

[68] Yad, Ishut 12, 16, based on Ket. 96b.

[69] Ket. 107b. Mielziner in *The Jewish Law of Marriage and Divorce* p. 100 note 5 points to a parallel to this law in Bishop's *Marriage and Divorce*, fourth ed., Vol. II, p. 612.

[70] Ket. ibid., Yad, Ishut 12, 19.

ligation the wife retains her earnings for her own support. The wife's earnings are also drawn upon for her support before the court acts on her petition for alimony.[71] According to certain views, the husband may say to his wife: Get your maintenance out of your earnings — but he must add the difference, if the earnings do not suffice for her maintenance.[72] The husband may even stipulate in the marriage agreement to be altogether freed from the alimentation obligation—and naturally forfeit the wife's earnings. Such a stipulation was not uncommon in olden times, especially in the case of husbands who continued their studies after marriage.[73] It is not an infrequent experience even in modern Jewish life. When such a condition of marriage does occur today, however, the husband seldom — or rather never — challenges his alimentation obligation, if the wife is compelled to depend on his support.

The Talmud does not cite a ketubah clause stipulating the husband's alimentation obligation. Yet it is not to be assumed that the Talmudic ketubah had no such clause, even though alimentation is elemental in marriage, like marital union. Rather must it be taken as an insignificant omission, for in the levirate ketubah of Talmudic days we do read the clause: "I, so-and-so, take unto myself so-and-so as my levirate bride

[71] The view of Asheri that the court deducts the wife's earnings whenever it is called to supply her maintenance. Maimonides is of the opinion that no calculation is made as to her earnings until her husband returns — if it is a case of desertion — or until it becomes a case of permanent alimony instead of a temporary matter. See Yad, Ishut 12,16.

[72] Ket. 70b. but see Yad, Ishut 12, 16 and *Kesef Mishna* thereto.

[73] Tos. Ket. 4, 7; Jer. Ket. 29d, Ket. 56a. R. Meir contests this view, for it would permit a stipulation contrary to Biblical law.

to support and maintain her properly." [74] The inference from this is apparent, that the ordinary ketubah also had an alimentation clause. But its form is not known to us. In post-Talmudic ketubot the formula reads: "and I shall give thee . . . and thy sustenance and thy clothing and thy needs. . . ." In some ketubot there is a repetition of the alimentation clause in the following form: "and I shall serve and honor and support and maintain thee in the manner of Jewish husbands who serve and honor and support and maintain their wives in truth.[75] The former must be taken to be the original Jewish ketubah clause, stipulating the alimentation obligation in conjunction with the clothing and conjugal union, even in the Biblical order. The latter is taken by David Kaufman[76] to be of Byzantine origin, adopted in the Jewish ketubah from a non-Jewish source. It stipulated originally that the husband shall honor and support his wife and that the wife shall honor and obey her huband. The church emphasized the latter part of the provision, while the synagogue, with but scanty instances where the latter half of the provision is also included,[77] has perpetuated the former half of the clause, the part specifying the husband's duties by his wife, for the ketubah is essentially an instrument to safeguard the wife's rights, not the husband's. Thus it was that without intention to reiterate the alimentation

[74] Jeb. 52b.

[75] The repetition is omitted in the ketubah ed. Abrahams in *Jews' College Jubilee* Volume, Saadya ketubah ed. Gaster in MGWJ, Fostat ketubah of 1030 in REJ, Schechter ketubah in JQR. The repetition is retained in the R. Hai ketubah and the R. Gershon ketubah, the *Sefer Ha-shetarot, Mahzor Vitri*, Yad, and modern ketubot.

[76] MGWJ, 1897, pp. 217 f.

[77] Kaufmann points to such instances; contained also in the Karaitic ketubah.

clause, the alimentation duty was mentioned again in a phrase which, while adopted from a foreign source, beautified the style of the deed[78] and sounded well when recited aloud by the *Hazan.*[79]

[78] *Shita Mekubezet* quoting RITBA ad Ket.63 לשופרי דשטרי

[79] Cf. Adret, Responsum 629, *Hagahot Maimoniyot, Ishut* 10, 7.

CHAPTER X

Sundry Obligations

The husband must provide medicine and medical service for his wife in case of illness. The mishna treats this as a separate marriage obligation,[1] but in truth it is only an extension of the alimenation obligation, just as support today is understood also to include doctors' bills.[2] There is no record in the Talmud or in post-Talmudic writings of a special clause specifying this obligation in the marriage writ, and one feels inclined to believe that no such clause ever existed — probably because medical aid was taken to be included in the alimentation clause of the ketubah.

The law, however, is sensitive to a distinction between medical aid and support. Food or clothing represents current expense, but medical aid may represent a hospital bill or a doctor's fee for a protracted illness. The average husband who can well provide for current household expense may find himself at the point of ruin because of a large bill for medical treatment. Therefore the law distinguishes between current medical expenses and a lump sum medical bill, that which is of no definite amount and that which is set down at a definite figure. The Babylonian Talmud teaches that the husband must pay all medical expenses whether of the one kind or of the other; the Palestinian Talmud teaches that whereas the husband must pay for

[1] Mishna Ket. 51a. Jerushalmi omits from this mishna the provision for medical service .

[2] Tos. Ket. 4, 5. See Rashi Ket. 51a, s. v. חייב.

current medical service, he cannot be forced to pay a lump fee for his wife's medical treatment. He can be expected to give medicine only as he gives food.[3] It is agreed by both Babylonian and Palestinian traditions, however, that when the wife in her widowhood is supported out of her husband's estate, the heirs are obligated to supply her with current medical aid in the same manner as they must give her her food, but need not pay any lump sum for medical service. In such an eventuality she draws on her ketubah.[4]

Medical service is different from maintenance in another respect. One can gauge how much maintenance may cost, but no one can estimate how much a husband might have to spend to cure his wife's illness. Is it not possible for a husband to be economically ruined by a chronically ailing wife? What is he to do? Since the law permits the husband at his pleasure to divorce his wife, he may in this case say to his wife: Here is thy divorce and thy ketubah, go and cure thyself.[5] This is his privilege according to the older law, but the later tannaim declared it a moral misdeed for the husband to divorce his wife while she is sick —

[3] See Ket. 52b, and Jer. B. B. 17a, Jer. Ket. 29a. The difference between them consists in the fact that the Babli takes the statement of R. Simeon b. Gamaliel (Tos. Ket. 4, 5) to refer to the case of a widow demanding medical service out of her husband's estate, while the Jerushalmi interprets it to refer to the case of a wife demanding medical service from her husband. *Itur* decides with the Palestinian tradition, Cf *Shita mekubezet*, Ket. 51a; R. Asher and R. Nissim (Ket. 52b) and Maimonides decide with the Babli and they wish to read in the Jerushalmi נכסי בעליך instead of בעליך. Cf. Bloch, *Sha'are Torat Hatakanot*, II p. 112, Yad, Ishut, 14, 17, and *Eben Haezer*, 79

[4] Ket. ibid.

[5] Tos. Ket. 4, 5, Ket. 51a.

he may not divorce her, they say, until she is recovered.[6]

Piracy, highway robbery, bedouin attacks upon towns, and ancient methods of warfare made slavery and captivity a danger to which every one was subjected, and more especially women. A ransom was required to redeem the captive or the slave. Where the family could not raise the required ransom, the community paid it out of its charity funds. To redeem the captive was one of the most sacred duties of the community. The community was naturally interested to place the responsibility of redeeming a captive on some member of the captive's family. In the case of a girl, the law of the more remote past placed the obligation of paying ransom upon the father as long as she was unmarried and upon the husband after marriage.[7]

Later halakah does not recognize a legal obligation on the father to pay ransom for his daughter,[8] although one may well assume that his moral obligation was never denied by the law.[9] Why the law was lenient with the father in his duties by his daughter, one can account for only by a general conjecture. Daughters were an unwelcome burden to fathers. They were all liability and no asset. Marrying off a daughter at the cost of a large dowry after cheerless years of raising her was enough of a burden, which parents willingly

[6] Sifre, ed. Friedmann, 214, p. 113. See *Magid* ad Yad, Ishut 14, 17.

[7] See Appendix A. Evidently, according to R. Jose b. R. Judah, who gives the father the right to the use of his daughter's mulug (Tos. Ket. 4, 1, Ket 47a), his duty to pay ransom for his daughter should be taken for granted, if we follow out the amoraic scheme of the correspondence between the fruit of mulug and ransom.

[8] Ket. 47a.

[9] See Ket. 47a.

or unwillingly had to carry. The law therefore felt that to add burdens upon the father would be unjust. If the father is able and willing to pay the ransom for his daughter, he may do so as prompted by his conscience, but let not the court force him to do it. Rather that the community pay the ransom. Furthermore, the Talmud gives the impression that daughters were accounted as belonging more to their mother than to their father[10] — perhaps as a survival of the old matronimic system. Which adds a reason for the absence of a legal obligation in later halakah on the father to pay ransom for his daughter.

The husband's obligation to pay ransom for his wife grew in strength with the development of the law. Originally he had only a statutory obligation, probably imposed on him by the community; later he assumed a contractual obligation also by virtue of his marriage writ wherein a specific clause formulated that obligation. He paid ransom, therefore, both as a duty to the community and as an obligation to his wife. If he was an Israelite, he inserted into the ketubah the clause: If thou be made captive I shall redeem thee and take thee back to me as wife.[11] If he was an Aaronite he entered the following variant into the ketubah: If thou be made captive I shall redeem thee and cause thee to return to thy land.[12] For it is prohibited to a

[10] Among others, the *ketubat bnan nukban* proves this point, for it is as a concession to the mother that the father supports the daughters out of his estate.

[11] Ket. 51a.

[12] Ibid. The Babylonians interpret the words "to thy land" as to thy home town; the Palestinians (Jer. Ket. 29a) interpret it as to any inhabited part of the world. Their reading in the Mishna (according to Lowe, *The Mishna on Which The Palestinian Talmud is Based*, Cambridge 1883) is למדינתא instead of

priest to have a captive woman as wife because of the possiblity that she has been defiled by her captor — therefore after redeeming her he cannot take her back as wife.

According to the older social conception, the betrothed was in every sense the wife of her husband. According to the older usage the ketubah was written at betrothal. Hence the older halakah imposes on the husband the obligation of paying ransom for his wife from the moment of betrothal. However, as the bond of betrothal weakened and the betrothed maiden was considered as still belonging to her father's household, and as the writing of the ketubah was in the course of time shifted from betrothal to nuptials, the newer law taught that the groom is not obligated to pay ransom for his betrothed; that his obligation commences only with nuptials.[13]

The Babylonian tradition has it that the husband is compensated for the duty of paying ransom by the privilege he enjoys of using his wife's mulug. The Palestinians have no knowledge of such a compensation. Whatever is offered in the Babylonian Talmud to prove that the tannaim had in mind a correspondence between ransom and the fruit of mulug is highly speculative. One feels quite at liberty to conclude that the Palestinian tradition is more correct in this case.[14]

Two tannaitic traditions are submitted in the Talmud as to the maximum amount a husband is required to pay as ransom for his wife. According to one tradition, the first time the wife is made captive, her hus-

למדינתך. Cf. Maimonides, *Mishna Commentary*, Ket. ibid., Yad, Ishut 14, 18.

[13] See Appendix A.

[14] Cf. above p. 116.

band must pay a ransom of even ten times her value as a slave; after that only her market value as a slave.[15] According to the second tradition, the first time he must pay a ransom even equal to ten times the amount of her ketubah; after that only an amount equal to her ketubah. R. Simeon b. Gamaliel permits the maximum never to reach beyond either the woman's ketubah or her market value, considering overpayment of ransom a menace to the community.[16]

The first part of the ransom clause is to a certain extent limited by the second part, that is, the payment of ransom is obligatory on the husband provided he can take his captive wife back unto himself — or in the case of a priest, provided the only bar to his taking her back is the captivity. In a prohibited marriage, therefore, the ransom clause is of no effect.[17] If at the time of the marriage there was no objection to his taking her back after captivity, but the objection to it developed later, as for example, where the husband or the wife vowed not to live together — in other words, if the clause in its fullness was valid at the time of the marriage but was no longer valid at the time of the occurence of the captivity, R. Eliezer teaches that the duty to pay ransom does obtain, while R. Judah believes that the obligation is nullified. The former traces the obligation to the moment of its inception, the latter to the time of its execution.[18]

[15] There is also an opinion that the husband need not pay more than one ransom. Cf. Tosafot Ket. 52a s. v. רצה.

[16] Ket. 52a-b. See Tosafot Ket. 52a, s. v. והיין

[17] Ket. ibid. According to Abaye, if a priest entered into a prohibited marriage, his ransom obligation remains valid, because he does not specify that he would take back his captive wife.

[18] Tos. Ket. 4, 5, Ket. 51b, 52b.

Annulling the ransom obligation by a common agreement between the contracting parties is not definitely permitted or prohibited in the Talmud itself, but post-Talmudic authorities declare such an agreement void, since the community is also an interested party, or as they put it, "the woman shall not be permitted to be lost among the Gentiles." [19]

The ransom obligation does not survive the husband, because it depends upon the condition of the husband's being able to take the captive back as wife, which condition cannot survive him. The heirs or the *levir* have no ransom obligation by the widow. She must spend her ketubah for that purpose. The older halakah teaches, though, that the obligation does fall upon the heirs if the woman was made captive before her husband's death. That is, the obligation survives him, if the discharge of it was possible in his lifetime.[20]

The ransom clause in the ketubah is among the oldest and is recorded as part of the marriage writ in Temple days. But there is hardly another citation of this clause in the Talmud, for apparently it was not a popular clause, and people omitted it from the ketubah so long as its provision was a matter of statute in Jewish law. In post-Talmudic days we have two instances of ketubot containing the ransom clause and both are Palestinian.[21] In modern days it has completely disappeared with the disappearance of the ransom problem.

[19] Tosafot Ket. 47a, s. v. זימנין.

[20] The older halakah is represented by the first tradition cited in Ket. 52a; the later halakah is found in the second beraita cited ibid. and Tos. Ket. 4, 5, and Jer. Ket. 29a.

[21] Ketubah Jerushalmit, ed. Berliner, and a ketubah apparently also of Palestinian origin, ed. Asaf in *Hazofeh* Vol. 10, p. 29.

To provide burial for the wife when she dies is another of the husband's obligations. Historically it goes back to the earliest Bible days, for thus we find that Abraham provided burial for Sarah and Jacob for Rachel and Leah.[22] Yet the rabbis speak of this obligation as a rabbinical institution.[23] As a ketubah clause it goes back to Temple days and it reads, "If thou die, I shall bury thee."[24] This obligation, it is declared by the rabbis, does not depend upon its specification in the ketubah; it falls upon the husband as a matter of statute, even if unexpressed in the writ. Hence, it was seldom, if ever, entered into the ketubah, in order to avoid foreshadowing such a gloomy prospect upon the couple at the height of its joy.[25] Not a single marriage writ is known to us containing this burial clause.

Under the provision of the burial clause, the husband is required to prepare burial for his wife in accordance with the local custom and as befits his position or her position — giving her the advantage of the social station of either.[26] The poorest husband, however, must provide a grave and a funeral procession, which shall include two flutes and two wailing women.[27]

[22] Gen. 23, 19; 48, 7; 49, 31.

[23] Ket. 47b, Yad, Ishut 12, 2, Duschak, *Das Mos-talmud. Eherecht*, p. 77.

[24] See Mishna Ket. 46b, Tos. Ket. 4, 2. In these sources the formula is not given, nor is the formula recorded in amoraic quotations of these tannaitic texts. Only the reading of the mishna in the Palestinian Talmud as given by Lowe records the formula.

[25] Cf. RABIH, *Mishpete Ketubah, Jahrbuch d. juedisch-literarischen Gesellschaft*, Hebrew section, Vol. III, p. 11.

[26] Tos. Ket. 4, 2, Ket. 48a.

[27] Ket, 46b.

In return for this obligation, the husband is heir to his wife's property.[28] The correspondence between succession and the duty to provide burial is logical even as it is traditional among the tannaim.[29] From this premise follows the conclusion that the husband's duty of burial does not continue after his death upon his heirs or his estate,[30] since his right of succession does not continue after his death.[31]

If the husband refuses to bury his wife, or if he is gone to a distant land, the court provides for her burial out of his estate.[32] Should the wife's father or even a stranger defray the burial expenses, the court will refund them out of the husband's estate.[33] The court is more liberal in the provision for burial than for maintenance,[34] because delay in burial that may be occasioned by litigation and restrictions would be a disrespect to the dead.

The older halakah imposed the obligation of burial upon the husband from the moment of betrothal,[35] but with the weakening of the bond of betrothal and with the shifting of the writing of the ketubah to the time of nuptials, the law freed the husband from the duty of providing burial for his betrothed — as it denied him the right of succession — until nuptials.[36]

Tannaitic sources record what is supposed to be

[28] Ket. 47b.

[29] Ibid. and Ket. 95b.

[30] Ket. 80b, 95b.

[31] See p. 138 above, note 26.

[32] Ket. 48a, 100b.

[33] Jer. Ket. 28d. An opinion is cited that only the father is reimbursed but not a stranger, but see Yad Ishut 14, 24.

[34] See p. 158 and note 69 above.

[35] See Appendix A.

[36] See p. 137 above, note 24.

a ketubah clause which reads, "The obligation which thou hast borne prior to this day shall fall upon me." [37] If this is the reading and the intent of this clause, it should mean that the husband obligates himself to pay the debts which the wife incurred prior to the marriage. The Talmud, however, makes no such deduction from this clause. And indeed the halakah teaches that the husband is not obligated to pay the debts incurred by his wife prior to the marriage, unless the money so borrowed is to be found in the husband's possession.[38] At any rate whatever claim may fall on the husband is not based on any ketubah specification, but is reducible to the question whether an attachment may be made of the woman's property to pay her debt after that property has been delivered into the husband's keeping. In fact, the husband is not held legally bound to pay the debts which the wife incurred after marriage,[39] unless she was forced to borrow for her maintenance in the event he failed to meet his alimentation obligation.[40] There is a tannaitic opinion that the husband must pay for the purification sacrifices which the wife owes to the altar, and another tannaitic opinion that he must pay for every kind of sacrifice which is due from the wife. This especial obligation is what the Talmud seems to infer from the supposed ketubah

[37] Tos. Ket. 4, 11, B. M. 104a, Nazir 24a, Nedar. 35b. The translation of this clause is based on the interpretation of it given by Rashi (Nazir ibid. s. v. דתניה but Rashi is differently interpreted by Tosafot Nazir and B. M. ibid. s. v. הנ'), and RABD commentary ad Sifra ed. Weiss, p. 72d. Cf. Fisher, *Urkunden*, p. 81, note 2.

[38] See B. B. 139a, Tosafot B. M. 104a, s. v.״הנ, Yad, Malveh, 26, 12 and Magid commentary quoting geonic authority.

[39] Tosafot ibid., Yad, Malveh 26, 9. See also B. K. 87a. EH, 91, 4.

[40] See Ket. 107b and Rashi ibid., s. v. חנן and p. 158 above.

clause.[41] And yet, one wonders in the first place how such an obligation is contained in the literal wording of the clause, and in the second place why does the clause limit itself to such a minor detail of the many possible debts and levies that may be borne by the married woman?

If we add to the above difficulties the fact that the texts recording this clause are in a hopeless confusion,[42] we feel compelled to give to this clause an entire-

[41] In addition to the references given in note 37, Cf. Sifra, ed. Weiss, p. 72d, Jer. Jeb. 14a, Sotah 17d, Ket. 29a. That the obligation applies only to a certain kind of sacrifice is the accepted view, while R. Judah applies it to all sacrifices. Cf. Sifre, ed. Horovitz, p. 13, and Sifre Zuta, ed. ibid., p. 234. Tos. Ket. 4, 11, citing the opinion of R. Judah is correct in adding "even if she ate prohibited fat or desecrated the Sabbath." The comment of ר"ש on Mishna Nega'im 14, 12 is incorrect, therefore, as applied to R. Judah.

[42] There seem to be two original texts. First, Sifra, end of chapt. 4, ed. Weiss, p. 72d which states the view of R. Judah that the husband must bring a sacrifice for his wife in accordance with his own station and that at divorce he is freed from such obligation by a specific clause in the *Shober*. Since the *Shober* may be written either by the wife or the husband, (Ediyot 2, 3) the clause may read either ואחרן דיאיתיין לי עלך מן קדמת דנא as the Sifra has it, or ואחריות דאית ליך עלי מן קדמת דנא as Nedarim 35b quotes. Second, Sifre 8, ed. Horovitz, p. 13, simply states the view of R. Judah that the husband must pay for any sacrifice which the wife offers on the altar. This view is based on a Biblical inference and has no connection with any clause. There is no opposition to R. Judah's view under the first heading but there is a disputant against his view under the second heading. Mishna Nega'im quotes a combination of R. Judah's statements, namely the first part of Sifra and that of Sifre.

In view of this, the amoraic citations of these sources can easily be explained. (a) Nedarim 35b and Nazir 24a should be corrected in accordance with Sifra as is done by R. Nissim, or should be taken as a citation of Mishna Nega'im with the

ly different interpretation from what tradition has given it. The clause is not a ketubah clause. No ketubah has yet been found containing such a clause, and no definite record of such a ketubah clause can be produced. The Tosiphta, which of all texts does seem to convey the impression that such a ketubah clause existed, is unreliable for evidence, because it is not submitted to us in its original form; it has the marks of scribes' emendations, and its correct reading is uncer-

addition of the second part of Sifre which the Mishna omitted. (b) The same is true of B. M. 104a whose reading in the Muenchen MS and others (See *Dikduke Soferim*) is exactly that of Sifra. Supposing the reading in our Talmud text is correct, even then the inference from the clause is to be understood as follows: Since the cancellation clause reads, "The obligations which thou hast borne (or which I have borne — depending upon who writes the *Shober*) shall be annulled" (See RABD, Sifra), it proves that such obligations did exist prior to the cancellation. Hence, the sacrifice of the wife must be offered by the husband, and naturally in accordance with his station. Cf. Tosafot Nazir 24a, s. v. חג״ and R. Asher and Tosafot commentary on margin of the Wilna ed. of the Talmud, Nedarim 35b. (c) The Jerushalmi quotations are those of the Sifra, Jer. Sotah adding the halakah contained in the Sifre.

The Tosifta is the only difficult text, and let it be granted that it is destined to remain difficult despite our effort at an explanation. It begins by quoting Sifre and adds the Sifra deduction from the clause. But in citing the clause, it assumes that the husband wrote it — which is not impossible — and gives the further impression that the clause is part of the ketubah. It infers the view of R. Judah that the husband must pay for all the sacrifices that his wife offers, from the clause — supposedly a ketubah clause — instead of inferring it from a verse in the Bible, as the Sifre does.

What appears clear from this investigation is, first, that Sifre and Sifra are the sources for Mishna, Tosifta, Babli and Jerushalmi; second, that in the sources R. Judah cites the clause only as a *Shober* clause, not as a ketubah clause, and proves from it only that the husband is relieved of certain sacrificial obligations at divorce.

tain. Furthermore, it seems to be based on earlier tannaitic sources where the clause is definitely cited not as of a ketubah. In the original tannaitic source the clause is recorded as reading, "(I do hereby annul and cancel . . . .) and the obligations which thou didst owe unto me prior to this day,"[43] and it is a clause written by the wife at the time of divorce in the special instrument which she gives to her husband as token of the full payment and hence cancellation of the ketubah. That instrument was written either on a separate parchment or on the margin of the ketubah itself and was called *Shober,* or writ of cancellation.

[43] The words in parenthesis are my own additions in accordance with the evident intention of the text in Sifra and in accordance with the interpretation of RABD, Asheri, and Tosafot (the two latter ad Nedar. ibid.).

CHAPTER XI

Provision for the Widow and Orphaned Daughters

The continuous and unbroken tradition since Biblical days gives the female members of the household, wife and daughters, no right of succession to the family estate.[1] In the more primitive scheme of succession, the female members of the family were considered part of the estate and as remote from the legal personality of an heir as the slave.[2] Whereas by Mosaic enactment the daughters were admitted to succession in the event no male issue remained,[3] the wife was not recognized as heir even under such conditions. This is implied in the Biblical provision[4] that the daughter of a priest who is widowed or divorced without issue by her Israelitish husband shall return to her father's house and eat of his bread. Her return to her father's house is equal to exclusion from the husband's family and, naturally, to denial of any right of succession.

Furthermore, not only is she denied succession, but by the implication of this Biblical law she is denied maintenance during her widowhood out of her husband's estate. The converse seems to be implied, that if issue has remained, she would be expected to eat of her husband's bread. This establishes clearly the Biblical provision for the widow — if there is no issue,

[1] Cf. p. 121 above. Gen. 15, 3 and 21, 10 omit any possibility of the wife's sharing in the estate.

[2] Cf. Nowack, *Lehrbuch*, I, pp 348 f.

[3] Numb. 27, 7-8.

[4] Lev. 22, 13, Gen. 38, 11.

she is completely excluded from her husband's family, without claim upon his estate for her maintenance; if there is issue, she is supported by the heirs.

In the light of these Biblical implications, a step forward in the development of Jewish law is evident in the ketubah clause of Papyrus G, which reads: "If on the morrow or any other day As-hor shall die without male or female issue by Miphtahya, his wife, Miphtahya shall have power over his house, his property, and possessions, and all that he has on the face of the earth." Freund correctly interprets this clause to provide not that the wife shall succeed him, but that she shall be admitted to the enjoyment of his estate without restriction; for, he points out, the term "inherit" is not used in this clause, as it is used in the next clause in the Papyrus.[5] It must also be pointed out that the inference cannot be drawn from this clause that if issue remain she would be denied this right of the use of his estate. On the contrary, no special provision is necessary on housing and maintaining the widow when she remains with issue by her husband — this is even Biblically granted. The provision of the clause adds to the Biblical law that even if no issue remains her maintenance during her widowhood is assured her out of the estate.[6]

[5] Cf. Freund GES, pp. 45-46.

[6] Nowhere in the Talmud is any distinction drawn between the widow with issue by her husband and the one without issue as regards her rights over her husband's estate or her personal independence. The Talmudic law, therefore, continues the tradition of the Papyri. The Biblical distinction between the one case and the other is strictly applied only to the question of the right of the priest's daughter of eating of the heave offering after being widowed by an Israelitish husband. If widowed without issue she may; otherwise she may not. Cf. Sifra ed. Weiss, p. 97c-d, Jeb. 69-70, Kid. 4a, 18a.

In the earliest rabbinic times, the reform of the Biblical law such as is seen in the Papyrus was already fully in vogue, and no distinction was drawn in the matter of maintenance of the widow whether she had issue by her husband or not. Thus the ketubah formulated the provision for the widow in the following clause: "Thou shalt dwell in my house and be supported out of my estate as long as thou shalt dwell in widowhood in my house[7] . . . . . and when thou marriest another thou shalt take all that is provided for thee in thy ketubah and go."[8] The Talmud, drawing its legal deductions from the ketubah clauses, treats this clause in two separate halves, and does not even indicate that it constitutes a positive and a negative condition of the same clause;[9] but the relation of the two

[7] Ket. 52b, 103a, Jer. Ket. 29b, Tos. Ket. 11, 5. For variants of this formula see Fisher, *Urkunden,* p. 98 and *Hazofeh* Vol. 10, p. 30, note 1.

[8] Mishna Jeb. 15, 2, Eduyot 1, 12, Tos. Eduy. 1, 6, Ket. 53a, Jer. Ket. 29a, Jer. Jeb. 14d. See Fisher, *Urkunden,* pp. 101-102 for variants.

[9] The second half of the clause is never found in direct connection with the first half, and Rashi, among others, takes the second half to refer also to the instance of the divorcee for whom it is specified that as soon as she is permitted to remarry her ketubah becomes due. See Rashi, Ket. 53a, s. v. שאין. The context in which the second half of this clause is referred to in Ket. ibid. raises the suspicion that the amoraim also understood it in that light. There is no evidence that the tannaim, in particular the Shamaites, who make use of this part of the clause (Jeb. 116b), understood it to provide for anything else but the release and the payment of the ketubah of the widow. It is hardly conceivable that this part of the clause would apply to the divorcee, since her ketubah is paid at the validation of the divorce, without reference to her remarrying. Why set the conditions of remarrying, an indirect evidence for the validity of the divorce, when the validity of the divorce may be made the condition in a more direct manner? That the second half com-

halves to each other is evident on the face of it, and therefore we include them in the one clause. It is an old ketubah clause, which underwent some modifications during the Talmudic period.

Our formula is probably the original formula employed by Jews everywhere to stipulate the provision of maintenance for the widow. In tannaitic days, however, it was in use only among the people of Jerusalem, following whose example it was also adopted as the formula for the Galileans. They were the more liberal element of the Jewish people "who were more concerned with the honor of their wives than with the security of their estates."[10] The Judeans were more practical and less romantic. The support of a widow for an indefinite period of time might consume the entire estate and leave nothing for the heirs. They revised the formula, therefore, to read: "Thou shalt dwell in my house and be supported out of my estate during thy widowhood until the heirs will agree to pay thee thy ketubah. . . " The Galilean usage left the choice to the widow whether to remain in her husband's house and be supported by his heirs or to collect her ketubah and forego support; the Judean usage left the same choice to the heirs. Probably it was a sign of approval of the Galilean usage that R. Judah I stated in his will: "Move not my widow from my house."[11]

plements the first and applies to the widow is evident in the reproduction of that clause in the Ketubah Jerushalmit, ed. Berliner.

[10] Ket. 52b. Cf. Jer. Ket. 29b.

[11] Gen. R. 96, 5; 100, 2; Jer. Ket. 35a; Jer. Kela'im 32a. Babli, Ket. 103a, reports that he asked his sons to honor his wife who was their step-mother. This may be a paraphrasing of the Palestinian account. The Palestinian Talmud sees in his request a plea with the community not to deprive the widow of

Economic conditions tended to favor the Judean usage; family ideals pressed for a recognition of the Galilean usage. There was no decided victory for either. In Babylonia as in Palestine the use of the one formula or the other was a matter of local custom. Sura, Mehasia, and their environs under the influence of Rab used the Judean formula; Nahardea and its suburbs under the leadership of Samuel used the Galilean.[12] Because Rab's influence seems to have reached a wider territory and because of economic pressure exerted, the Judean custom was the more general one. Yet because of Samuel's superiority over Rab in civil jurisprudence, the Gaonim have ruled that any locality that has no definite traditional practice in the matter is bound by the Galilean formula of the ketubah.[13]

Where the Judean custom prevailed, the heirs had the choice at any time of paying the widow the ketubah and sending her out of her former home. Where the Galilean custom prevailed, the heirs could not pay off her ketubah and free themselves from the burden of supporting her until the second half of the clause was fulfilled, namely, when she entered upon a second marriage. The law interpreted this part of the clause, however, to the advantage of the heirs. "When thou shalt marry another" was construed to mean "when thou

the house of the Nasi, which was community property. A slight variant of this reason is given also in Gen. R. 100, 2. Evidently both the Babylonian and the Palestinian Talmud did not find the correct explanation for the particular wording of Rabbi's will. Is it not possible that it contained a request that the Galilean custom prevail in the case of his widow as against the Judean?

[12] Ket. 54a.

[13] See Alfasi and R. Nissim, Ket. ibid., Tosafot Ket. ibid. s. v. ושמואל, Ginzberg, *Geonica*, II, p. 34, Yad. Ishut 18, 1.

hast set thy mind on marrying another." [14] Therefore, in amoraic days it was taught that if the widow paints and powders, if she accepts a proposal for marriage, or if she has illicit relations with men, she forfeits her maintenance from her husband's estate.[15]

Even in tannaitic days it was declared that when the ketubah is presented to the court for payment, the alimentation obligation on the heirs comes to an end.[16] Furthermore, if she has sold the ketubah, or, according to certain views, even part of the ketubah, that amounts to its being presented for collection, and her support ceases.[17]

The widow may waive her claim to support; even an indication that she means to waive that claim frees the heirs of that obligation. Her waiving or cancelling her ketubah for the benefit of the heirs, however, does not cancel her right to alimentation.[18] An amora teaches

[14] This explains the addition of the word, לכשתתפיסי, to the formula by Tosifta Eduy. 1, 6.

[15] Ket. 54a. These leniencies toward the heirs evidently apply to the localities where the Galilean custom is employed, for according to the Judean usage the heirs need find no excuses for ceasing to support her. Thus, receiving proposals as a ground for the discontinuance of her support is cited by Samuel, who adheres to the Galilean custom. The amoraim do not link up these leniencies with the use of the word לכשתתפיסי in the clause, but the connection is apparent.

[16] Ket. 54a. Jer. Ket. 34b. The Babylonian Talmud submits this tradition in the name of Samuel, the Palestinian in the name of Rab. If the Jerushalmi is correct, it must be understood that the intention of this law is to cancel the alimentation obligation from the time of the demand of payment to the time of actual payment of the ketubah, for Rab subscribes to the Judean custom which gives the heirs the privilege of casting off the burden of alimentation on the payment of the ketubah.

[17] Tos. Ket. 11, 1, Ket. 97b.

[18] Jer. Ket. 34b.

that if the woman waived her ketubah while her husband was alive, that waiver is complete and also cancels the clause of alimentation of the widow.[19]

Under the alimentation clause, the widow is entitled to a dwelling and maintenance. Both of these items are specifically mentioned in the clause. In normal conditions the widow continues to live as she had lived during the lifetime of her husband, uses the gold and silver vessels and the male and female slaves of the household, as though her husband were not dead but sojourning in a distant land.[20] She also eats and drinks according to her portion during the life of her husband; even her portion of wine is not diminished.[21] Neither can the widow force the heirs to alter this arrangement, nor can the heirs force her to submit to another arrangement. Should she, therefore, desire to live with her parents and to receive her alimony in cash from the heirs, they may restrain her, unless she offers the plea that because she is a young woman and the heirs young men it is not proper for her to live with them. Likewise, the heirs cannot force her to live with her own family at the expense of the estate.[22] The heirs cannot sell the house occupied by the widow, and should they do so, the sale is void. If the house is out of repair, they are not obliged to repair it. If uninhabitable, the loss is hers. She cannot even repair it at her own expense, for so long as the terms of the clause cannot be fulfilled by what was left by her husband, the provision for a house is automatically cancelled. In like manner if the dwelling contained in the estate is

[19] Ket. 53a.
[20] Tos. Ket. 11, 5, Ket. 103a, Jer. Ket. 35a, Jer. Ket. 32a.
[21] Ket. 65a, Jer. Ket. 34a.
[22] Ket. 103a, Tos. Ket. 12, 3, Jer. Ket. 29d.

no more than a hovel and cannot be called a "house" as specified in the clause, the widow has no claim on the estate for living quarters. In such cases she finds her own living quarters and is supported by the heirs.[23]

The levirate woman is supported out of her husband's estate for a duration of three months; thereafter she is supported by the *levir*. The reason for this provision of the law is as follows:The widow without issue by her husband cannot enter upon a levirate marriage sooner than three month's after her husband's death. After that period, because she is Biblically commanded to enter upon the levirate marriage, she is treated by the law as though she had accepted a proposal for remarriage. Therefore, the estate is freed from the obligation of supporting her. If her marriage to the levir has been delayed for a considerable time, she is supported by him, if the delay is due to him; and she supports herself, if she is the cause of the delay.[24]

Medical treatment is part of her sustenance and is paid for by the estate. R. Simeon b. Gamaliel teaches, however, that only current medical expenses are paid by the estate as part of her support, but a lump sum medical bill must be paid by the widow herself out of her ketubah.[25] The heirs have no obligation to pay ransom for the widow in the event she was made captive. If the woman was captive even before her husband's death, according to one tradition the heirs must pay her ransom as an obligation that had fallen on the husband prior to his death; according to another tradition

[23] Ket. 54a, 103a. Cf. *Geonica*, ed. Ginzberg, Vol. II. p. 33. Nahmanides and Adret understand from Jer. Ket. 29b that under such circumstances the heirs must rent a house for the widow.

[24] Tos. Ket. 6, 7, Jer. Ket. 29d.

[25] Tos. Ket. 4, 5, Ket. 52b, Jer. Ket. 29a. Cf. p. 163, note 3 above.

the heirs need not pay, as the husband's ransom obligation came to an end with his death, since the necessary condition of taking her back as wife can not be met.[26] At her death, her burial expenses are paid either by her heirs or out of her ketubah; her husband's estate is not taxed with that expense.[27]

As against the continuance of the husband's obligation to his wife in the estate, most of his rights over her come to an end with his death. One may conjecture that it was not so in the very remote past. As we find traces in the Bible of the heirs admitted to the full ownership of the persons of the concubines of the testators, it is not altogether impossible to think of a similar condition to have existed in respect to his wives. But we have no record of such a condition. Our earliest records declare the person of the widow independent of the heirs. Only her labors belong to the heirs in exchange for her maintenance, and she is expected to do the work she had done before — for her husband — save the personal attentions, mixing his drinks, washing his face, hands and feet, and making his bed.[28] She can retain her earnings for herself if she waives support from them;[29] and anything she comes by without labor, a find or a gift, is wholly her own.[30]

If the husband has left no estate, the widow has no claim upon the children — even her own children —

[26] Ket. 52a, Tos. Ket. 4, 5. From this law the inference is drawn by Alfasi that the heirs are not entitled to the use of the widow's property, for the right of fruit is granted in exchange for the obligation of ransom (according to the Babylonian tradition) and where ransom is not paid usufruct is not enjoyed. Cf. Yad, Ishut 18, 8. See pp. 166, 168 above.

[27] Ket. 81a, 95b.

[28] Ket. ibid. and 96a, Jer. Ket. 34a.

[29] Jer. Ket. ibid.

[30] Ket. 96a. As to usufruct, see note 26.

for support. If the husband divided his wealth among his children during his lifetime, when legally there is no estate left by the husband, the widow is nevertheless supported by the children, by virtue of an Usha enactment.[31]

Jewish law does not enforce back payment of alimony for the widow, if she has not collected her alimony for several months or years. But the heirs must pay any indebtedness incurred by the widow for her own support during the period of their neglect to give her due sustenance.[32]

The clause providing for the alimentation of the widow, like the number of other clauses dealt with in previous chapters, such as ransom, burial, and *ketubat benin dikrin*, is not included in our present day ketubah and is not found in the mediaeval ketubot so far known to us, with the exception only of three, all apparently of Palestinian origin. In those we have an illustration of both the Galilean and the Judean formulae.[33]

The daughters being deprived of inheritance, if male children remained, were, like the widow, at the mercy of the heirs of their father's estate. The fortune of the widow and that of the orphan girl were so akin to each other that both the statutory and the

[31] Jer. Ket. 28d. The Usha enactment obligates the children to support their father and his wife in the event the estate of the former was deeded to them during his life. See Ket. 49b.

[32] Ket. 96a, Jer. Ket. 34b.

[33] The three ketubot which contain this clause are *Ketubah Jerushalmit*, ed Berliner, a ketubah edited by S. Asaf in *Hazofeh* Vol. 10, pp. 29-30 and the unpublished fragment of the Genizah, T-S 12.659 in which only the word ואנת is found, but which by its context may be definitely identified as the beginning of our clause. The Berliner ketubah follows the Galilean tradition, while the Asaf ketubah continues the Judean usage.

ketubah provisions for them run parallel throughout Jewish law.

The problem of the support of the orphan girl arises from the newer legislation, which declares the woman under certain circumstances independent of any master. Originally, the woman belonged to one master or to another, but never to herself. Unmarried, she belonged to her father; after his death to his heirs, or her brothers; married, she belonged to her husband; widowed, if without issue by her husband, she went back to her father; with issue, she belonged to her own children. By a series of changes in the law, the woman step by step gained her independence.

The decision which Moses rendered in the case of the daughters of Zelaphchad, because of the absence of male issue, that they succeed their father, establishes the first instance of the woman's independence. The supposition in this case is that she is dependent upon her father and upon her brothers, whether she be of age or a minor, but she is her own master when she has neither father nor brothers. In rabbinic legislation we find that when she is of age she is completely independent, even though she has both father and brothers. The rabbis rule also that if she is orphaned of her father, she is independent of her brothers, even if she is still a minor. They infer this from the Biblical verse: "And you shall take them (the Gentile slaves) as an inheritance for your children after you." From this verse they argue: "*Them* you give as inheritance to your sons, but you do not give your daughters as an inheritance to your sons." [34] Thus the orphan girl is by

[34] Sifra, ed. Wiess, p. 110a, Ket. 43a, etc. The specific application of the principle belongs to a later day, but the principle is probably of early tannaitic origin.

this final legislation an independent personality, and with her independence rises the question of her maintenance.

The solution was found in the formulation of an agreement between husband and wife to support the orphan girl out of the estate after her father's death, which agreement was set down in the ketubah in a clause designated as *ketubat benan nukban,* (KBN), which specified: "The female children which thou shalt beget by me shall dwell in my house and be supported out of my estate (and be clothed at my expense)[35] until they are married."[36] The terminus, until they are married, is easily understood, for with marriage she is provided for by her husband. Levi, one of the earlier amoraim, introduced another terminus: "Until they become of age," or "Until they become of age and it be time for them to be married."[37] This modification of the clause probably came about in this wise. The *bogeret,* or the girl of age — twelve years and a day old — was by rabbinic legislation declared independent of her father. In almost all cases she was then already a married woman. If in the exceptional case she was still unmarried, she was expected to take care of herself. Therefore the law yielded to the feeling that, as the *bogeret* would expect nothing from her father, she may expect nothing from his estate. The original formula of the KBN clause sufficed only until the unmar-

[35] The bracketed part is an addition found in Jer. Ket. 34d.

[36] Ket. 52b, Jer. Ket. 29a, 34d, Jer. Jeb. 14d, B. B. 131a. Variants are given in Fischer, *Urkunden*, p. 93.

[37] The question of the *bogeret* was raised before Levi's time. R. Elazar is quoted as maintaining that the orphan girl loses ner *benan nukban* privileges with her reaching majority. Ket. 53b. It was Levi, though, who formulated the ketubah clause in accordance with it. Cf. Tos. Ket. 4, 17, Jer. Ket. 29b.

ried *bogeret* was a case of more frequent occurence, as it was in the time of Levi. In accordance with Levi's modification of the clause, therefore, the KBN provision terminates either with the orphan's marriage or with her reaching puberty.

From the original terminology of the clause, one would judge that the KBN obligation terminates with the orpan's betrothal, not with her nuptials.[38] Furthermore, we have cause to believe that the original law imposed the alimentation obligation upon the husband from the time of betrothal.[39] If this is so, it stands to reason that the heirs' duty in that direction terminates with the orphan's betrothal, for then she is provided for by her husband. Hence it is fully in keeping with the older halakah when the later tannaim take it for granted that the heirs are freed of the KBN obligation from the moment of her betrothal.[40] The amoraim were not quite as decided on the question as the tannaim were, for in their day the *arusah* was so completely of her father's household and so fully independent of her husband that they could see no reason for discontiuning her alimentation out of her father's es-

[38] The expression עד דתילקחן or עד דתנסבן indicates betrothal, not nuptials. Compare the expression שאם תנשאי לאחר (Jeb. 117a) which the halakah interprets to mean "When thou art *betrothed.*"

[39] Cf. Appendix A. Mishna Ket. 97a, which states that if the betrothed is widowed of her husband she is not supported out of his estate, represents the later halakah. Even according to the codes, in accordance with Alfasi ad Ket. 53b and Samuel Hanagid, cited in R. Nisim ibid., and Yad, Ishut 19, 15, the husband must support his betrothed if she is orphaned of her father.

[40] See Ket. 53b: "How long is the daughter supported? Until betrothal."

tate.[41] Nevertheless, the final halakah declares betrothal, not nuptials, the terminus for the KBN obligation.[42] A rabbinic marriage, however — that is, a marriage concluded for the orphan minor girl by her mother and brothers who have only rabbinic authority for that transaction — is not accounted a terminus for the KBN provision even if that marriage included nuptials. Therefore, whenever she returns to her parental home before she has reached her majority, she is supported out of her father's estate.[43]

The KBN provision applies only where male issue remained, but has no validity if only female issue remained, for then the daughters are the heirs, not the charge of the estate.[44] The sons have only the right of succession but no alimentation privileges in the estate. If the estate, therefore, has only enough for the alimentation of the daughters, the sons are completely disinherited. Or, as the mishna puts it, "In a limited estate the daughters are supported and the sons go

[41] Ket. ibid. Twice is the question raised whether the betrothed is supported out of her father's estate, once by the editor of the Gemara and again by Rab Hisda. The latter's question is variously interpreted. See Alfasi and R. Nisim a. l. But Rashi's interpretation seems to be the correct one. The objection to it is that the amora raises a question which a tanna had already settled. See Tosafot ibid. s. v. ארוסה. Our exposition of it explains away the difficulty. While the tannaim could still permit themselves to consider the *arusah* as out of her father's household, the amoraim could not, because the bond of betrothal continually weakened in the process of development of Jewish law.

[42] Yad, Ishut 19, 10.

[43] See Ket. 53b and Alfasi ibid. and Yad, Ishut 19, 16.

[44] B. B. 139a.

begging."[45] According to one tanna, the estate is accounted to be a limited one if it cannot yield sustenance for the whole family for one year. The more general view defines a limited estate as one which is short of yielding, above all actionable encumbrances, enough sustenance for the family until both boys and girls reach majority. If a wealthy estate has depreciated to the point of becoming a limited one, the sons, once admitted to succession, cannot be sent begging but share in the benefits of the estate equally with the daughters until the estate is wholly consumed. If the estate has increased in value, the gain belongs wholly to the sons, because, even though set aside for the support of the daughters, the estate is owned by the sons.[46] Since title to the estate belongs to the sons, the halakah decides that if the sons have sold the estate, though it had been set aside to be used wholly for the support of the daughters, the sale is valid.[47]

By the terms of the KBN clause, the minor unmarried daughters are entitled, out of the estate of their father, to food, clothing, and domicile. They are also granted a marriage portion at their marriage, termed *parnasah,* but the latter is not part of the *benan nukban clause.*[48] It represents rather a continuation in the estate of the father's obligation to give his daughter dowry. The amount of *parnasah* was originally gauged by the dowry which the mar-

[45] Ket. 108b, B. B. 139b. Admon and Rabban Gamaliel oppose this view. But the halakah agrees with the view of the anonymous tanna. Cf. Tosafot Ket. ibid. s. v. אדמון, Yad, Ishut 19, 17.

[46] B. B. ibid., Jer. Ket. 36a, Jer. B. B. 16d.

[47] Ket. 103a, B. B. 140a.

[48] See Ket. 68b. See RSBM, B. B. 139b and Tosafot's objection thereto. Cf. p. 91, note 11.

ried daughters got from their father. But Rabbi standardized it at ten percent of the total of the estate.[49] If a smaller dowry was given her, she may after marriage claim the rest that is due her.[50] While the KBN obligation terminates with the daughters' coming of age, the *parnasah* obligation never terminates; the difference between the major and the minor in respect to *parnasah* is only that whereas the minor cannot give a legally valid consent to a smaller *parnasah* than is due her, the major can.[51]

Because *parnasah* is not included in the KBN, the father can leave instructions whether or not and how much to give to his daughters, in the same manner as he can will a house of widowhood to his daughter or a nuptial house to his son or a gift to a stranger.[52] But he has no power to alter the alimentation obligation to his minor unmarried daughters, because this is their right by virtue of a contract between him and their mother.[53]

The KBN clause is implied in every marriage contract, whether expressed or not. There are such cases, however, where no contract exists or where the contract is impeached. The *arusah* has no ketubah accord-

[49] Ket. 68a, Tos. Ket. 6, 1-4, Ned. 39b, Jer. Ket. 39d. Cf. *Bloch, Sha'are Torat Ha-takanot* II, 2. pp. 189-192. See pp. 101-102 above.

[50] Ket. 68a, Tos. Ket. 4, 17, 6, 7, Jer. Ket. 29b. The ruling is that if she was married as a minor, neither her own consent nor the groom's is valid. When she grows up, therefore, she can claim her full dowry. Alfasi, Ket. ibid. gives halakic decisions as to the need of her registering her complaint against the action of the heirs in giving her insufficient dowry.

[51] Ket. 68b and Alfasi ibid.

[52] Ket. 68b, Tos. Ket. 11, 6-7, Jer. Nedar. 39a.

[53] Ket. ibid., Yad, Ishut 19, 13, 20, 10.

ing to later usage;[54] the woman who has been forced by her husband prior to betrothal has no ketubah;[55] the woman who marries contrary to rabbinic law, as a matter of fine, has no ketubah;[56] the levirate woman has no ketubah from her *levir,* the old ketubah remaining in force;[57] and finally there is the woman who has waived her ketubah.[58] Is the KBN provision valid or invalid in such instances? Will the daughters begotten of such marriages be supported after their father's death out of his estate or not? The amoraim raise the question without offering a decision, but the decision in these cases has been rendered by post-Talmudic authorities.

The father cannot convey to his heirs any of the rights which he has in his minor daughter — as a result of the principle mentioned above that the daughters cannot be given as an inheritance to the sons. It is for this reason that, although the heirs support the minor orphan girl, they are not entitled to her earnings or to whatever indemnity she may receive for an injury or to what she may find.[59] The heirs do not take the father's place in this case; they just pay the father's debt.

The *benan nukban* clause stands parallel in one re-

[54] Ket. 54a, Jer. Ket. 29b. The halakah decides that the daughter born of the *arusah* has no KBN privileges. See Alfasi, Ket. ibid., Yad, Ishut 19, 14.

[55] Ket. ibid., Jer. Ket. 27d. Alfasi decides that the daughter born of the אנוסה has no KBN provision.

[56] Ket. 53b. (בת שניה). Here too Alfasi decides that the KBN does not apply.

[57] Ket. ibid. Here too the decision is in the negative.

[58] Maimonides decides that the KBN clause is also waived. See Yad, Ishut 9, 12, and *Magid* and *Migdal 'Oz* commentaries. Cf. Jer. Ket. 29b.

[59] Ket. 41b, 43a, Jer. Ket. 27b, 28b, 34d, Jer. Pe'ah 18b.

spect to the *benin dikrin* clause, and in another to the alimentation of the widow clause. This group of three have the same history and are always grouped together in the ketubah. Furthermore, since Talmudic days, those ketubot that include one clause include the other and those that omit them omit all three without exception. The proximity of *benan nukban* and *benin dikrin* is evident; one provides for the daughters, the other for the sons out of their father's estate. This parallelism is noted by as early an authority as R. Elazar b. 'Azariah, and on that basis the amoraim are inclined to believe that both of these clauses represent the enactment of one court.[60] The parallelism between the *benan nukban* clause and the provision for the widow appears to me more striking. Both provide for the women and arise with the newer condition of the woman's independence; both provide sustenance until they are married. It would not be surprising to find evidence that all three clauses were the institution of a single court, but surely the last two appear to represent one legislative activity. We are, however, without sufficient historical material on the subject, and the best conjecture we can make is that our clause belongs to the first century before the common era.[61]

[60] B. B. 131b. The Talmud finally rejects the suggestion that both were enacted by the same court and leaves us with the impression that the KBN clause is younger.

[61] That the clause belongs to the Temple days is evident from the fact that Admon cites it (Ket. 108b); that it is younger than the Book of Tobit is evident from the assumption in the book that the woman is not independent of her father after widowhood and apparently also after majority, while the clause, as was said, represents the general innovation of the law of giving the woman more independence. The rabbinic marriage of the minor girl, which is also based upon her independence of her brothers, is discussed by the Hillelites and Shamaites. Jeb. 107a. Our conjecture, therefore, is that it belongs about the time of Hillel. Cf. Appendix A.

CHAPTER XII

PROVISIONS AS TO DIVORCE

Divorce in Biblical terminology is synonymous with driving out. As a physical fact, it was beyond the control of the law; the woman was divorced — driven out — whether in keeping with or in violation of the law. Hence, even when divorce was conceived of as a legal decree, the invalidation or annulment of a divorce, if the instrument and the formalities connected with it were in accordance with the prescription of the law, was unknown in the Jewish law.

The Bible restricts divorce in two instances, in the case of the husband falsely charging his wife with antenuptial unchastity[1] and in the case of rape.[2] With reference to both the Bible says: "He shall not be at liberty to send her away all his days." And one would expect that by this prohibition the Bible actually deprives the husband of the power to divorce his wife. Yet it is a prohibition that does not invalidate the divorce if he act contrary to the law. By the evidence of Josephus[3] and the Mishna,[4] with sufficient cause he may divorce her. By the ruling of the tannaim, if without sufficient cause he divorces his wife, in either of these two instances, he is compelled to remarry her, but the divorce is not invalid.[5] In the same manner, the protest in the New Testament against divorce does not

[1] Deut. 22, 19.
[2] Ibid. 22, 29.
[3] *Antiquities,* Bk. 4, Ch. 8.
[4] Ket. 39a.
[5] Makkot 15a.

challenge the husband's power, but restricts his right. "Let no one put asunder what God had joined together"[6] expresses only a prohibition. If the husband's powers were prescibed, no matter what good cause he might present, he would be helpless to divorce his wife except by a court decree, which is unknown in Jewish law. When the New Testament, therefore, permits divorce on grounds of fornication and the like, it reflects on its prohibition of divorce as a mere pointing to sin, not as an annulment of the act. If the Church has declared divorce void, it has gone far beyond the teachings of the New Testament and has departed from its root — Jewish law.

The ancient law, both Jewish and Babylonian, also recognized the husband's right to divorce his wife at his pleasure, without cause at all. Sometimes the term for divorce is synonymous with hate, which means that the husband's displeasure with his wife was suffiicent cause for divorce. The natural interpretation of the verse in the Bible dealing with the bill of divorcement seems to be that the Bible took it for granted that the husband divorces his wife "because she finds no favor in his eyes." Philo and Josephus[7] so

[6] Matthew 19, 6. Cf. Amram, *The Jewish Law of Divorce*, Philadelphia 1896, p. 36 for a fuller discussion of the New Testament legislation on divorce.

[7] Cf. *Special Laws* Ch. 5. English ed. of Young in Bohn's Library, Vol. III. pp. 310-11. *Antiquities*, Bk. 4, Ch. 8. I do not agree with Amram that the interpretation of Philo and Josephus of this Biblical verse (Deut. 24, 1) is equal to the teaching of the Hillelites against the Shamaites. Exegetically perhaps, but halakacally no. The discussion between the Shamaites and the Hillelites centers on the question whether the Bible expresses a moral judgment about the case of groundless divorce. Both grant, however, that the husband's will alone makes a divorce legal.

undersood the Biblical verse. In the fact that Joseph "was minded to put her (Mary) away privily" there is also evidence that the husband was not required by law to show cause for divorcing his wife.[8]

Beyond the legal side of divorce, however, Jewish law raises the question of its moral propriety. Of the latter, we have two standards, the halakic and the agadic, or the actual Biblical or rabbinical prohibition and the appeal to a higher sense of rectitude. The agadic protest against divorce is included in the story of creation, where husband and wife are declared to be one flesh,[9] and is clearly voiced by Malachi in the words: "For I hate him who puts away his wife, said the Eternal God of Israel."[10] The rabbis repeatedly denounce divorce, and declare the effort to bring about peace between husband and wife as among the loftiest of noble deeds.[11] And the very *raison d'être* of the ketubah is conceived by them as a deterrent to divorce. The halakic verdict on divorce is contained in the well known rabbinic discussion as to the interpretation of the Deuteronomic verse which is the basis of our law of divorce. The Shamaites draw from it a Biblical prohibition against divorce, unless it be for the cause of

[8] Cf. Amram ibid., p. 35.

[9] The New Testament interpretation of this verse (Gen. 2, 23-24) is correct insofar as it reveals the ideal of marriage in the Old Testament and its inference is correct that divorce is a compromise with conditions. That is merely an agadic statement. But to formulate a law on this basis — prohibiting divorce — is clearly no longer an interpretation of the old but an addition to it. Blau in the *Juedische Ehescheidebrief*, Vol. I. p. 59 finds the root of the New Testament prohibition against divorce in the halakah of the Zadokites, which may also have been the source for the Shamaites.

[10] Malachai 2, 16.

[11] See Ned. 66b, Gittin 90a-b.

adultery. The Hillelites find in the verse a permission to divorce one's wife on the slightest cause, "even if she scorched his porridge." R. Akiba reads into the verse the husband's freedom to divorce his wife if only "she find no favor in his eyes." [12] The New Testament follows the Shamaites, but Jewish law has decided with R. Akiba. It is therefore a continuous unbroken tradition among Jews to give the husband full freedom to divorce his wife without cause.

To discourage divorce is the business of the ketubah in general, as conceived by the later rabbis, but the ketubah sometimes also makes special provisions to that end.

According to the legislation of Hammurabi, the divorce price upon the husband is the return to his wife of the dowry which he had received and an additional settlement on her of his own property.[13] No mention is made of the forfeiture of the mohar which he had paid to the father, but that may be taken for granted, else the return of the mohar to the husband would be stipulated. Nor is any mention made of the return of mattan to the husband, but on the contrary, the additional settlement of the husband's property on the wife appears to be synonymous with the forfeiture of the mattan. Thus Babylonian law set down the divorce price as follows, forfeiture of mohar, mattan, and dowry. The Bible is silent on the question of dowry and mattan, but specifies the forfeiture of the purchase price in the case of the master freeing his slave-wife, which is the exact parallel to the forfeiture of

[12] Gittin 90a. The interpretation of this Mishna given by Holdheim in *Ma'amar Ha-ishut*, Ch. 2, and by Zeitlin in JQR XIV p. 130 are both artificial.

[13] CH 138-140.

mohar in the case of the husband divorcing his wife.[14] As to mattan, we have no evidence from the Bible at all; and as to dowry, we may conjecture that no special provision for its return was necessary, for, as we have seen above, the Biblical dowry was really mulug, the private property of the wife.

Papyrus G devotes a special clause to the divorce price on the husband, which reads: "If tomorrow or any later day As-hor shall stand up in the congregation and say: I divorce my wife Miphtahya, her marriage settlement shall be forfeited and all that I have delivered unto her she shall give back." According to this reading, he forfeits the mohar, but not the mattan nor the dowry. There is another reading which substitutes for the last part of the clause "and all that she brought with her she shall take away," [15] according to which reading, he forfeits mohar, mattan, and dowry.

While this papyrus clause is not found in the rabbinic ketubah, its provisions, as yielded by the latter reading, have been adopted in toto in rabbinic legislation. "He shall pay the ketubah" is the standard rabbinic phrase for the divorce price on the husband. It means that he must pay the mohar and forfeit the marriage coin;[16] he must pay the mattan and forfeit all gifts that he had given her; he must return the dowry as of the value at the time of the marriage[17] and

[14] Exod. 21, 11.

[15] See p. 28, note 24 above. The latter reading agrees with Talmudic law.

[16] Cf. Jer. Ket. 34c.

[17] According to geonic enactment, if the dowry retained some of its original use, he need not pay for depreciation, so long as she can take her own dowry articles with her. See p. 100, note 32 above.

her mulug as of the value at the time of divorce.[18]

A Palestinian amora reports a local usage in his day of inserting in the ketubah a clause specifying a special divorce price. The clause read: "If he divorces .....if she divorces. . . . "[19] It is unfortunate that the amora cited the clause by its beginning and does not give it in full, since therefore we do not know what divorce penalty was prescribed in it. But it is certain that the penalty was severer than required by statute,

[18] This follows from the fact that the husband has no share in the mulug save the right of usufruct. Appreciation or depreciation is her gain or loss.

[19] Jer. Ket. 30b, Jer. B. B. 16c. The word שנא is taken here as a technical term for divorce, and it differs from other terms used for divorce which designate driving out, in that it presupposes the natural cause for divorce, a dislike of each other and a desire to be released of the bond of marriage. It is probably so used in Deut. 21, 15; 24, 3 and in Papyrus G. Cf. Freund GES p. 16, note 1. Some translate the word, *Sone,* literally, to hate, and would complete the clause as follows: If he hates her, he shall add to her ketubah three dinarim a week; if she hates him she shall lose her ketubah, in accordance with the law of "rebellion." Cf. Fischer, *Urkunden,* pp. 116-17. I cannot agree with this view because the execution of the disciplinary methods prescribed for rebellion does not depend on the legality of a monetary agreement, (*tenai momon*) since it is a court enactment (*tenai bet-din*). See B. B. 131. Besides, hate or honest revulsion is not granted in the Talmud (Ket. 63b) to be a case of rebellion.

I would rather complete this clause as follows: If he divorces her she shall take all that is written in the ketubah; if she divorces him she shall take only half of her ketubah. The first clause is completed in accordance with the halakah and on the basis of a ketubah clause providing for the widow, as stated above, p. 177 and note 8. The second half of the clause is completed in accordance with another ketubah clause, reading: If this one shall be married to that one and will be displeased with his companionship, she shall take half of the ketubah. (Jer. Ket. 31c) See further on this matter, p. 204.

for the amora cites it as an instance of a clause that is binding even though its specifications are contrary to statute.

An extra penalty on the husband is stipulated in Papyrus G for a specially obnoxious form of divorce in the following clause: "And if he shall rise up against Miphtahya to drive her away from the house of As-hor and his goods and his chattels, he shall pay the sum of twenty kebhs and this deed shall be annulled." [20] What is meant by the words, "he shall rise up . . .to drive her away from the house of As-hor, his goods and his chattels?" There is no exact parallel to it in the Talmud.[21] The only logical interpretation of it one can give is to account it a case of high handed action in driving away the wife without appearing in the congregation, that is, without court action. The special offense against the wife for which a higher penalty is prescribed may be understood in one of two ways. First, as a remnant of the past, driving out without court action was effective in the dissolution of the marriage, but it was no longer used except in the dismissal of the slave-wife. The wife by being driven out was degraded in such a manner as though she were a slave. Hence the fine of twenty kebhs, which is the exact fine imposed on the husband for elevating a slave-wife to the position of co-mistress with his legitimate wife. Second, in accordance with the newer law, driving out did not constitute divorce.

[20] See note 25 on p. 28 above.

[21] J. N. Epstein in *Jahrbuch d. jued.-lit. Gesellschaft,* Vol. VI, p. 371 claims that the papyrus clause previously mentioned represents the case of *mored* while this clause deals with the ordinary divorce. This interpretation looks impossible in view of the fact that this clause prescribes severer penalties than the former one.

Therefore the marriage was not dissolved. But being driven away from her husband's house and goods and chattels, she was deprived of domicile, support, and companionship without being freed to marry another. Hence the severer penalty. If the latter is the intention of the papyrus clause, it has its counterpart in the rabbinic statute concerning the rebellious husband.[22]

The woman cannot divorce her husband according to Jewish law. This arises from two historical foundations. Divorce in its original form was driving out of the house. The husband is the owner of the house; it is he who brings his wife to his home, it is therefore he who drives her out of his house. The wife cannot drive the husband from the house which is not hers but his. Even when divorce became a social formality by decree or writ it was still impossible to give the wife the power or right to give her husband a bill of divorcement. For one reason because of the more ancient tradition, and for another reason because the bill of divorcement was primarily intended to free the one who was divorced to marry another. Since only the woman is restricted against marrying another before she is freed from her husband, she is the only one who can be divorced. The husband, according to Biblical law, can have a number of wives.[23]

It should be logically possible, however, for the

[22] Neither of these interpretations is impossible, yet I feel that the former is the more logical one. The word *letarekutah* is the Aramaic equivalent for "to divorce her" and the implication in it is that divorce is carried out and is not merely a denial of rights to a woman who continues as wife. The distinction we draw later between שונא and גרש further adds to the probability of the first interpretation of our clause. Cf. Deiches in *Hashiloah* 1907, p. 515 and Freund in WZKM, Vol. 21, p. 170.

[23] The only Deuteronomic mention of the bill of divorcement is in connection with remarriage. See Deut. 24, 1-3.

woman to leave her husband, that is to free herself, even though she cannot divorce him.[24] Such a possibility is assumed in Code Hammurabi[25] and in a number of instances in the Bible.[26] From the earlier portions of the Bible it would appear that if she justified her action before the court she was even permitted to marry another,[27] but the later law did not permit her to remarry without the bill of divorcement.

Papyrus G provides for the possibility of the wife divorcing her husband as for the husband divorcing his wife, and it prescribes the terms of such an eventuality by a ketubah clause. Thus we read: "If tomorrow or any later day Miphtahya shall stand up in the congregation and say: "I divorce (*Sanaiti*) As-hor my husband, the price of divorce shall be upon her head; she shall return to the scales and she shall weigh for As-hor the sum of five shekels (6 ?) and two d.— and all which I have delivered unto her she shall give back, both string and thread, and she shall go away whither-

[24] The term for divorce is *Garesh* or *shalah* in Hebrew and *Tarek* in Aramaic. These terms go back to the original conception of "driving out," and such a term cannot be employed in connection with the wife's initiative in the divorce proceedings. The term *Sane* goes back to the conception of desiring to be separated, or *Hitpater*, to be freed, and applies to the woman as well as to the man.

[25] CH 142. See Sachau, *Syrisch-romische Rechtsbuecher*, p. 38.

[26] Exod. 21, 7-11 is one case where the Bible provides for the woman's right to leave her husband. This evident point in the Bible cannot be circumvented by the remark of the Mekilta (a. l.) that she still needs a bill of divorcement. This was the ruling of rabbinic law, but does not reflect Biblical law. One also gets the impression of the woman's freedom to leave her husband from Hosea 2, 4-15.

[27] Follows logically from Exod. ibid.

soever she will." [28] According to some interpreters, this clause directly indicates that the wife had the power of divorcing her husband as the husband had of divorcing his wife;[29] but others infer from it only the right of the woman to demand a divorce from but not to issue a divorce to her husband.[30] To me it appears that this papyrus takes Biblical legislation as its background, in the following manner: The bill of divorcement was an instrument that only the husband could use. The more ancient method of driving out, which was still effective,[31] could also be used by the husband only. But the third method of dissolving the marriage in the presence of the court could be employed by either the wife or the husband. It consisted of a declaration before the congregation of the formula: "I divorce (synonymous with I hate) my husband or my wife." Apparently, if no punitive measures were sought, the court declared the marriage bond dissolved merely on the grounds of either party refusing to continue living with the other.[32]

[28] See p. 27, note 21.

[29] See Sayce and Cowley in the introduction to the papyri.

[30] Freund, GES, p. 16, and WZKM, 21, p. 174.

[31] Hence Papyrus G, which contains a clause specifying a fine against the husband for "driving out" his wife (*Tarek*), does not provide for the possibility of the wife driving out the husband, but it does provide for husband and wife equally for the case of *sane*, or being displeased with each other and therefore separating.

[32] The material for that kind of divorce, namely by standing up in the congregation and pronouncing a certain formula, is very scant. CH 141, 142 and Meissner, *Beitrage z. altbabylon. Privatrecht*, Leipzig, 1893, p. 72 prescribe divorce in that form, but in Jewish law this form is not known except in the papyri and remnants of it are found in the fact that Targum Jonathan requires a court for divorce (ed. Ginsburger, p. 341, ad Deut. 24, 1) and so does Karaitic law.

In Talmudic times, only the bill of divorcement survived as the method of dissolving a marriage, and by its historical character could be issued only by the husband, not by the wife. Josephus reports that members of the Herodian family, following the Roman law and custom,[33] executed divorces by the bill of divorcement being issued by the wife, and that the Jewish courts made vehement and emphatic protest against it.[34]

Yet, while in form, the husband executed the divorce, in essence Talmudic law recognizes the woman's right to divorce her husband, or to be more exact, to institute divorce action, and if her petition is granted, the court forces the husband to issue the bill of divorcement. Thus, the Mishna reports that, "In former days it was said that three women are granted divorce together with the full payment of the ketubah: She who says to her husband, I am unclean to thee; she who states, Heaven is between me and thee; and she who asserts, I am taken away from Jews." [35] The three instances given in the Mishna represent situations where the court may be fully convinced that the woman will not live with her husband, hinting at conditions that make it impossible for her to continue as his wife, but not stating any definite ground for divorce.[36] The later tannaim restricted her in that free-

[33] *Code Justinian*, Bk. 5, Title 17, Const. 6.

[34] *Antiquities*, Bk. 15, Ch. 7, Sec. 10 and notes by Whiston. See also *Antiquities* Bk. 18, Ch. 7 and Amram, *The Jewish Law of Divorce*, pp. 60-61

[35] Nedar. 90b, Jeb. 112a.

[36] The Talmud takes "I am unclean to thee" to mean that she was violated, "Heaven is between me and thee" that she charges him with masculine incompetency, and "I may have no relation with Jews" to be a vow which prohibits her to live with a Jewish husband. The exact definition of these terms is

dom and demanded that she show cause sufficient to warrant a dissolution of the marriage. The tannaitic restrictions against the wife's forcing a divorce were further continued in their legislation concerning the *moredet,* the rebellious woman; but that legislation imposed only punitive measures on her, and did not deny her the final right of getting her divorce. Even in amoraic days, we have the legal opinion expressed that the woman who has an honest revulsion of feeling toward her husband may force her husband to divorce her.[37]

The Palestinian Talmud cites two ketubah clauses, similar in nature to the papyrus clauses, which provide for the case of the woman forcing the divorce. One of these clauses has been referred to above, reading, "if he divorces . . . . . if she divorces" [38] without mentioning any procedure or penalty. Another clause is recorded in the following context. A woman permitted herself to be kissed by a man, and her husband presented it to the court as a case of unfaithfulness. Her relatives contested that there was no evidence for unfaithfulness. The ketubah was brought into the case and therein was found the following clause: "If this one be married to that one, her husband, and she be displeased with his companionship (shall seek divorce), she shall take half of the ketubah." Whereupon R. Abin concluded that "Because she permitted herself to be kissed by him, it is as though she brought action for divorce

not reliable, but the Mishna appears rather to legislate that she must bring clear charges and prove them both as to their verity and as to their hindrance in their common life.

[37] See p. 148 above.

[38] See p. 198 and note 19 above.

(*sen'at*), and she is entitled to only half of the ketubah." [39]

None of the ketubah clauses here mentioned, relative to divorce either at the instance of the husband or the wife, is recorded in the post-Talmudic ketubah. By statute, if the husband divorces his wife without justifiable cause, he loses all that he gave her in gifts and must pay her the mohar, dowry, and mulug. If the wife forces a divorce without justifiable grounds, she must return all gifts which her husband had given her, she has no claim upon her husband for any of the ketubah obligations and guarantees, she can only take what she finds left of her dowry and mulug in whatever condition they may be.[40]

The final halakah did not alter the ruling in the case of the husband divorcing his wife, but it raised strenuous objections to the above ruling in the case of a wife forcing her husband to divorce her. It sees great danger to the community that a wife should be able to force her husband to divorce her merely on the grounds of a change of heart towards him. It favors the opinion of some scholars, therefore, who maintain that no matter what fine may be imposed on the woman in such a case, she cannot get her divorce without the free will of her husband.[41]

[39] Jer. Ket. 31c. It appears that R. Abin in concluding that "It is as if she brought action for a divorce (*sen'at*)" assumed that the specification of the clause, "she be displeased with his companionship" was synonymous with the other clause, "If she divorces." On this basis one has the suspicion that: first, "If she divorces" implies only a change of heart toward her husband and nothing else as a cause for the divorce, and second, that the fine imposed was the loss of half of the ketubah. See J. N. Epstein in *Jahrbuch d. jued-lit. Gesellschaft*, VI, p. 369.

[40] Yad, Ishut, 14, 8.

[41] See Magid ad Yad ibid., Tosafot Ket. 63b-64a, EH 76, 2.

There is no telling what Jewish law today would be in the matter of giving the wife an equal chance with her husband to free herself from him, had we the power to enforce Jewish law upon Jews. Without such power, the law cannot even hear the woman's case, for the court cannot divorce; the court can only compel the husband to divorce, if its force is effective. On the other hand, should a non-Jewish court compel the husband to divorce his wife, or should other methods of compulsion be used except that of Jewish law, the divorce would be invalid even if executed wholly in accordance with the rabbinic requirements, because it would be an instrument made out by one who acts not as a free agent.[42]

[42] Gittin 88b.

CHAPTER XIII

Fines and Forfeitures

In the case of divorce without justifiable cause, the subject treated of in the previous chapter, we have seen that if a fine was imposed, either by statute or by a specific ketubah clause, it was imposed on the plaintiff. In the case of divorce on justifiable grounds, if a fine is imposed, it is on the defendant. The ketubah is in all cases, except in that of rebellion, the only bone of contention. If the husband is fined, he pays the ketubah in full, which amounts to a loss of his investment in the marriage, such as mohar, mattan, and gifts. If the wife is fined, she loses part or all of her ketubah. We shall now take up the penalties in connection with the various grounds for divorce, and we shall turn first to the fines and forfeitures imposed on the wife when the husband presents justifiable cause for divorce.

Cruelty is ground for divorce. "It is a meritorious deed to divorce an evil wife."[1] But a wife's cruelty to her husband is not penalized in the Jewish court, for, as the Talmudic dictum has it: "A man assaulted by women has no cause for action."[2] The cruel wife, therefore, loses none of her ketubah rights.

Sterility is a justifiable cause for divorce.[3] If the husband has no children by another wife, the divorce is mandatory upon him.[4] The law assumes, however,

[1] Jeb. 63b.
[2] B. M. 97a.
[3] Jeb. 64a.
[4] Ket. 77a, Yad, Ishut 15, 7.

that, unless otherwise proven,[5] sterility is not due to a defect in the wife, but to sexual incompatibility. Hence, according to Talmudic law, even as according to Hammurabi,[6] the wife suffers no loss of her keubah.[7]

Sterility is established after ten years, and according to others after two or three years of childless marriage,[8] provided during the entire period there was no miscarriage, and husband and wife have been living together, both in good health.[9] All these conditions apply only to the first and the second marriage of the woman, but do not apply to the third marriage after she has been divorced from two husbands on account of sterility. She may not marry a third unless he has children or another wife. If she does, without giving him suspicion as to her sterility, he may divorce her on two counts, on sterility and deception. In that case,

[5] Her statement as to his physical fitness for connubiality is given more credence than his statement. Her being proven sterile after being divorced from him does not reflect retroactively on her condition prior to the divorce. If the husband wishes to marry another wife to prove that he is not sterile, she may object to a second wife. See Jeb. 65a, Yad, Ishut 15, 9.

[6] CH. 138.

[7] Tos. Jeb. 8, 4, Jeb. 64a. According to R. Hananel and R. Tam she forfeits the mattan — Cf. *Or Zaru'a*, 653 — but most authorities declare that she gets all that the ketubah calls for. See Yad, Ishut 15, 8.

[8] Jeb. 64b. According to certain views, and partly evident also from the Talmudic discussion of the subject, the question of childlessness has no bearing on a marriage outside of Palestine, for the sinfulness of living in a foreign land may be the cause of childlessness. Cf. *Or Zarua* ibid. Most authorities, however, recognize childlessness as a ground for divorce in any country Cf. *Itur*, I, p. 71c.

[9] Jeb. 64a.

the law fines her to the extent of totally losing her ketubah.[10]

The standard ground for divorce in all systems of law is unfaithfulness. In Jewish law unfaithfulness is possible only of the wife, not of the husband, because where polygamy is permitted another woman cannot cause a breach of the marriage vow. Unfaithfulness

[10] See Jeb. 65a, Tos. Jeb. 8, 4, Yad, Ishut 15, 14, *Itur*, p. 70b. *Itur* suggests, with evident hesitancy, that she loses both mohar and mattan. Asheri is of the opinion that she loses mohar only. See Asheri Ket. 11, 25-28. Tosafot Ket. 65a seems to agree with Asheri in full, treating this case as that of *Ailonit*. R. Meir of Rothenberg is cited in Mordecai Ket. 280 (apparently misquoted in Asheri Ket. 13, 18) as of the opinion that the expression in the Talmud, "she shall be divorced without the ketubah" implies also the loss of mattan. R. Meir would apparently apply his rule also here. It would also seem from his decision that in this and similar cases — except for rabbinically prohibited marriages — the husband must return the zon-barzel as of the value it had at the time of the marriage. The direct application of this rule of R. Meir is intended for the case of the woman who refuses to follow her husband in establishing their domicile in Palestine, and it is extended to every case where the Talmud orders a divorce without the payment of the ketubah. As for me, I fully agree with that scholar in the case cited, but I heartily disagree with him in all other cases, including that of deception as to sterility. In these cases where the loss of the ketubah is due to deception, or the legal — though not the formal — annulment of the marriage, the husband's right to the use of the zon-barzel is based simply on the permission granted him by the woman. Hence, he cannot be asked to pay for the zon-barzel as of the time of the marriage except on the basis of the ketubah, and that is cancelled because of deception. Otherwise is the case of the woman who does not follow her husband to Palestine, where the marriage is valid and the question is only as to the extent of the fine. It appears therefore logical that this case of the sterile woman, like the case of the *Ailonit* (as reasoned by the Talmud, Ket. 101a) is subject to the forfeiture of the zon-barzel and the loss of her mulug except the *bla'ot*.

is distinctly, therefore, a cause for divorce which the husband alone can present.

There are three shades of unfaithfulness. All three are treated alike by the law in the matter of fines. In all cases, the husband has a religious duty to divorce his wife;[11] but if the testimony is defective, he must pay her the ketubah in full;[12] and if the case is proven by due legal process, she loses her ketubah completely.[13] The ketubah obligations, such as redemption, burial, medicine, sustenance, *bnin dikrin* and *bnan nukban* privileges are cancelled.[14] Of the mohar and mattan she gets nothing; of the dowry and mulug she takes only what she finds. The husband need not pay for any loss or depreciation even if the last thread of it is destroyed.[15]

The first case is that of adultery. If she is caught in the act, and testimony to that effect is given by at least two witnesses, the husband may not continue to live with her. Divorce is mandatory, with the total loss of the ketubah.[16] If there is no evidence for adultery save her own confession, she loses the ketubah, but divorce is optional with the husband, because there is

[11] Sifre Numb. ed. Horovitz, p. 23, Jer. Ket. 25a, Kid. 66a, Alfasi ibid., Ket. 9a, Asheri ibid., Yad, Ishut 24, 17-18, Isure Bi'ah, 18, 11, *Itur*, p. 69d.

[12] Yad, Ishut 24, 17, based on Kid. 66a. Cf. *Magid* ibid.

[13] Ket. 101a, Jer. Ket. 30b, 31c. The term היוצאת משום שם רע is taken by Maimonides (Yad, Ishut 24, 15) to represent the last of the three cases, but I can see no reason for his opinion. Ket. 101a takes this term to be synonymous with זינתה. Rather it looks to me that it represents divorce on grounds of unfaithfulness and includes all of the three classes.

[14] Ket. 35b, 54a, Jer. Ket. 27d.

[15] Yad, Ishut 24, 7, *Itur* ibid. based on Ket. 101b.

[16] Sotah 31b, Kid. 66a reports the view of Abaye that one witness is sufficient for this case. Raba opposes this view and the halakah decides with him. Cf. Jeb. 24b and Tosafot thereto, Yad, Ishut 24, 18 and *Itur* ibid.

cause to suspect that her self-condemnation was prompted by her desire to free herself from her husband.[17]

The second case is that of the *sotah*. Biblical law gives the husband the right to command the wife (a command of jealousy — *kinnui*) to avoid secret relations with a co-respondent. When the command is given in the presence of witnesses, she becomes a *sotah* on the testimony of witnesses to the effect that she was seen in hiding (*setirah*) with the co-respondent. Although there is no testimony as to illicit relations between them, the wife becomes prohibited to her husband. In Temple days, she was put through the ordeal of the "cursed water." [18] If the ordeal revealed her guilt, she was an adulteress; if found guiltless, she returned to her husband's house. With the abolition of the cursed water by R. Johanan b. Zakkai,[19] the possibility of the *sotah* returning to her husband came to an end. Hence, she is divorced with the total forfeiture of her ketubah.[20]

The third case is that of testimony presented to the effect that the wife was found in a compromising position, without evidence, however, of illicit contact. The instances cited in the Talmud are, a man coming out of her room and she putting on her undergarments; or in privacy with a man and sputum found on his or her bed; or in the company of a man in a hiding place; or kissing or hugging a man; or being on each other's lap; or being with him behind locked doors.[21] On such testimony, the husband has cause to divorce her with the

[17] Cf. Nedar. 90b, Yad, Ishut ibid.

[18] Numb. 5, 11-31.

[19] Sotah 47a.

[20] See Yad, Ishut, 24, 24, based on Sotah 2b.

[21] Jeb. 24b, Jer. Ket. 31c.

total loss of her ketubah.[22] However, divorce does not become mandatory in this case unless, in addition to these circumstantial evidences, there is rumor — continuously persisting for the duration of a day and a half — that the wife is having illicit relations with the co-respondent.[23] According to another view, divorce is never mandatory in this third case, so long as there is no testimony of actual adultery.[24]

Another legitimate cause for divorce is the wife's laxity in certain religious observances. Divorce on such grounds is never compulsory[25] but optional with the huband, and he cannot sue for forfeiture of the ketubah unless he has given her warning in the presence of witnesses and she has disregarded it.[26] Under this heading we consider two classes, the violation of Biblical commands and the breach of accepted Jewish customs. Of the first kind, the Mishna cites the following examples: laxity in tithing or heave offering of dough, or in ritual cleanness, or in fulfilling of vows.[27] Laxity in such observances in a measure also involves the husband, hence not only divorce but also a penalty is justifiable. The wife's private religious conduct may be a matter of concern to the husband, but does not count as

[22] Yad, Ishut 24, 15 based on Maimonides' interpretation of Jeb. 24b, which is supported by the context of Jer. Ket. 31c.

[23] This is the view of Rashi and *She'eltot.*

[24] The view of R. Hananel, and R. Tam and Maimonides. Cf. Tosafot Jeb. 24b, *She'eltot* 134, Yad, Ishut 24, 15 and *Magid* commentary to Ishut 24, 16.

[25] Sotah 25b.

[26] Ket. 72a, Jer. Ket. 31b, Tos. Ket. 7, 7, Sotah ibid., Yad, Ishut 24, 14. See *Itur* p. 69b where the Jerushalmi is differently quoted from the reading in our text.

[27] Ket. ibid.; the Talmud also adds, going about without head cover.

a cause for divorce under penalties.[28] The violation of Jewish customs is illustrated in the Talmud by the following misdemeanors: appearing in public places with exposed shoulders or arms or uncovered head, bathing in men's bathing places, weaving in the market place, indulging in conversation with men or flirting with them, acting familiarly with her slaves or neighbors, being loud mouthed on matters private, or cursing her husband's parents in his presence.[29] For such misdemeanors and religious laxities, the husband may divorce her at the total forfeiture of her ketubah.[30]

The woman is expected to be sociable and neighborly, else she makes her husband also objectionable in his surroundings. If the wife, therefore, has restricted herself by a vow not to lend or borrow household utensils, not to attend weddings or funerals, not to make any new clothes for his children, or if she has restricted herself to the life of a nazarite, the husband may divorce her with the total loss of her ketubah.[31] Even if it was within the husband's power to annul these vows and he failed to do so, he still can blame her and not himself; and on the ground that her vows are in themselves objectionable, he may divorce her with due forfeiture of the ketubah.[32]

[28] Cf. *Itur* p. 69d, *Tur Eben Haezer* 115.

[29] Ket. 72a-b, Gittin 90b, Sotah 25b, Tos. Ket. 7, 6-7, Tos. Sotah 5, 9, Jer. Ket. 31b, Jer. Sotah 16b, Numb. R. 9, 8.

[30] The Talmud only states that her mohar and mattan are forfeited, but does not say anything concerning the dowry. From the context of Ket. 100b-101a it appears, however, that the husband is not held liable for loss of or damage to the dowry. On this inference rests the decision of Maimonides in Mishna Commentary Ket. 72a, Yad, Ishut 24, 10. See also R. Nisim Ket. 101a, *Itur* 69a, *Tur Eben Haezer* 115 f.

[31] Ket. 71a, 72a.

[32] The forfeiture in this case seems to be exactly the same as in the case of the woman who refuses to follow her husband to his rightful domicile. See note 45 p. 218.

Misrepresentation is ground either for the annulment of a marriage[33] or for penalized divorce. It may be one of two kinds, either deception, with knowledge by the wife of the true facts, or error due to conditions beyond the knowledge of the wife. The discovery of physical defects in the wife that had not been known to the husband, such defects as would make a priest unfit for services in the Temple, or such defects as a bad odor from the body or mouth, excessive perspiration, a wart on the face, a masculine voice, oversized or misplaced breasts, epilepsy or irregularity in menstrual periods, constitute legal grounds for divorce together with the wife's forfeiture of her entire ketubah.[34] Because marriages were made in olden days be-

[33] Misrepresentation where a specific stipulation was made at the time of the marriage completely annuls the marriage. Where no specific stipulation was made the marriage is not dissolved except by a divorce. It is understood to be a rabbinical divorce by some or a doubtful divorce by others, because it is a matter of doubt whether the husband would have refused to marry his wife had he known of her defects or her vows. See Ket. 73b.

[34] Ket. 72b, 75a, 77a, Tos. Ket. 7, 8-9. The forfeiture involved in these cases as in the other cases of deception include the loss of her mohar and mattan. As to the dowry, neither the Talmud nor the codifiers have given a definite verdict. R. Nisim, Ket. 101a and *Itur* p. 69a seem to indicate that she also loses her dowry guarantees of the ketubah as in the case of unfaithfulness.

The logic of the case of deception leads me to believe the following forfeitures were intended by the Talmudic and post-Talmudic authorities. The mohar and mattan are completely cancelled, as is every other ketubah obligation, because the ketubah is based on a marriage of no legal validity. Hence, whatever dowry articles are left, she takes, but what was destroyed or lost she cannot claim payment for from her husband on the basis of the ketubah, because there is no valid ketubah. If she claims it on the basis that he used her dowry, he retorts

tween brides and grooms who had not seen each other, the husband's carelessness in failing to notice such defects was no defense to the wife, who should have made known to him her physical defects. The woman who enters her husband's home burdened with intolerable vows, such as that she shall eat no meat or drink no wine or wear no ornaments, and has not made those vows known to her husband, also loses her ketubah on account of deception.[35]

If on entering the nuptial chamber the husband finds himself deceived as to the bride's virginity, he has a valid cause for divorce and forfeiture of the ketubah, provided he has had no private meetings with her prior to nuptials and provided also that he reports his complaint to the court immediately upon the first con-

that he used it rightfully with her permission. This rule should hold good for the woman who was found non-virgin, *ailonit,* or sterile. The mulug, however, is not based on the ketubah, because the mulug is not entered into the ketubah. The husband is entitled to the use of it by her consent even though the marriage was not valid. Therefore, she cannot claim depreciation through legitimate use. But can she claim damages from him for a destructive use of her mulug, so that at the time of her divorce her mulug has become worthless? Technically the question should be formulated: Is she entitled to *bla'ot* of her mulug, i. e. the loss of the mulug capital beyond the legitimate use of it? The answer to this question will be the same as the answer to the same question in the case of the *ailonit.* If the *ailonit* is granted *bla'ot* the cases here treated will also warrant giving the wife the *bla'ot;* and those who deny *bla'ot* to the *ailonit* will deny it also to the woman who was deceptive in matters of her physical appearance or her vows. According to *Itur* ibid., the woman who has no regular menstrual periods does not lose her mattan.

[35] Ket. 72b, Tos. Ket. 7, 8, Physical defects and intolerable vows are treated by the law as strictly parallel in their effects upon the ketubah.

tact with her.[36] If the possiblity of adultery between the time of betrothal and nuptials is involved, the divorce becomes mandatory upon the husband;[37] if that suspicion does not seem plausible, divorce is optional[38] and the forfeiture is the only question in the case. Her denial of the charge without testimony in her behalf[39] is insufficient against the husband's personal statement. Her defence may be either that she was violated after betrothal[40] or that loss of virginity was due to accident without male contact.[41]

The standard case of marriage under misunderstanding, not deception, is that of the *Ailonit*, the she-ram, in Talmudic terminology, designating a sexually abnormal woman with masculine elements in her physical make up. That condition is often not established until the age of twenty, so that there is no suspicion of wilful deception on her part. Divorce in that case is mandatory only in so far as she is of necessity sterile, but if the husband has children by another wife, divorce is optional with him. But because the marriage was based on error, the woman forfeits her mohar; the dowry is given back to her without obligation on

[36] Ket. 3b, 11b, 12a, Jeb. 111b, R. Meir makes 30 days the time limit.

[37] Ket. 9a, Yad. Isure Bi'ah, 18, 10, 11. Jer. Ket. 25a.

[38] Should the husband, however, not divorce his wife, he would have to write another ketubah for her with a mohar of one hundred zuzim only.

[39] Ket. 10a. According to some authorities, her denial is insufficient only with respect to the question of the mohar but not to the other ketubah obligations. Hence, if the husband cannot prove his charge he must even pay her the mattan. See Alfasi Ket. ibid. But see Asheri.

[40] Ket. 12b.

[41] Ket. 13a, in which case her mohar is reduced to one hundred zuzim.

the husband to pay for loss or depreciation; the other ketubah obligations are cancelled. The husband must pay her the mattan and, above the normal use of her mulug to which he was entitled, he must pay for loss or destruction of the capital value of the mulug.[42]

Finally, the husband has certain rights of domicile. The place of marriage is assumed to be the domicile of the couple, unless otherwise specified in the ketubah. He may move from a foreign country to Palestine without her consent.[43] Within Palestine, three geographical divisions are recognized, Judah, Galilee, and

[42] Ket. 100b-101a. Basing themselves on a beraita quoted in Ket. 101a which teaches that "*mema'enet* and her conpanions" do not forfeit the mattan, Alfasi, Maimonides, Asheri, Itur and others agree that the *ailonit* forfeits only her mohar but not her mattan. They count the *ailonit* as companion to *mema'enet.* RABD does not find the *ailonit* included in the implications of that beraita and therefore rules that the *ailonit* forfeits both mohar and mattan. Whatever is left of her dowry is given back to her, but the husband need not pay for loss or destruction or depreciation. What is left of her mulug belongs to her, but for loss or destruction beyond that which is due to his legitimate use of it the husband, theoretically conceived, should pay. But the question arises as to how far may the husband's legitimate use of his wife's mulug go? According to R. Kahana (Ket. ibid.) his right of fruit does not entitle him to exhaust the capital value of the mulug, while according to R. Nahman he may use the mulug until there is nothing left of it. If the view of R. Nahman is correct, then there is no such conception as "loss or destruction beyond the legitimate use of it." Hence, while Alfasi decides that the husband must pay for loss or destruction of mulug beyond the legitimate use of it, Itur (63d, 69c) declares that there is no such thing, for the view of R. Nahman prevails. Cf. Asheri Ket. 101a, Yad, Ishut 24, 1-3. Of the other terms of the Ketubah, the *ailonit* has no KBD or KBN because she has no children. She gets her support as long as she is with her husband, but she does not collect payment for back alimony. See Tosafot B. M. 67a.

[43] Ket. 110b, Jer. Ket. 36b, Tos. Ket. 13, 2.

Transjordania. He cannot move from one to the other without her consent, but he can move from one city to another of similar size within any one division.[44] In so far as he is within his right of domicile, if she does not follow him, he has cause for divorce with the total loss of the ketubah.[45]

So much for the grounds on which the husband may sue for divorce. The wife has similar rights. These rights were protected by the Jewish court when it had the power to enforce its decree by fine or imprisonment or suitable corporal punishment. We turn now to a brief account of the grounds on which the wife may sue her husband for divorce.

Denial of conjugal union to the wife is valid ground for divorce. As we have seen above, the tannaim have formulated a disciplinary method of breaking the will of the "rebellious husband" who denies his wife the right of marriage. This method cannot apply, however, if the husband had fortified his cruelty by a religious vow not to give his wife marital satisfaction, for the law will not compel him to violate his vow. In such a case, the vow itself becomes the ground for divorce. According to the Shamaites, the vow is valid cause for divorce if it prohibits marital union for a period in excess of two weeks; the Hillelites say, even in excess of one week.[46] If the vow specified no term of prohibition, Samuel teaches that the

[44] Ibid.

[45] Asheri Ket. 13, 18 (see also 11, 25-28) teaches that she loses mohar but not mattan. *Itur* p. 70b suggests that she also loses mattan. R. Nisim (Ket. 110b) declares it to be a case of total forfeiture of the ketubah. Mordecai cites R. Meir of Rotenberg in the opinion that she forfeits mohar, mattan, and mulug including the *bla'ot*, but not her dowry.

[46] Ket. 61b, Tos. Ket. 5, 6.

husband is given a week or two for the purpose of seeking an annulment of his vow; Rab teaches that the wife has the right of being freed without any delay.[47] The penalty on the husband is the full payment of the ketubah.

If the husband has denied his wife conjugal relation on account of ill health, he is given six months' time to cure himself. If his health is not restored, the wife may demand a divorce and the full payment of the ketubah.[48] Sexual contact in an unnatural manner, if insisted on by the husband, constitutes ground for divorce.[49] The sterility of the husband is no ground for divorce, if judged on the basis of the religious duty to beget offspring, for the woman has no such religious obligation. It is a cause for divorce, if the woman demands it on the basis that in her old age she would remain without the support and comfort of a child.[50] If the divorce is granted her on this ground, she receives her ketubah in full, except for the mattan, which she forfeits.[51]

Wife beating is considered in the Talmud either one of two cases. Either it is assault upon which she obtains redress at the court in the same manner a stranger would,[52] or it is chastisement for the purpose of discipline, which is the husband's prerogative as head of the family. The Talmud again and again sets up standards of kind, affectionate, and considerate

[47] *Gemara*, Ket. ibid. See Yad, Ishut 14, 6. *Itur* 71a.

[48] Yad, Ishut 14, 7.

[49] Ket. 48a, *Itur* 71a.

[50] Jeb. 65a-b, Nedar. 91a.

[51] R. Hananel and Alfasi Jeb. ibid., Yad, Ishut 16, 10, Asheri Ket. end of Chapter 6. R. Tam opposes this ruling and believes that she gets her ketubah in full. Cf. Tosafot Jeb. ibid.

[52] Tos. B. K. 9, 14.

treatment of a wife, but does not recognize wife beating as a ground for divorce. However, post-Talmudic authorities have ruled that the husband who is accused of wife beating is given command by the court to cease that ugly practice and, if he disregards it, he is compelled to divorce his wife and pay her the full ketubah.[53] Imprisoning a wife out of jealousy is a vulgar form of discipline, but does not constitute a cause for divorce.[54]

Non-support, as we have seen above, calls for certain disciplinary measures by the court, but does not constitute a cause for divorce unless such measures have proven futile. Rab, however, is of the opinion that "A person cannot live with a serpent in one cage," and, therefore, the wife is entitled to a divorce and her ketubah without delay.[55] If the husband has cut off his wife from support by a vow prohibiting her the use of his possessions, the vow itself becomes a cause for divorce. In the case of an Israelite he is given one month, a priest is given two months; and thereafter, if the prohibition continues, he is compelled to divorce her and pay her the ketubah in full.[56] A vow prohibiting her the enjoyment of fruit, even though he names a single kind of fruit unknown or distasteful to her, constitutes a cause for divorce, so long as the vow specified a duration in excess of one day in the case of an Israelite or two days in the case of a priest. Likewise, a vow prohibiting her the use of

[53] See Iserlis note to EH 154, 3.

[54] Gittin 90a, Tos. Sotah 5, 9, Jer. Sotah 17a.

[55] Ket. 63a, 77a. Jer. Gittin 50d supports the view of Rab. Asheri cites *Halakot Gedolot* as making Rab's view the final halakah, but Alfasi and R. Hananel oppose the view of Rab. See Asheri and Alfasi Ket. 77a.

[56] Ket. 70a, Tos. Ket. 7, 2-3.

ornamented garments or cosmetics constitutes ground for divorce, in the case of poor people if it made the duration of the prohibition indefinite, and in the case of wealthy people if it specified a duration of thirty days. In the same manner, if he has prohibited her wearing shoes for a period of three days in a village or twenty-four hours in a city, or if he has prohibited her the use of the bath house for a period of two weeks in the village or one week in the city, he is compelled to divorce her and pay her the ketubah.[57] Also if he prohibits her visiting her parents for a period of two months while they live in the same city or for a period of two consecutive holidays when they live in another city,[58] she may demand her divorce and her ketubah. Further causes for divorce within the same category are, restricting her social liberties, such as to attend weddings and funerals, to lend to or borrow from neighbors household utensils, or to make new garments for her children,[59] ordering her to do useless labor such as pouring water over a dung hill[60] or to be totally idle[61] or to be vulgar — as to let strangers taste her cooking, or to talk to strangers on private matters.[62] According to certain rabbinic opinions all these constitute ground for divorce not only if the restriction was made by a vow pronounced by the husband but even if the vow was pronounced by the wife and the husband failed to annul it when it was in his power to do so.[63]

A husband's unattractiveness, either due to phys-

[57] Jer. Ket. 31b.
[58] Ket. 71b.
[59] Ket. 71b, 72a, Tos. Ket. 7, 4-5.
[60] Ket. ibid., Tos. Ket. 7, 6. See *Itur* 71a.
[61] Ket. 59b, Ta'anit 31a.
[62] Tos. Ket. 7, 6.
[63] Ket. 71a, Jer. Ket. 31b.

ical defects, a bad odor from the mouth or nose, the loss of a limb or arm or eye, or due to his vocation, such as a copper miner, a tanner, a dung gatherer, is valid cause for divorce. According to R. Meir it is valid even if the husband's physical defect or vocation was the same at the time of the marriage; she may demand a divorce on the claim that she cannot endure it any longer.[64] Leprosy is ground for divorce, and divorce is not optional but mandatory.[65]

According to the opinion of R. Ami, the wife has valid cause for divorce if her husband has married a second wife in addition to her.[66] The opposite opinion that "a man may take many wives so long as he is able to support them" has prevailed in Talmudic law and, therefore, a number of post-Talmudic ketubot have the special provision —"That if he marry another wife in addition to this one, he will release her (the present bride) by a valid instrument of divorcement."[67] This clause is found, naturally, in those countries where the enactment of R. Gershon, prohibiting polygamy, was not honored. Where polygamy was prohibited it was not necessary to make provisions against it in the ketubah.

Finally, the wife has certain rights of domicile. If the husband wishes to move to a new city contrary to her rights, she may object. She may even insist on living in Palestine against the husband's wishes to live in a foreign land.[68] If her insistence upon her rights

[64] Ket. 77a-b, Tos. Ket. 7, 10-11. R. Simeon b. Gamaliel includes also the loss of an arm, leg or eye.

[65] Tos. Ket. 7, 11, Ket. 77b.

[66] Jeb. 65a.

[67] See the Sephardic ketubah, ed. Gaster MGWJ, p. 586, and others.

[68] Ket. 110b, Yad, Ishut 13, 20. According to the Palestinian

in this matter brings about a separation between the couple, the wife is entitled to divorce and the payment of the ketubah.[69]

Talmud, Jer. Ket. 36b, the wife can insist only on remaining in Palestine if Palestine has once become the couple's domicile, but she cannot force her husband to move to Palestine from a foreign land.

[69] Although Talmudic law regulates this matter (Ket. 110b etc.), because of insecurity of life in mediaeval days, and therefore the frequent flights of husbands from one place to another, which exposed the wife to dangers of *'agunah* and being separated from her kin, it is not infrequent that the mediaeval ketubah makes special restrictions as to the husband's right of domicile, together with the provision that if he violates that clause he shall divorce her with the full payment of the ketubah.

CHAPTER XIV

FINES AND FORFEITURES (Continued)

The fine of the ketubah in connection with groundless divorce was treated in a previous chapter, and to that was added in the last chapter a study of the effect upon the ketubah of the legitimate and valid grounds for divorce, both when the husband sues or the wife sues for divorce. But these by no means exhaust the list of fines and forfeitures of ketubah provisions found in Jewish law. We still must consider the fines and forfeitures in prohibited marriages, either when the prohibition existed at the time of the marriage or when it developed later; also reduction or cancellation of ketubah provisions in imperfect marriages; and a number of statutory forfeitures.

Marriages that constitute Biblical incest are legally invalid. Hence, the ketubah has no legal force whatever. Husband and wife are total strangers to each other, and whatever claim they have against each other is not a matter of domestic relations but a matter of torts or equity or the like.[1] The Biblical prohibitions that do not constitute incest, however, do not invalidate the marriage, but make divorce compulsory and also cause forfeitures of the terms of the ketubah.

Marriages restricted by a Biblical negative prohibition — a widow marrying a high priest, a divorcee marrying a lay priest, a male or female bastard or *Natin* marrying an Israelite, a divorcee remarrying

[1] Tos. Jeb. 2, 2-4.

her husband after she had been married to another man — are penalized in the following manner.[2] If the

[2] Jeb. 84a, 85b, Ket. 100b, Tos. Jeb. 2, 3. In this group should also be included the case of an adulteress who was not divorced by her husband or, having been divorced, was remarried by her husband in defiance of the Biblical injunction against it. But the Talmud thinks this case a matter of dispute between Rabbi and R. Simeon b. Elazar (Jeb. 85b). According to Rabbi it does belong to this category, according to R. Simeon b. Elazar it belongs to the category of "*Sheniyot*" in penalty, even though it represents a violation of a Biblical law. See Yad, Sotah 2, 16.

The Mishna also puts in this category the case of a levirate woman who was freed from her *levir* by the ceremony of *Halizah* and thereafter married a lay priest. The prohibition of such a marriage is only rabbinical, but in penalty it belongs to the category of the violation of a Biblical law. The Talmud justifies it by saying that her becoming rabbinically unfit to eat of the heave offering is to her like a stigma upon her social position and therefore she would be likely to treat that marriage with as much gravity as a Biblically prohibited marriage. R. Obadiah Bartenora (Jeb. 9, 3) states that since the *Haluzah* is Biblically prohibited to marry a high priest, her marriage to a lay priest is also treated as though it were a Biblical prohibition. *Tosafot Yom-tob* concludes, however, that the marriage of a *Haluzah* to a priest in respect to penalties belongs to the category of "*Sheniyot*", but the Mishna included it in the class of Biblically prohibited marriages by sheer habit of phrasing. Cf. Yad, Ishut 1, 7, and *Magid* thereto.

The case of a woman who has her menstrual flow at the time of intercourse (Nidah 12b) seems to belong also to this category. The prohibition is Biblical in the sense that so long as the flow has occurred with three consecutive intercourses she is accounted a perpetual *nidah*. Wherefore, if the condition was not known to the husband at the time of the marriage, she loses mohar and mattan (according to Maimonides, but Nahmanides and Itur teach that she does not lose mattan) and dowry and all other ketubah provisions. It appears also that he need not pay for the loss of the *bla'ot* of the dowry but he must pay for the loss of the *bla'ot* of the mulug. See R. Nisim, ad Alfasi Shabuot, at the beginning of chapter 2. What the penalty should be if the husband knew of the condition at the time of

condition of the prohibition was known to the husband at the time of the marriage, he must pay his wife the ketubah in full, but he owes her no support during his life, no redemption, and neither the *ketubat benin dikrin* or the *ketubat benan nukban* provisions.[3] If the condition of the prohibition was not known to him, he is freed from the payment of the mohar but must pay the mattan.[4] He need not pay for the depreciation or destruction of the dowry, but is liable for the loss to the mulug beyond the measure of legitimate use of it.[5] All other ketubah clauses are cancelled.

Those marriages which are prohibited by a Biblical positive precept, such for instance as the marriage of a high priest to a non-virgin, who, however, had not been previously married, are not subject to any forfeitures whether the husband knew of that condition or not.[6]

the marriage is not given in the codes, but apparently it would be the same as in the cases of Biblically prohibited marriages. See Yad, Ishut 25, 8 and *Magid* thereto.

[3] Ket. 52a, 101b, Jeb. 85a, Jer. Jeb. 10b. Whether the husband needs to pay back alimony is a matter disputed among authorities. Maimonides, Yad, Ishut 24, 4, rules that the husband must pay. Tosafot B. M. 67a and other authorities argue that since he owes no support he is also under no obligation to pay back alimony. See *Magid* ad Yad ibid. Maintenance during widowhood is not forfeited by her.

[4] Ket. 101a as interpreted by Alfasi and Asheri. *Itur* p. 70c quotes an authority who maintains that she loses mattan also and *Sha'ar Hehadash* commentary thereto identifies this authority with RABD, who maintains that the *ailonit* loses mattan also. This is very likely in view of a note of RABD to Alfasi ibid.

[5] Alfasi and Asheri ibid., Yad, Ishut 24, 8. *Itur* opposes the ruling that the husband has to pay for the *bla'ot* of mulug because it is the husband's right to use up the mulug until there is nothing left of it. See note 42, p. 217.

[6] Yad, Ishut 24, 4 based on Jeb. 85b. While there is no ketu-

There are certain Biblical prohibitions against husband and wife living together. Divorce is then Biblically compulsory. If the woman marries a second husband on flimsy testimony of the death of the first and then the first husband appears to claim his wife, he is Biblically commanded to put her away because of her defilement by the second husband.[7] If the divorcee discovers her bill of divorcment to have been void after she was remarried to another husband, she may not remain the wife of the first.[8] If the woman who was to enter into a levirate marriage married a stranger on grounds that by error were calculated to give her full permission to do so, she cannot remain his wife.[9] In all these cases, because the woman is at fault, she is fined to the extent of losing her mohar, mattan, dowry, and every other ketubah privilege. Even for the loss of the *bla'ot* of the mulug she has no recourse.[10] To compel the husband to divorce her in accordance with the Biblical injunction, the law has deprived him of his

bah forfeiture, as a measure that will tend to bring about a divorce between them, the law frees the husband from the alimentation obligation and compels him also to pay for the use of his wife's property. The absence of any forfeiture in this case — where the condition was unknown to the husband — is difficult to understand, because it at least falls in the category of deception as to virginity, which is treated above.

[7] Jeb. 87b.

[8] Jeb. 91b, Gittin 79b-80a.

[9] Ibid.

[10] Yad, Gerushin 10, 7, R. Nisim, Ket. 100b, R. Asher Ket. 11, 25-28. But *Itur* p. 70d groups these cases among the instances in which the mattan is not forfeited. The loss of the dowry and mulug is complete, including *bla'ot,* but she takes only what is left. Rashi Jeb. 87b, s. v. *Bla'ot* seems to believe that she cannot even take with her what is left of her dowry or mulug. See *Nimuke Yosef* and *Tosafot Yom-Tob* ad Jeb. ibid.

rights over his wife's earnings and of his right of succession to her.[11]

Severer forfeitures are prescribed for the rabbinically prohibited marriage.[12] Three reasons are given in the Talmud for the greater severity. The rabbinically prohibited marriage does not leave a stain of impurity or inferiority upon the husband, wife, or the offspring. Hence, greater restriction is necessary all around. Again, the woman is liable to inveigle the man to marry her in defiance of a rabbinic prohibition, since neither she nor her children will suffer any blemish through it. Hence, the penalties are largely directed against her. Lastly, rabbinical prohibitions might be treated with levity but for the greater penalties.[13] In a rabbinically prohibited marriage, the wife forfeits her mohar but not her mattan, alimony during his lifetime or after his death, redemption, burial, the KBD and the KBN provisions.[14] The husband does not have to pay her for the dowry as of the time of the marriage, but if completely lost, he must pay her the value of its *bla'ot,* or the estimated residue of the dowry at the time of the divorce. Her mulug is completely lost. She takes only what is left of it, with-

[11] Jeb. ibid., Yad, Gerushin ibid.

[12] With the exception of the *Haluzah* marrying a lay priest. See note 2, p. 225.

[13] Tos. Jeb. 2, 2-4, Jeb. 85a-b, Jer. Jeb. 10b. What the Babli quotes in the name of Rabbi, Tosephta quotes in the name of R. Meir. The Talmud takes the second reason to be either an interpretation of the first or of the third. See Rashi and Tosafot Jeb. 85a at bottom.

[14] Tos. ibid., Ket. 101a, Alfasi Ket. ibid., Yad, Ishut 24, 2, *Itur,* p. 70c. For alimentation of the wife or for support of the widow see Jer. Jeb. 10b, R. Asher Ket. 11, 25-28. For the KBD and the KBN provisions, see Jer. ibid., Ket. 53b and Alfasi and R. Nisim thereto.

out claim upon the husband for any payment whether for use, loss, or complete destruction.[15] So long as they are married, the husband's rights are in no way curtailed.[16] And this arrangement of penalties holds good whether the husband had knowledge of the condition of the rabbinic prohibition or not.[17]

The rabbinically prohibited marriages here treated represent "secondary incest" or degrees of relationship akin to but at least one step removed from incest, termed *"Sheniyot l'arayot."* But there are other forms of rabbinically prohibited marriages. Thus, a woman found childless in two marriages may not marry a third husband who has no children, and if she does, divorce is mandatory[18]— as we have seen above. But no fine is prescribed in this case except for deception. If the husband, therefore, knew of this condition prior to the marriage, he must at divorce pay her the ketubah in full despite the fact that from the very beginning it represented a rabbinically prohibited marriage.[19] Some marriages are rabbinically prohibited on grounds of public safety. One who divorces his wife because of rumors of improper conduct[20] or because of intolerable vows[21] may not remarry her. One who is named as co-respondent in a case of unfaithfulness of a wife to her husband[22] may not marry that woman after she is divorced. A judge or a witness instrumental in declaring a woman free to remarry on testimony of her

[15] See Ket. 101a and Alfasi thereto.
[16] Tos. Jeb. 2, 2-4.
[17] Alfasi ibid. Yad, Ishut 24, 2, 4.
[18] See pp. 207-208 above.
[19] See Tosafot Jeb. 65a, s. v. חצא quoting geonic authority.
[20] Gittin 45b, Jeb. 25a.
[21] ibid.
[22] Jeb. 24b.

husband's death may not marry her.[23] A pregnant or a nursing woman may not be married.[24] In some of these instances the rabbinic prohibition makes divorce compulsory, but no fine or forfeiture is prescribed for any of them.[25]

Jewish law recognizes the expediency of contracting a marriage sometimes for persons who have no legal power to enter into a contract. Such marriages are legally imperfect. They represent a social sanction for marriage companionship without a marriage contract, or a rabbinic marriage. Such marriages are performed in the same manner as the legal marriages with a writ and the conveyance of dowry, but the writ does not carry the legal force that a legally valid marriage represents.

Thus, a minor boy has no power to enter into a contract and therefore cannot contract marriage. His physical and moral welfare may require it. No rabbinic marriage has been provided for him, but it is possible for the father to select a wife for him, as no doubt it often was the case that a father married off his boy while a minor. If that marriage was dissolved before the husband reached majority, the wife was entitled to none of the terms of the ketubah. But if he retained her after he reached majority, she was entitled to the full mohar and all other ketubah obligations, but she had no claim on her husband for mattan, apparently because the obligation of mattan has its inception with the first intercourse, at which time he was a minor and not really married to her.[26]

[23] Jeb. 25a-26a.

[24] Jeb. 36b.

[25] Maimonides decides in all these cases that the divorce is not compulsory. See Yad, Gerushin 10, 12-15.

[26] Ket. 90a, Yad, Ishut 11, 7.

The minor girl who is married by her father is her husband's wife in the full legal Biblical sense, because the Bible gives the father the right to marry off his daughter; hence, the father, not the girl, is the contracting party. After the father's death, the rabbis gave the mother and the brothers the right to marry off the minor girl, for the sake of placing her under a reliable and most often loving master. That marriage is a rabbinic marriage, but has the validity of a Biblical marriage for all purposes.. She can free herself from her husband, however, by *Mi'un,* by a declaration that she no longer desires her husband, as well as by the bill of divorcement. If the husband gives her a bill of divorcement, he has to pay her the full ketubah.[27] But if the girl dissolves the marriage by *Mi'un,* which is synonymous with an annulment of the marriage, she forfeits the mohar but not the mattan; she forfeits the dowry and the mulug to the extent that the husband need not even pay for the destruction of the *bla'ot;* she loses her maintenance if uncollected.[28]

An insane person has no legal power to enter into a contract. Hence, whether the husband was insane or the wife at the time of the marriage, the marriage has no legal effect, although they may in all propriety continue to live together as husband and wife, and therefore

[27] Ket. 100b, Jeb. 113a, Jer. Ket. end of Chapter 11. The husband's rights in such a rabbinic marriage is disputed between R. Eliezer and R. Joshua, the former denying him all the rights, the latter granting him all the rights. Rabbi finds the opinion of the former more acceptable, yet the halakah decides with the latter. See Ket. 101a, Jeb. 107b-108a, Yad, Ishut 22, 4.

[28] Ket. 100b-101a, 107b, Jer. Ket. 34c, Yad, Ishut 24, 5, *Itur* 70c. Tos. Ket. 11, 4 cites the opinion of R. Eliezer that she is entitled to her *bla'ot* and to be reimbursed for the fruit which the husband took from her property. This follows from his position that the minor is legally not married in any sense.

the statutory ketubah obligations usual for other marriages do not apply. If the husband is sane and the wife insane, he has none of the rights in his wife which a valid marriage entitles him to, but he must pay mohar or mattan or whatever else he promised her, not on the basis of the ketubah but on the basis of a promise for a consideration.[29] If the husband is insane and the wife is sane, he owes her absolutely nothing and his rights as a husband are doubtful.[30]

A deaf mute is according to Jewish law a person below the level of legal responsibility, therefore his contract has not full legal validity. Unable thus to enter into a marriage contract, yet evidently in need of companionship, he is given the right to enter into a rabbinic marriage. Thus the marriage of two deaf mutes or a normal person with a deaf mute is Biblically invalid but has rabbinical validity. The deaf mute woman is by rabbinic ordinance not entitled to any mohar at all, in order to make marriage to her easier on the man. Yet if a normal man married a deaf mute woman and gave her a ketubah of ever so large an amount, he must pay that amount on divorce — not as a ketubah but as mere promise for a consideration. On the other hand, he has no claim on her for any of the rights of a husband. Similarly, if a normal woman married a deaf mute husband, he is entitled to all the privileges of a husband while she has no claim on him at all. If the court entered into an agreement with a normal man on behalf of a deaf mute woman for the con-

[29] Jeb. 113a, Tos. Ket. 1, 3, Jer. Ket. 25b.

[30] The doubt arises from this fact. On the one hand, the marriage of an insane person is of no legal effect; on the other hand, the wife being sane, her grants are valid. Is or is not the right to her earnings, the yield of her property or of succession to be taken as an implied grant by her in the very fact of her accepting him as husband?

sideration of his marrying her, that agreement is binding. Without specific stipulation, or in the case of the marriage of two deaf mutes to each other where stipulation has no legal power, the ketubah terms do not apply,[31] and the husband has no legal rights over his wife's property.

The final group of forfeitures are those which we should term statutory forfeitures due to certain conditions of the marriage which in no way reflect against the legality or the propriety of the marriage. According to Biblical law one who forces a virgin must marry her and can never divorce her, and he must pay to the girl's father fifty shekels, the price of her virginity. As indicated above, this fine of fifty shekels represents the original mohar; hence no mohar is due after that is paid. Nor did the rabbis enact a special mohar in this case, to be paid to the wife at divorce, in order to discourage divorce, because the Biblical law that he shall not be able to send her away all his days was deemed a sufficient check. In view of the fact, however, that the woman may demand a divorce without violation to any Biblical law, and furthermore because it is always possible for the husband to make his wife so unhappy that the demand for a divorce will come from her, R. Jose b. R. Judah is of the opinion that the husband must assume a mohar of a hundred zuzim.[32] Mattan, dowry, alimentation, redemption, burial, and the other ketubah obligations, however, are in no way affected,[33] except for the *ketubat*

[31] Jeb. ibid., Alfasi and Asheri thereto, Jer. Ket. ibid., Yad, Ishut 11, 4, 6 and *Magid* ad 4.

[32] Ket. 39a, Tos. Ket. 3, 6.

[33] *Sheyare Korban* commentary to Jer. Ket. 27d (end of chapter 3, section 5) quotes authorities in a decision that the KBD is forfeited and even mattan and dowry.

benin dikrin and the *ketubat benan nukban* obligations, concerning which the Talmud leaves us in doubt as to whether they are in force or not.[34]

In a levirate marriage, the ketubah of the deceased husband remains unpaid and is taken over by the *levir* at the time of the marriage. The *levir* assumes on his own account all obligations which have their inception with his marriage to the deceased brother's wife, such as alimentation, redemption and burial. But he has no obligation, save as administrator of his brother's estate, to pay the mohar, mattan, and dowry. These are obligations of the deceased brother and must be paid out of his estate. By a rabbinic enactment, however,—as preventive of divorce — the mohar obligation is imposed upon him personally as well, so that if the deceased brother's estate is insufficient for the payment of the mohar, the *levir* must pay the mohar up to the amount of one hundred zuzim out of his own.[35] Whether the *ketubat benin dikrin* and the *ketubat benan nukban* obligations fall upon the *levir* is a question which the Talmud itself does not decide. The inception of these obligations is in the ketubah made out between the deceased brother and his wife; the fulfillment of them is possible only by the children begotten by the *levir*. Hence, the original KBD and KBN clauses are of no effect. It remains therefore a matter of doubt whether the *levir*, who does not write a ketubah of his own, does or does not imply these obligations in his marriage.

[34] Ket. 54a, Jer. Ket. ibid.

[35] See Jeb. 38a and Maimonides Mishna Commentary thereto, Jeb. 52b, Ket. 80b, Jer. Jeb. 5d, Jer. Demai 25c. If the *levir* divorced her and remarried her, he still does not have to make a new ketubah, for he remarries her on the terms of the ketubah that had been in force prior to the divorce. He is at liberty, though, to make a new ketubah with new terms, and these are binding.

Since the matter remains doubtful, post-Talmudic authorities rule that these obligations cannot be enforced.[36]

If the woman sells her ketubah to a stranger, the woman loses none of the ketubah obligations — except that the buyer collects the mohar, mattan, and dowry when the ketubah becomes payable, that is, when she is divorced or widowed. The same is true when the wife sells her ketubah to the husband himself. There is no curtailment of any of the ketubah obligations, except mohar, mattan, and dowry — and by rabbinic enactment, to prevent divorce, he must give her a new ketubah for a mohar of a hundred zuzim. But if the woman gives her ketubah as a gift to her husband or waives it, the entire ketubah is cancelled, including the KBD and the KBN clauses and alimentation of the widow[37] and — according to certain views — support and redemption and burial

[36] Ket. 53b treats of *ketubat benan nukban* but *ketubat benin dikrin* is not mentioned, but *Shita mekubezet* ibid. points out the logic of treating the KBD together with the KBN in this case. See Alfasi Ket. ibid. and Yad, Ishut 19, 14.

[37] Ket. 53a, Yad, Ishut 17, 19 and *Magid* thereto, Yad, Ishut 19, 12 and RABD thereto. Rashi opposes the ruling that the wife loses alimentation. She forfeits only alimentation in widowhood, according to him. RABD opposes the ruling that the KBN is forfeited.

CHAPTER XV

THE LIEN

By ketubah clauses and statutes, the law provided not only for the several obligations treated of in the preceding chapters but also for proper security that these obligations would be met when they mature. The principal ketubah obligations to be considered are the mohar and mattan and dowry, maturing at divorce or at the husband's death.[1] They are by nature similar to a loan with the wife as creditor and the husband as debtor, and the security which the law has provided for the payment of an ordinary loan is also provided for the payment of these ketubah obligations.

Security for a loan, in Bible days, was vested in the person of the debtor or his children or his possessions. In the event of the debtor's default, the creditor owned the debtor's person or his belongings. As may well be expected, as the social sense was refined, the person of the debtor or his children were no longer put at the disposal of the creditor for the payment of his debt, and the debtor's property was all that could be attached. It is probably at this stage of development that the "pledge," another Biblical institution, came to be the security for the loan. The pledge was property of value equal to the loan given by the debtor to the cred-

[1] See note 8, p. 239. In the case of death the ketubah is payable immediately according to the Judean usage, while according to the Galilean usage it is not payable until the widow remarries. If the widow was under obligation to enter a levirate marriage with her husband's brother, the ketubah is not at all payable during widowhood.

itor, out of which he might collect his debt in the event of the former's default. The creditor had to hold possession of the pledge in order that the debtor might not sell it or give it away. This method was evidently cumbersome and inadequate in a more developed commercial age, and therefore, the Jews adopted — probably from the Hellenic legal system — the idea of a lien. A lien on the debtor's property meant that the law held that property *as a pledge* on behalf of the creditor without need for the creditor to have actual possession of it. The lien was thus a direct descendant of the pledge[2] and is an early ancestor of the mortgage. It differs from the latter in this respect that while the mortgagor has no personal obligation to the mortgagee, the debtor, in the Jewish system of law, carries that obligation himself despite the lien on his property. Until the debtor is personally insolvent the lien has no legal effect.[3]

A lien is effected by the insertion in the note of indebtedness of the clause, "All my property be security for thy loan." According to certain authorities, every note of indebtedness carries a lien with it, for the omission of the lien clause is considered only a scribal error.[4] There is no security, save the debtor's solvency, with a loan unrecorded in a note of indebtedness. All judgments issued by the court carry with them the security of a lien on the debtor's property. Any purchaser of the debtor's property subsequent to the date of the lien buys it subject to the lien, and the creditor can collect payment from it if the debtor is in-

[2] This is the historic rendering of the legal dictum *Sh'ibuda d'oraita,* the principle of lien is Biblical, maintained by R. Johanan and R. Simeon b. Lakesh and Ulla — B. B. 175b.

[3] Gittin 48b.

[4] B. M. 12b-14b, Ket. 51a.

solvent. Likewise, the debtor's estate goes over to his heirs subject to all liens on it.

Except when the lien clause is especially modified also to include movable property, as will be shown later, the lien rests only on the debtor's realty but not on his personalty. The purchaser of movable property, therefore, buys it without any encumbrance whatever. The heirs likewise come by the movable property of the estate without any encumbrance. The heirs differ from the purchaser only in one respect, that they take over the testator's personal obligations as well as his liens, but need not pay them except out of realty. Therefore, while the buyer must pay only loans secured by a lien, the heirs must pay even loans unsecured by a note, if they inherited realty, "in order not to discourage lending."[5]

It was Simeon b. Shetah's reform of the ketubah which made it in every sense a note of indebtedness, and therefore, the lien clause was introduced by him in the ketubah in the same manner as it was employed in the loan. He permitted the husband to use his wife's mohar, or rather to give her a mohar of credit. That represented a debt, and to secure that debt he caused the ketubah to have the standard lien clause, "All my property shall be guarantee and security for the payment of thy ketubah."[6] It is likely that in the mind of Simeon b. Shetah this clause was to protect the mohar only, but since the husband's freedom to use his wife's nedunya extended beyond the limits of safety to the interests of the wife, the lien clause was taken to cover the dowry also. Later on the mattan also needed pro-

[5] Arekin 22a, Ket. 91b, 92a, B. B. 157a, 176a. See also Tosafot Ket. 81b and 86a.

[6] Ket. 82b.

tection, for either it was a credit mattan, or it was used by the husband as the dowry was, and therefore the mattan too was included in the lien clause. Hence, probably since Hadrianic days, the lien clause in the ketubah covered the triple obligation of mohar, mattan, and dowry. Since that day there is hardly a single instance of a ketubah with the lien clause omitted, although its omission would be of no legal significance.[7]

It is not certain from Talmudic evidence whether Simeon b. Shetah gave the husband the option to give either a cash or credit mohar, or made a credit mohar and the lien clause mandatory. If his intention was to make marriage less burdensome on men, he probably made it optional; on the other hand, if he meant, as the later rabbis understood it, to discourage divorce, he probably made it mandatory. It is certain, however, that the later generations of tannaim capitalized the institution of Simeon b. Shetah to discourage divorce and, therefore, not only made the lien mandatory but also declared that no payment of the ketubah was possible, except with the wife's expressed consent, so long as the husband and the wife continued in a married state. They expressed this principle in a legal dictum, "The ketubah does not mature during life."[8] In the

[7] Tos. Ket. 2, 2, Ket. 51a. The lien clause of the post-Talmudic ketubah reads, with various slight modifications: נכסין. . . . . אחראין וערבאין לפרוע מנהון שטר כתובתא דא נדוניא דין ותוספתא דא.

[8] The dictum—"*Lo nitena ketubah ligbot me-hayim*" (Ket. 81a-b), as suggested above (Note 10, p. 129), is of some antiquity and its original intention was to give the husband a right of tenancy over his wife's ketubah so long as he lives, so that the KBD provision does not operate until the father's death. Was that principle derived from any ketubah clause? Possibly from the reading of the KBD clause itself. But the commentators of the Talmud (Ket. 81a) seem to connect it with the

same spirit is the law formulated that, while the husband may assign to his wife a certain parcel of realty for the security of her ketubah and such parcel thereby falls practically under the woman's control, the lien is nevertheless in no wise removed from the other properties of the husband.[9] If a purchaser wants to buy

clause of the Shamaites — "when thou marriest another, shalt thou take what is provided for thee in thy ketubah and go." The connection between this principle and the Shamaitic clause is rather far fetched, but it is not impossible. The clause sets a terminus for the maturing of the ketubah — outside of the possibility of divorce — namely, the husband's death and the woman's subsequent freedom to remarry. So long as he lives, therefore, the ketubah is not due.

To the later tannaim, however, this simple interpretation of the dictum was not acceptable, because to them the law was clear that the husband is the first heir of his wife. How can he then be expected to give the ketubah to anyone after his wife's death, so long as he is alive? They therefore applied it to the case of the *levir*. The *levir's* case is a problematical one. The wife is a widow and yet not free to marry another. The *levir* is the successor to his brother, yet he cannot touch his property because of the lien for the payment of the wife's ketubah. The Mishna (Ket. 80b) teaches that the *levir* cannot pay the widow's ketubah, but must hold the deceased brother's property as totally mortgaged to the wife. So does a beraita (Ket. 81a) stress that point. (As for this stringency with the *levir*, the reason is not clear, but see Rashi and Tosafot in comment upon this beraita.) When the amoraim asked themselves the question, why is not the ketubah payable by the *levir* at any time, they answered by the general and misunderstood use of the principle that the ketubah does not mature during life. In the Talmud itself the application of this principle is strictly limited to the case of the *levir* in relation to the ketubah of his deceased brother's wife. Post-Talmudic authorities have adopted this principle in all marriages, in the sense that no ketubah matures, and no payment can be made of it, so long as the couple is alive and in a married state. Cf. Yad, Ishut 16, 3.

[9] B. B. 49b, Ket. 51a, 55a, Gittin 41a, Jer. Jeb. 8a, Jer. Shebi'it 39b, Cf. RShBM B. B. 50a, s. v. ואחת.

realty from the husband free from the wife's lien, he must obtain a written waiver from the wife and that waiver must be reinforced by a *kinyan* or a legal form of conveyance. And yet the waiver is not valid unless there is positive proof to the effect that the wife did not grant it under coercion from or to please her husband.[10] The lien is considered as removed from the husband's property only in one instance, which is accounted to be a case of "leniency with which the law treats the ketubah"— namely, if the husband deeds his property to his children during his life with his wife's consent, and leaves her ever so small a parcel as security for the payment of the ketubah, the lien is attached to that parcel and the rest of the property is free from the lien encumbrance.[11]

Despite the apparently unrelenting character of the lien, the payment of the ketubah when matured was circumscribed by a set of limitations according to the earlier rabbinic law. So far did this extend that the wife's security became insufficient, and the later Talmudic law and subsequent geonic law were put to the task of strengthening the security for the ketubah by modifications of the lien clause, as well as by special enactments. The limitations were twofold in nature, first because of the limitations of the lien in general, in loans as well as in ketubot, and second because of the special "leniency with which the law treats the ketubah."

Every lien is effective only against realty, not against personalty. Movable property has not sufficient stability to warrant the creditor to rely on it for the

[10] Ket. 95a.

[11] Tos. Pe'ah 1, 16, B. B. 132a-b, Jer. Pe'ah 17b, and end of chapter 3.

payment of his debt. However, because, as explained above, a loan carries with it a personal obligation in addition to the lien, the movable property in the possession of the debtor himself is placed at the disposal of the creditor for the satisfaction of his claim. The lien of the ketubah, like the lien of a loan, is effective only against realty. But unlike the latter, the personalty in the possession of the husband cannot be attached for the payment of the ketubah,[12] not to speak of the personalty of the estate held by the heirs.[13] The law concedes, however, that any personalty which

[12] The tannaitic text of Tos. Ket. 12, 2 cited in Ket. 56b, which is taken to represent a discussion as to whether or not under special conditions movables can be assigned for the payment of the ketubah, is in all likelihood misunderstood by the amoraim. The words *ketubat isha* probably refer to alimentation, not to the mohar; and R. Jose's retort לפי שאינן קצובין means that the sum of the obligation is not fixed, for it is exactly the same expression that he uses in Gittin 51a in that sense. R. Jose is not opposed to the principle that movables cannot be attached for the payment of alimentation, but to the further explanatory remark that it is a special enactment for the benefit of society.

That movable property in the hands of the husband cannot be attached for the payment of the ketubah is rather a strange law. Is not the ketubah a debt, and why shall the husband not be made to pay it if he has the wherewithal? Possibly this law has come about through a loose rendering of an older tannaitic dictum. The tannaim taught (Ket. 80b, 84a) that movable property *of orphans* (i. e. of an estate in the possession of the heirs) cannot be attached for the payment of the ketubah. The amoraim omitted the words "of orphans" and just cited (Ket. 81b, etc.) the dictum as "movable property cannot be attached for the payment of the ketubah." One reading in Yad, Ishut 16, 15 has it that the divorcee who seeks payment of her ketubah from her husband can obtain it even from his personalty, but almost all authorities oppose him on the basis of Nedar. 65b and Kid. 65b. Cf. *Magid* ad Yad ibid., R. Nisim and Asheri ad Nedar. ibid. and Tosafot Ket. 81b.

[13] Ket. 51a, 55a, B. B. 150b.

the woman may have seized during her husband's life as security for her ketubah she is permitted to retain in satisfaction of her claim,[14] but if she has seized it after her husband's death, when it had already come under the jurisdiction of the heirs, she is compelled to return it.[15] A further concession is made that certain movables, because so staple and so integral a part of the household in certain localities, are treated as belonging to the immovable class in respect to the wife's right to count on them for the payment of her ketubah.[16] And still another concession is made that the dowry represents a claim superior in nature to the claim of mohar and mattan, because it is based on actual value received by the husband. Therefore, the claim of the dowry is in every respect equal to the claim of a note of indebtedness. The lien is effective only against realty, but the personal obligation is invoked in respect to the dowry and is actionable against personalty in the possession of the husband himself.[17]

At about the middle of the amoraic period, commerce demanded that the lien clause be modified to include also movable property, for the lien on immovable property was no longer sufficient for the increased volume of credits plus the decrease in holdings of realty

[14] Ket. 84b-85a.

[15] Ket. 96a representing the view of Rabina as interpreted by Alfasi and corroborated by Yad, Ishut 18, 11. Cf. Tosafot Ket. 84b and Tosafot Ket. 96a and *Hagahot Maim.* ad Yad ibid. The case of a silver cup cited in Ket. 98a is taken to represent the first instance, as having been seized by the wife before her husband's death.

[16] Ket. 67a.

[17] See Ket. 55a and Magid ad Yad, Ishut 16, 5 at the end. The personalty of the estate in the possession of heirs is not attachable even for dowry, because it is not attachable even for a regular loan, as was stated above on p. 238.

among the Jews. Rabbah is the amora who saw the possibility of legislation which would make movable property also subject to the lien. He based his stand on the older law, which declared that when movable and immovable property are conveyed together, the legal form of conveyance of the immovable suffices for both. From this law he drew the inference that as conveyance of land also covers conveyance of chattels, so may the lien on land also cover the lien on personalty, for is not the lien a form of conveyance? Hence he ruled that if the lien clause reads "Movable by way of immovable property,"[18] personalty as well as realty thereby become subject to the lien, and the creditor would then be entitled to collect his debt from either, whether in the possession of the debtor himself, his heirs, or even if conveyed to a purchaser. From the Talmudic references it does not appear that this clause was generally used in the note of indebtedness in the amoraic period and there is no evidence that it was at all used in the ketubah. It is, however, frequently found as a ketubah clause in post-Talmudic times, and has the effect of making the lien in every respect applicable to movables as well as to realty.[19]

Two objections developed against this clause. In the first place, it tied up the husband's movable property to such an extent that he could not use it in commerce, for the purchaser could buy it only with the encumbrance of the ketubah lien. In the second place, the lien on movables depended upon the validity of the

[18] B. B. 44b, Ket. 27a. The efficacy of a lien on movables when the debtor has no land is denied in the Talmud, ibid. but see Tosafot ibid.

[19] See *Magid,* Ishut 16, 8. See also RABIH in *Mishpete ketubah* in *Jahrbuch,* Vol. 3. Hebrew section p. 18, but see also EH 100, 1.

lien on realty. Hence, when the husband had no realty, even his personalty was no security for the payment of the ketubah. These two considerations, and the latter most valid in geonic times when Jews owned very little realty, prompted the geonim to legislate in defiance of Talmudic law that debts and ketubot are payable out of movables, a bold enactment which is ascribed to R. Hunai of the eighth century.[20] This geonic enactment did not go as far as the Talmudic formula of "movable by way of immovable property"; for it did not place a lien on movables, and therefore the husband could sell movables without encumbrance, and therefore also the wife could not collect payment of her ketubah from the purchaser of her husband's movables. But it declared the movables owned by the husband or left by him in his estate to his heirs subject to the payment of the ketubah.[21] As an exact parallel to the geonic enactment, post-Talmudic authorities introduced into the ketubah as in the other writs the formula, "both immovable and movable property[22] during my life and after my death."[23] This formula has the

[20] Cf. Letter of R. Sherira, ed. Levine, pp. 105, 108; JQR, N. S., Vol. 10, pp. 310 f. The enactment is quoted in all geonic sources. *Hagahot Mordecai* gives the date of the enactment as 708, but reliable sources fix it at 787.

[21] It is certain that the husband's personalty in the hands of a purchaser who had bought it from the husband himself cannot be attached for the payment of the ketubah because the geonic enactment did not place a lien on movables. One may still wonder whether the movables sold by the heirs after their father's death can be attached for the ketubah. The logic of the situation requires that it shall be, but the legal decision is against it. See EH, 100, 1.

[22] See *Hemdah Genuzah*, 65, Yad, Ishut 16, 8.

[23] "During my life and after my death" was originally a standard phrase in contracts giving perpetual validity to the terms contained in them. It goes back even to the papyri, D-3-8.

same effect as the geonic enactment, except that it bases its legality on contract instead of legislation.

A by-product of the geonic legislation is the modification of another Talmudic law, for which Maimonides is in the main responsible.

According to Talmudic law, if the husband's property improved after his death, that increment of improvement, *Shebah,* is not subject to the payment of the ketubah. Likewise, if the property improved after it was sold to a purchaser. Again, property which was to be owned by the husband but title to and possession of it did not materialize until after his death — technically termed, *Ra'ui* — cannot, according to Talmudic law be attached for the payment of the ketubah.[24] With the geonic enactment, however, or with its equivalent, the formula "Both immovable and movable property during my life and after my death," the increment of improvement and anticipated additions to the estate are also subject to the payment of the ketubah.[25]

In Talmudic days it was customary to insert in writs also the formula, "Even from the cloak on my back" as an addition to the lien clause.[26] By this formula the creditor's personalty even unto the last he owned was subject to the payment of his debts. Evidently, this formula had no legal significance, because by statute alone the creditor can take off the cloak of the debtor's back for the payment of his debt. Nor did the formula imply that the debtor's cloak can be at-

The Talmud cites it (B. B. 153a) as a phrase of rare occurrence in deeds. See *Jahrbuch* Vol. 6, pp. 364-5.

[24] Bekor. 52a, Yad, Ishut 16, 5.

[25] See Maim. Commentary to Mishna Bekor. 8, 7; *Kesef Mishna* ad Yad, Ishut 16, 7, but see EH 100, 2.

[26] B. B. 44b.

tached even after it was sold, for a lien on movable property is impossible according to Talmudic law except by way of immovables. It was therefore no more than a nice scribal flourish which had its stylistic value. It was taken over into the ketubah very readily, but in the ketubah it had a legal function. According to Talmudic law the ketubah is not payable out of movables even in the possession of the husband, while with the insertion of the above formula into the ketubah, it puts at the disposal of the wife the movables owned by the husband for the payment of her ketubah. However, with the geonic enactment or its equivalent ketubah formula, the phrase "Even from the cloak on my back" served no more than an ornamental purpose in the ketubah also.

The amoraim felt the necessity of adding another modification of the lien clause. The date of the writ is also the date for the lien, and that means that the lien is effective only against property owned by the husband at the time of the lien, but not against property bought by him subsequent to that date. To the minds of the amoraim that constituted insufficient security for the woman. Therefore, they inserted in the ketubah also the formula, "property that I did acquire or that I shall acquire" [27] as an addition to the lien clause. By virtue of this stipulation, the lien was effective against any realty owned by the husband at any time during his married life, so that even if he bought a

[27] B. B. ibid. and Ket. 82b. The importance of this clause lay in the fact that property acquired by the husband after marriage could be taken for the payment of the ketubah even from the purchaser, on the basis of the lien. If it remained in the possession of the husband or in his estate, it could be taken on the basis of the husband's personal obligation, without the stipulation of this clause.

parcel of realty and resold it, the wife could take it away from the purchaser to satisfy her ketubah claim. This formula was probably also in use in other writs, as it was in the ketubah, and constitutes part of the lien clause in all post-Talmudic instruments.[28]

Still another weak point in the lien clause was detected in post-Talmudic days, and a remedy to it was offered by the insertion of another formula into the lien clause. The Talmud rules that the ketubah, when paid out of realty, is paid only out of the poorest kind of realty in the possession of the husband or his heirs.[29] This limitation applied to the mohar and mattan only, but not to the dowry, which was payable out of the realty of medium quality.[30] Chivalry, it was felt, required a better treatment of the wife's claim in respect even to her mohar and mattan, and therefore, post-Talmudic authorities coined the new formula, "Out of the choicest of my property," and added it to the lien clause, thereby making the ketubah, even the mohar and mattan, payable out of the best realty of the husband or his heirs.[31] The formula is now generally used in ketubot as well as in writs of indebtedness.

It was not unusual for the wife at the time of the marriage to demand a guarantee for her ketubah above the lien inserted in it. She required the husband's father to endorse the lien as guarantor, so that in the

[28] While the lien is also on property acquired by the husband after marriage, in respect to that property, however, all creditors whose writs are dated prior to the date of its purchase are treated equally without regard to the priority of the debt, as will be shown later. See Yad, Ishut 17, 6.

[29] Gittin 48b, Ket. 55a, Tos. Ket. 12, 3.

[30] Jer. Gittin 46c. See *Magid*, ad Yad, Ishut 16, 3.

[31] See *Hagahot Mordecai*, Ket. 311.

event of the default of the husband, she could collect her ketubah from the father-in-law. Such a guarantee was also mentioned in the ketubah and was binding.[32] The guarantee of a stranger, not the father-in-law, may also be entered into the ketubah, but it is binding only in respect to the dowry and not in respect to the mohar and mattan, since the latter represent no investment based on the guarantee.[33] The guarantee of a stranger is binding for the entire ketubah only if he is entered into the writ as an *'Areb kablan,* a guarantor in the absolute, offering his guarantee for the ketubah whether the husband be able to pay it or not.[34] Whenever the guarantor is made to pay the ketubah, in case of divorce, the husband must vow not to remarry his wife, else he might be divorcing her only to extract money from the guarantor.[35] The same vow is required from the husband when the wife collects payment of her ketubah out of property that he has donated to the Temple, for the protection of Temple property. But no such protection is offered to the purchaser, in case the wife collects her ketubah out of property sold to him by the husband, because he should have taken proper precaution against such an eventuality before he entered into the purchase.[36]

To intensify the effectiveness of the lien, rabbinic authorities have introduced into the ketubah, as well

[32] B. B. 174b, Yad. Ishut 17, 9. However, a *Kinyan* is necessary, according to Maimonides.

[33] 'Arekin 23b, B. B. ibid., Yad. ibid. According to Maimonides even a *Kinyan* does not validate the guarantee. RABD disputes it. As to the validity of a guarantee in respect to dowry, Cf. *Magid,* Ishut, 17, 9 and *Hagahot Maim.* ad Yad, Ishut 17, 7.

[34] B. B. ibid.

[35] B. B. 173b.

[36] 'Arekin 23a-b.

as into the writ of a loan, a number of legal formulae, some of amoraic, some of geonic, and some of post-geonic origin. A third century amora, Rab Hisda, records the use in the lien clauses of the formula, "Not as a promise based on speculation nor as a stereotyped form."[37] He cites it in connection with the effectiveness of a lien on movables by way of realty, but it may have been in use in writs generally. And probably it was,[38] for it touches a halakah that had its origin in that generation of scholars. That law teaches that a promise recorded in a writ is not binding, if it is *Asmakta,* based on speculation. The lien in general may be taken as a promise based on speculation, for the debtor may assume that the lien would never be resorted to, because he would be sure to pay his debt on maturity. Likewise, the husband may have granted the lien for the ketubah on the speculation that he may be able to pay it or that he may never divorce his wife and in addition may survive her, and thus would never have to pay the ketubah. To obviate such a possible repudiation of the writ and at the same time to testify that the writ is a truly binding instrument, the ketubah contains the Talmudic formula, as an addition to the lien clause, that it is "Not as a promise based on speculation nor as a stereotyped form."

The mere statement in the ketubah that it is not *Asmakta,* however, would not cover the full legal requirement. One requirement of the law to counteract *Asmakta* is to convey the rights contained in the promise by the *Kinyan,* by the legal formality of conveyance.[39] Where the actual taking possession of the prop-

[37] B. B. 44b.
[38] See Tosafot ibid.
[39] Nedarim 27b.

erty involved in the promise of the lien is impossible, the formality of conveyance is carried out by the *Kinyan Sudar*,[40] that is, the recipient of the promise or the lien gives the maker thereof a garment or vessel of ever so insignificant value, which object may be immediately returned to the giver, and when the maker of the promise or the lien accepts that gift, the conveyance is concluded. And furthermore, it is not necesssary that the recipient himself give the object of the *Kinyan;* the witnesses to the contract can act in his stead. Therefore with every ketubah, the *Kinyan Sudar* is executed by the witnesses, who record this fact in the formula, "And we have executed the *Kinyan* .... with an object fit for legal conveyance." [41] This formula too is amoraic in origin, and continues to the present day in the ketubah as well as in other writs.

Another legal subterfuge to offset the weakness of the *Asmakta* which the Talmud suggests, is to specify that the conveyance involved in the promise or the lien shall take effect "from this moment" [42] and shall not be suspended until the conditions of the promise or the lien are fulfilled. As a matter of additional precaution, the ketubah has also adopted this Talmudic suggestion and contains as part of the *Kinyan* formula the addition, "that it be effective from this moment." As part of the *Kinyan* formula, this addition served another purpose. The *Kinyan Sudar* is not effective for conveyances projected into the future, because, as said above,

[40] See note 5, on p. 33 above.

[41] B. M. 41a, B. B. 136a. The usage of the witnesses acting on behalf of the guarantee is referred to as a halakic decision of R. 'Amram Gaon by RABIH in *Mishpete Ketubah, Jahrbuch,* Vol. 3. Hebrew section, p. 20.

[42] B. M. 66b.

the object of conveyance may be returned to the giver, so that at the time in the future when the conveyance is consummated, the object of conveyance is no longer in the possession of the grantor.[43] Hence, the declaration that the conveyance is made as of this moment helps to establish the validity of the *Kinyan.*[44]

Some ketubot resort to an additional precaution against the *Asmakta,* suggested by Talmudic law. According to the amoraim, the possibility of the *Asmakta* is excluded in all writs made out before a recognized court,[45] apparently because the actions of a person before the court are assumed to be more stable and positive. Hence, the husband is declared in the ketubah as having accepted the people before whom he caused the ketubah to be written and to be attested to as constituting a recognized court, and this declaration is made by the brief addition to the *Kinyan* formula of the words, "before a recognized court."

In addition to the above, some ketubot record the fact that the groom took an oath that he would fulfill the terms of the ketubah and annul none of its provisions. But the more prevalent precaution against the annulment of any of the ketubah terms is what is technically called *Bitul Moda'a,* voiding any declaration of annulment. A contract or a promise or a lien can be annulled by the grantor stating before witnesses — of course, not in the hearing of the grantee — that his contract or promise or lien is made unwillingly, under coercion, or as a matter of temporary expediency, and

[43] Nedar. 48b.

[44] See Tosafot B. M. 66a at bottom and R. Nisim, Nedar. 27b below.

[45] Nedar. 27b. According to Rashi the several precautions together exclude the possibility of *Asmakta;* others believe that any one of these enumerated here suffices. See R. Nisim ibid.

on the testimony of the witnesses to that effect, the instrument is declared void. To counteract such a possibility, the grantor is required to state in the instrument that he voids all such possible annulments of the instrument, that he declares the *Moda'a* of no effect.[46] Another remedy to this weakness is suggested by R. Solomon b. Adret of the thirteenth century, that the grantor shall agree to declare the witnesses before whom the *Mada'a* may or might be made as legally incompetent to testify.[47] The ketubah has recourse either to one, the first of these methods or to both, to annul any possible voiding of the lien or its terms.

The total of the extra precautions to guard the validity of the lien resolves the lien clause into the following formula: "And as for the security of the ketubah, dowry, and mattan, I have assumed for myself and for my heirs after me that they be paid of the choicest of the property and possessions that I have under the sky, both what I did acquire and what I shall acquire, immovables and movables, the movable by way of the immovable property .... during my life and after my death, and even out of the cloak on my back, from this day and forevermore. And we (witnesses) have carried out a legal conveyance with an object fit for that purpose, to confirm all that is herein above entered and specified, that it be effective from this moment, that it be not as a promise based on speculation nor a mere form blank, but as though executed before a recognized court and having the power and validity of all

[46] See for instance a ketubah taken from a Sephardic Mahzor edited by M. Grossberg at the end of his "*Hebel Menaseh*" London 1900. The practice of administering an oath to the groom is recorded in the Sephardic ketubah ed. Gaster, MGWJ, Vol. 54, p. 586.

[47] See Novelae of RSBA ad Gittin 34b.

the ketubot executed in accordance with the Jewish custom and prescription of the sages of blessed memory, voiding all declarations of annulment and discrediting the testimony of witnesses thereto."[48]

[48] Variants, to be sure, are not lacking, but what has been here set down as the formula represents a composite one. Our present day Ashkenazic ketubah is much simpler than that, omitting the precautions against *Moda'a.* In connection with the forgoing it may be worth while to compare RABIH, *Mishpete Ketubah,* Meldola, *Hupat Hatanim,* Duran, TShBZ, Vol. 3, 301.

As has been seen in many instances of this chapter, where the lien of the ketubah is somewhat inferior to the lien securing a loan, some ketubot add the following formula, "He has accepted all this as loan and debt" — referring in some instances to dowry alone and in others to all the ketubah obligations.

CHAPTER XVI

Payment

When the wife seeks payment of her ketubah, she is required to present testimony that the ketubah has not already been paid. The writ itself serves as testimony. In the absence of the writ, she has no claim. Where ketubah-less marriages are permissible, she collects mohar without writ or proof, but she cannot claim mattan and dowry without sufficient proof of her claim.[1] In the case of divorce, she must present the bill of divorcement even for the claim of mohar.[2] The bill of divorcement, however, is not required at a time of persecution, such as the Hadrianic persecutions known to the tannaim, when it is dangerous to preserve a religious document.[3] If the wife produces two bills of divorcement and one ketubah, only one ketubah is paid, the assumption being that the husband had divorced his wife and remarried her on the terms of the one ketubah. If she produces two divorces and two ketubot, both ketubot are payable. In the case of one divorce and two ketubot, or in case the wife presents two ketubot at her husband's death, she may collect payment on either, if their terms are different, but she can collect payment on the one latest in date only, if the terms of the two ketubot are the same. If at the husband's death the wife presents a divorce and a ketubah, the ketubah is immediately payable, but the ques-

[1] Yad, Ishut 16, 21-22.
[2] Ket. 89a.
[3] Ibid.

tion arises whether the divorce represents another ketubah or not. In which matter the law decides that if the divorce is dated prior to the ketubah it represents another ketubah which was unpaid and, therefore, she is entitled to two ketubot; but if the divorce is later in date than the ketubah, it represents only a remarriage on the basis of the one ketubah, and only the one ketubah is therefore due.[4]

A very old usage in Jewish law required the woman demanding payment of her ketubah to take an oath that she had not been paid and that she had not concealed any of her husband's property.[5] The oath is required only when payment of the ketubah is to be made by the court in the husband's absence, or by the heirs out of his estate, or by a purchaser of the husband's property on the basis of the lien, but is not required when the husband himself pays the ketubah — unless she admits having received part payment, or the husband can show some kind of proof, even if inconclusive, that the ketubah had been paid.[6] In all cases where the oath is required for the payment of the ketubah, if she died prior to taking the oath, her heirs have no claim on the ketubah.[7] Articles of her dowry she may take without an oath, and likewise she may collect payment without oath out of realty assigned to her by the husband for the special purpose of securing her the payment of the ketubah.[8] A waiver of the requirement

[4] Ket. 89b, 90a, Yad, Ishut 16, 29-30.

[5] Ket. 105a. Authorities of Temple days are connected with this usage.

[6] Ket. 87a, Yad, Ishut 16, 14-18. See also Yad, Ishut 16, 4 based upon the view of R. Simeon cited Ket. 88b.

[7] Shebuot 48a.

[8] Ket. 55a, Yad, Ishut 16, 3; 18, 9 and *Magid* comment on latter.

of the oath is provided for by the law in a ketubah formula, stating on behalf of the husband, "Neither vow nor oath may I or my heirs or my representatives impose upon thee or thy heirs or thy representatives."[9] This formula exempts her from the oath in all circumstances, except when she invokes the lien to get payment of her ketubah out of the purchaser of her husband's property, for the husband cannot waive the purchaser's right of protection of his property.[10]

The old practice of administering an oath to the wife, through an enactment of Rabban Gamaliel, of the first century, yielded to the newer usage of administering a vow to the woman, stating in substance that if her claim is not true she prohibits to herself by vow the use of certain things, as the payee of the ketubah may designate.[11] According to Samuel, the enactment of Rabban Gamaliel did not completely do away with the oath. It was discontinued in the courts, but it remained in use in private settlements of ketubah claims. According to Rab, the oath was really discontinued, even in private settlements. It remained only a matter of rare and accidental occurrence, when the woman burst forth with an oath on her own initiative. This latter amora found vows a poor substitute for the oath, because people treated vows lightly, and therefore his court made it practically impossible for the widow to collect payment of her ketubah.[12] Post-Talmudic law, however, decides against this authority and continues the practice of administering a vow to the wife when

[9] Ket. 86b, Tos. Ket. 9, 3.

[10] Yad, Ishut 16, 20 and *Magid* thereto.

[11] Gittin 34b. The vow cannot be administered to a woman who was remarried, for her second husband may annul it. See Yad, Ishut 16, 12 and *Magid* ad Ishut 16, 11.

[12] Gittin 35a.

the ketubah is presented for payment, unless the husband inserted the waiver of the oath or vow into the ketubah.

The widow may sell her husband's property for the payment of her ketubah without a court order, provided she has proven her claim according to the methods and prescriptions given above, but she must call in a committee of three laymen to appraise the value of the property.[13] If she has been divorced and collects payment of her ketubah in the absence of her husband, she cannot sell his property except through the court. Although the law honors no claim, even though valid, against minor orphans, and suspends payment of it until they become of age, unless it is a loan on which interest grows,[14] the claim of the ketubah is honored against minor orphans. Two reasons account for this. In the case of the widow, until the ketubah is paid, her alimentation is a tax on the estate. In the case of the divorcee whose ketubah had not been paid until the husband's death, she is given special consideration in order that she might have better chances for remarriage.[15] Whenever the court is called upon to sell the husband's property for the payment of the ketubah, a public announcement of the proposed sale is made. That announcement is made daily, at the time laborers go to work and at the time they return for a period of thirty days, giving the boundaries and the description of the parcel, the price set for it, and the purpose of the sale.[16]

The ketubah has a statute of limitation. If it re-

[13] Ket. 97a-b, 98a, B. M. 32b, Yad, Ishut 16, 13 and *Magid* thereto.

[14] 'Arekin 22a.

[15] Ibid., Jer. Gittin 46d, Yad, Malweh 12, 3.

[16] 'Arekin 21b, Ket. 100b, Yad, Malweh 12, 8.

mains unpaid for twenty-five years after maturity, it is cancelled. This statute applies only to the widow who resides with her parents, on the assumption that her lack of attention to the payment of the ketubah is evidence that she has waived it. It does not apply to the divorcee. Nor does it apply to the widow who resides with the heirs or who has preserved her ketubah instrument. Nor does it apply to the dowry, which is never cancelled until paid.[17]

In Jewish law as in common law, a lien of earlier date supersedes a lien of later date, so that the lien of later date can be invoked only after the former one has been satisfied. The ketubah and the note of indebtedness are alike in this ruling, that the earlier lien is first honored.[18] If a lien of a ketubah and of a note of indebtedness dated on the same day are presented for execution, the note of indebtedness is given priority to the mohar and the mattan of the ketubah, but the dowry of the ketubah and the note represent equal claims.[19] Sometimes, according to certain authorities, the ketubah claim is honored prior to the note of indebtedness, due to the special consideration which the law wishes to give the woman in order to make marriage safer for her. Such a case is illustrated in the Mishna by money of an estate which is in the keeping of a borrower or a trustee, on the return of which, according to certain views, the wife has prior claim on it for the payment of her ketubah.[20] If the husband has

[17] Ket. 104a-b, Yad, Ishut 16, 21-24, Magid, Ishut 16, 23. Whether the mattan has the statute of limitation is a matter of discussion among the amoraim, cited Babli Ket. ibid., Jer. Ket. 35b and Jer. Gittin 46c.

[18] Ket. 93b.

[19] Ket. 86a, Yad, Ishut 17, 4, 7.

[20] Ket. 84a.

to meet a note and pay his wife's ketubah and has both realty and money, the note must be paid out of the money and the ketubah out of the realty, for the wife would not be able by law to attach her husband's money for the payment of her ketubah, while the holder of the note would.[21]

If two or more ketubot of the same date are presented for payment, according to certain authorities, the husband's estate is divided in proportion with the claims to meet the obligations. According to others the manner of division is the following: The lowest claim is taken as the common denominator and that amount or an equal fraction of it is given to every claimant. Thereby one ketubah is paid in full and is put out of the way. The next lowest claim is taken as the new common denominator, and the division of the estate is repeated in the same manner until the estate is exhausted or the claims satisfied.[22]

The oath, or the vow that was in vogue as requisite for the payment of the ketubah, was employed as much for the protection of other creditors as for the protection of the estate. Therefore, whenever payment is made on one claim while others remain in part or entirely unpaid, the recipient of payment must take an oath to the truth of his claim as a protection to the other claimants. If one ketubah is paid and other ketubot or notes, for one reason or another, remain unpaid, the holder of that one ketubah must take the oath or the vow to prove her claim to the satisfaction of the other claimants.[23]

[21] Ket. 86a, Yad, Ishut 17, 4.

[22] See Yad, Ishut 17, 8 based on an interpretation of Ket 83a. Cf. *Magid* thereto.

[23] Ket. 93b.

The question of the priority of a claim arises only with respect to the lien. Therefore it affects only realty owned by the creditor prior to the date of the lien. It does not affect movables, because there is no lien on movables. Even the geonic enactment did not change the status of movables in that respect, for the enactment did not make movables subject to lien. The only condition in which the lien may apply to movables is with the insertion of the clause, "movables by way of immovables" in the writ. And in such an instance movables too are subject to the question of the priority of claims. Since, therefore, there is no priority with reference to payment out of movables, any claimant may retain what he chances to seize of the movables of the creditor's estate — else a division of the movables is made in proportion to the claims, or in graded order, as given above. However, the note of indebtedness is given priority to mohar and mattan of a ketubah, even out of movables.[24]

Property bought by the creditor after the date of the lien is not subject to the lien. Therefore priority does not apply to it. But if the creditor inserted in the writ the clause, "that I did acquire or that I shall acquire," the lien also extends over the property acquired after its date. However, in respect to such property, the date of the lien is not the date of the writ but the date of the purchase of the property, for prior to that date it was free from encumbrance. Hence all creditors prior to the date of the purchase have equal rights to it, and all creditors after the date of the purchase have the order of priority according to the dates

[24] Yad, Ishut 17, 3, 6, 7, Malweh, 20, 2. See *Kesef Mishna* ad Yad, Ishut 17, 3, 4.

of their writs.[25] This rule applies to the ketubah as it does to the note of indebtedness, but the note, of course, is honored first, as stated above. The increment of improvement of the creditor's property, or additions to the property from an expected source, are counted as property purchased later than the date of the lien in respect to priority.

The ketubah obligations other than the triple group of mohar and mattan and dowry are not covered by the lien clause of the ketubah. They are not obligations based on contract but on "court enactment," or *tenai bet din.* That accounts for the fact that they are not included in the ketubah lien, but one may still wonder why a statutory lien should not protect these obligations, as is the case with every court order. One reason offered in the Talmud is that the obligations are never fixed as to the amount, and therefore cannot be made a condition in any sale of property executed by the husband. Were all of the husband's sales to be subject to meeting such obligations, commerce would be seriously hindered. The Talmud applies this reasoning in connection with the alimentation of the widow and the orphaned daughters[26] and it may well serve to explain the other obligations, such as alimentation of the wife, ransom, and burial. Another reason may be added. These obligations do not exist until the need for them arises; and they are unlike mohar and mattan and dowry, which have the inception of their obligations with the moment of marriage. Hence property owned by the husband during his married life cannot be made subject to the payment of these other obliga-

[25] Yad, Ishut 17, 2, Malweh 20, 1.
[26] Gittin 48b, 50b, 51a, Tos. B. B. 6, 21.

tions, as it is made subject to the lien clause of the ketubah.

Since no written lien or statutory lien protects these obligations, they are not payable out of realty sold by the husband to a purchaser. On the other hand, since they are based on a "court enactment," all realty held by the husband himself or left in his estate to his heirs is drawn upon for the payment of them. And the law has made the necessary provisions to enforce upon the husband or his heirs the due meeting of these marriage obligations.

To obtain the wife's support from her husband, the court either attaches his property[27] or employs such methods as it sees fit to force him to earn a living for her.[28] In his absence from home, the wife may sell some of his property for her support or may apply to the court for such action.[29] Although the general court procedure in the case of selling a person's property in his absence to satisfy a claim is to make public announcement of the sale and the purpose of the sale, and to make the creditor swear to the truthfulness of his claim, neither oath by the woman[30] nor public announcement by the court is required to satisfy a wife's petition for alimentation;[31] but the husband's property is sold to the first buyer at the value appraised by the court. The wife is not even required to produce the ketubah, although the suspicion might arise that she

[27] Ket. 77a. See Yad, Ishut 12, 11 and *Magid* thereto. See p. 157 above.

[28] See Tosafot Ket. 63a at bottom, *Hagahot Maim.* ad Yad, Ishut ibid.

[29] Ket. 48a, 107a.

[30] Ket. 105a. Cf. Yad, Ishut 12, 16. The oath is supposed to be deferred until the ketubah be presented for collection.

[31] Ket. 100b.

had waived her ketubah and was therefore — according to certain authorities — not entitled to alimentation.[32]

For burial expenses the same method is employed as that for alimentation. Either the husband is forced to pay, or his property is sold for the amount necessary to cover the wife's burial expenses. The ceremonies of public announcement are not required.[33] The same method in every respect is employed to raise the ransom money needed in the case of the wife's falling into captivity, with the one exception, however, that public announcement is required when the husband's property is offered for sale.[34]

The obligations of *mazon ha'isha* and *mazon habanot* (KBN), or alimentation of the widow and the minor orphaned girls, commence, of course, with the husband's death. The security for these obligations is the realty of the estate so long as it is held by the heirs. But if they sell it, the buyer gets a clear title and the widow and minor orphan girls can have no recourse to it for their maintenance.[35] The movable property of the estate, even if held by the heirs themselves, is free from the encumbrance of these obligations.[36] However, if the widow has seized certain movables as security for her maintenance, whether she seized them prior to her husband's death or after it, she can draw her support from them.[37]

[32] So decided in Yad, Ishut 12, 18 in the face of a geonic controversy.

[33] Ket. 100b.

[34] Yad, Ishut 14, 20.

[35] Ket. 69a, Yad, Ishut, 18, 13.

[36] Ket. 51a, 69b, Tos. Ket. 4, 18; 12, 2. But see note 12, p. 242.

[37] Ket. 69a, Jer. Ket. 34b; Cf. Yad, Ishut 18, 10 and Tosafot Ket. l. c.

The widow herself may sell some of the realty of her husband's estate for her maintenance, at a price set by three laymen who are connoisseurs in land values;[38] or she may petition a court order for its sale. If the court handles the sale, only so much is sold as is necessary for her maintenance for a period of six months, and the purchase money is given to her in six equal monthly installments.[39] The realty of poorest quality is selected for such purpose.[40] The formality of public announcement is waived, but the widow is required to present her ketubah[41] and to take an oath or a vow to prove that she has not concealed any of her husband's property[42] — unless the ketubah specifies that "Neither I nor my heirs nor my representatives may impose an oath or a vow on you or your heirs or your representatives.[43]

The minor orphan girls get their support in the same manner as the widow. However, being minors, they cannot sell their father's property by themselves, but must ask for a sale by the court, and being in no position to conceal any of their father's property, they are not required to take the oath administered to the widow.[44] Their support can be drawn only from realty

[38] Ket. 97b, B. M. 32a.

[39] Ket. ibid., and Yad, Ishut 18, 21.

[40] Gittin 48b, 'Arekin 22a, Ket. 69a, 110a.

[41] Ket. 100b, and Yad, Ishut 12, 18; 18, 23.

[42] Ket. 87a, Gittin 34b, Yad, Ishut 18, 19. Some authorities maintain that no oath is administered to the widow demanding alimentation unless she also presents the ketubah for payment, else the oath is deferred until such time as she demands the payment of her ketubah. See RABD notes to Yad, l. c.

[43] Ket. 86b, Tos. Ket. 9, 3.

[44] Yad, Ishut 19, 11. The reference in *Magid* thereto of Ket. 69a is erroneous. That passage speaks distinctly of *parnasah*, which is treated as an obligation on the heirs but not on the

in the possession of the heirs, but not from realty sold by the father or by the heirs, and from no movable property at all. There is an enactment recorded in the Talmud and corroborated by actual court decisions to the effect that minor orphan girls can obtain their support even from the movables of their father's estate,[45] but the final Talmudic halakah decides adversely.[46] However, because of the geonic enactment that the ketubah and the loan shall be payable out of personalty as well as out of realty, or because of the usual insertion into the ketubah of the phrase, "both movable and immovable property," post-Talmudic law permits support of the widow and the minor orphan girls to be drawn also from movable property of the estate."[47]

Parnasah, or the marriage portion, of the orphan girls is considered an obligation falling upon the heirs themselves, not on the father. While it is not paid out

father, while sustenance for the minor orphan girls is definitely an obligation of the father. The inference from that passage would be the contrary, that the orphan girls are required to take the oath. The view of Maimonides is rather based on the logic of the case as here given, that in addition to their being minors there can be no suspicion that they have taken anything of their father's.

[45] Ket. 50b.

[46] Ket. 51a.

[47] Yad, Ishut 16, 7. As a corollary of this, the post-Talmudic authorities feel that as long as movables may be attached for the payment of the alimentation obligation of the widow and orphan minor daughters, the increment of improvement on the realty of the estate after the father's death and additions to the estate after his death, are also subject to the payment of these alimentation obligations, contrary to Talmudic law. When movable property is used for the maintenance of the minor orphan girls, the law of "a limited estate" when the girls have priority over the sons, does not apply, but both the male heirs and the minor orphan girls are supported alike. See Yad, Ishut 19, 18.

of realty sold by the father, it is payable out of realty of the estate sold by the heirs.[48] It is payable out of a better grade of realty, and no oath or vow is imposed on the girls when payment is made.[49] It is not payable out of movables — even in the face of the geonic enactment in respect to the ketubah.[50]

The *ketubat benin dikrin*, that is, the mohar, mattan, and dowry of the ketubah when presented for collection by the wife's heirs against their father's estate, was originally protected by the lien clause of the ketubah, for it was merely a case of the wife's heirs representing her in demanding payment of the ketubah. But with the newer conception that the *ketubat benin dikrin* clause gives the sons a special status in respect to the ketubah, as heirs of the father, the lien clause of the ketubah is not considered to apply to the *benin dikrin* clause.[51] Hence, payment is made only out of realty left by the father in the estate, but not out of personalty,[52] and the geonic enactment authorizing payment of the ketubah out of movables did not alter the ruling in the case of the *ketubat benin dikrin*.[53] Furthermore, the *ketubat benin dikrin* claim cannot be honored against property that was sold by the father, because their claim, as heirs, is limited to the estate.[54] However, it may well be assumed that if the heirs sold the estate in defiance of the *benin dikrin* claim of the wife's sons, the latter can collect payment of their claim even from the purchaser.

[48] Tos. Ket. 4, 18, Ket. 68b.
[49] Ket. 69a, Yad, Ishut 20, 6.
[50] See Ket. 50b, 69a-b, Yad, Ishut 20, 5.
[51] See pp. 128 ff above.
[52] Ket. 50b, 52b.
[53] Yad, Ishut 16, 7.
[54] Ket. 55a.

The order of priority of the several ketubah obligations is as follows. The ketubah itself is prior to all other obligations. Of the ketubah, dowry is prior to the mohar and the mattan. Then the alimentation of the widow is provided;[55] and then follows support of the minor orphan girls and *Parnasha;*[56] and lastly the *ketubat benin dikrin* is met. The rest of the estate is given to the heirs. The priority of one ketubah over another as to date has bearing only on the triple ketubah obligations, mohar, mattan, and dowry, secured by a lien, but has no bearing on the other obligations.[57] These obligations are met in the order given above, no matter how many widows or minor orphan girls or *ketubat benin dikrin* claims are in question, and no matter what the dates be of the writs on which those claims are based.

[55] B. B. 140b, Yad, Ishut 19, 21. However, Tos. Ket. 10, 1 and Jer. B. B. 16d and Jer. Ket. 36a state that support for the widow and for the minor orphan girls are the same level. On the basis of this Jerushalmi utterance, the decision is rendered by Tosafot (Ket. 43a, B. B. 140a) that the priority of the widow holds good only where widow, minor girls, and minor sons demand support; for it is only then that priority is invoked as between the minor boys and the minor girls. If the question of priority is not raised between the sons and the daughters, that is, if only sons or only daughters remain, the widow's claim to support is only equal that of the minor orphan girls or the minor orphan boys.

[56] Cf. Yad, Ishut 20, 11, based on B. B. 139a-b.

[57] Cf. Tos. Ket. 10, 1, Yad, Ishut 18, 14 and *Magid* thereto and Yad, Ishut 19, 21.

CHAPTER XVII

Special Clauses

Rabbinic law permits any agreement between husband and wife in the matter of their mutual relations, and such agreement is valid and binding, provided it is made in proper legal form and not contrary to Biblical law or public weal. In accordance with this, where statutory law or the standard ketubah formula did not fully cover the points of agreement between husband and wife, they resorted to special clauses. The special clause thus served as an addition to the ketubah. Sometimes it served as a forerunner of the standard ketubah clauses. Any timely need that had not sufficiently impressed itself upon social life was first met by individuals or localities by methods of their own choice. Any new need in marriage relations was equally met by ketubah clauses of individual or local creation. When a local usage was generally adopted it became the law. The special clauses that we shall here consider belong to both categories, as additions to the standard and as forerunners of the standard. We consider those as special clauses which have only local recognition, which are not binding (save as a matter of custom) unless specified in a writ. They are either part of the ketubah proper or part of the *tena'im*, the latter being a supplement to the ketubah written in a separate instrument or on the ketubah itself.

It would form a book in itself to exhaust all the special clauses employed in Jewish marriage contracts and, were these clauses given their social background, it would form an interesting book indeed. But, for our treatment of the subject, we must make our choice from the mass of clauses of only those that seem to have halakic import.

In the matter of succession to the husband or to the wife, we have seen above certain local usages which deviated from the Talmudic law. The Palestinian usage, the Shum enactment, and the Toledo *minhag* have been cited. The ketubot specify either of these customs by a brief clause, that "succession shall be in accordance with the *minhag* Toledo" or "succession shall be in accordance with the Shum enactment" or "in accordance with the usage of the people of Palestine." Sometimes they specify that "the local custom shall prevail in the matter of succession," having reference to either of the three usages, as may be employed in that locality.[1] Sometimes, however, they give the order of succession in detail. The Sephardic ketubah, for instance, following the Toledo usage, specifies, either in the ketubah itself or in the *tena'im* following the ketubah text, that: "If (God forbid) the bride shall die without issue during the lifetime of the groom, he shall return to the bride's heirs half of the dowry which she brought him... but if issue remain, then shall all go to the groom according to the law of the Torah,— namely, the husband succeeds his wife. If (God forbid) the groom die during the lifetime of the

[1] See the Sephardic ketubah and Benai Israel ketubah. The Palestinian custom is referred to as the custom of the people of Palestine or of the rabbis of Palestine, and reference is also made to the origin of this custom in the Palestinian Talmud. The Palestinian Talmud cites that usage as returning the entire dowry to the bride's father if she dies childless. So does a ketubah in the Cambridge University library, Egypt 1089, marked J-3-Y. The ketubah ed. Schechter and *ketubah Jerushalmit* ed. Berliner specify the return of only half of the dowry to the wife's father as a modification of the Palestinian usage.

above named bride without issue, she shall receive the full payment of her mohar, mattan, and dowry. Should issue remain, it shall be left to them or their guardian to choose either to pay her the ketubah in full or to divide the estate with her."[2] A local custom reflected in a ketuabh of Medona of the year 1800, a photograph of which is in the Alder collection of the Jewish Theological Seminary, is an interesting reversion to the original intention of the *ketubat benin dikrin.* It specifies that in the event the husband survives the wife and issue remains, the wife's dowry shall belong outright to her children, sons or daughters, so that their claim to it shall be prior to any other claim, ketubah, or note of indebtedness. The husband, however, remains the trustee of the dowry during his lifetime. His trust must not be questioned or challenged by the children at the penalty of their loss of all rights to the dowry. This entire provision applies only if the husband has remarried, else he is full heir of his wife's dowry.

In the event the husband dies without issue, the woman's property rights are not the only questions involved. It is more important to the woman to be free to remarry, and for that she needs the *Halizah.* Hence some ketubot record that the brother or brothers have taken an oath and obligated themselves to free her by

[2] I copied these clauses from a Livorno ketubah of the year 1789 in the Adler Collection at the Jewish Theological Seminary Library. The same is found in an Ancona ketubah, a Tunis ketubah, and a Ragusa (1793) ketubah of the same collection. An Ancona ketubah (1753) gives the woman the full payment at her husband's death whether with or without issue. Many ketubot mention the "Christian agreement into which they entered," presumably regulating their property rights in accordance with civil law. See the Milan, Gorizia, and Sinigalia ketubot in the same collection.

Halizah without demands or claims upon her;[3] others provide also, for that purpose, that the husband shall give her a conditional divorce, to become effective a moment before his death in case he falls seriously ill.[4]

Before polygamy was prohibited in the Ashkenazic communities and afterward in the Sephardic communities, where the ordinance did not have general recognition, the wife on her own account demanded the insertion of a clause in the ketubah obligating the husband to take no other wife beside her. It forms an important local usage and is part of the ketubah or the *tena'im* formula of various countries and times. It reads, "That he may not marry or take, during the wife's lifetime and while she is with him, another wife, wife-slave, or concubine except with her consent; and if he does . . . , he shall from this moment be obligated to pay her the ketubah in full and give her a bill of divorcement by which she shall be free to remarry."[5]

Closely allied with this clause is the clause specifying that the husband shall not retain in his house a female servant who is objectionable to the wife. Frivolity with servants was not an uncommon evil in olden times, and a wife had enough reason to object. The clause read, "He also agreed not to have in his employ a female slave that is objectionable to her. If he have such a slave, he shall free his wife by a bill of divorcement which shall be valid for divorce, even if

[3] Ancona ketubah of 1801 in the Adler Collection.

[4] Medona ketubah 1800.

[5] See Sephardic ketubah ed. Gaster and the ketubah ed. Abrahams in Jews' College Jubilee Volume. In MS form it is found in Adler Collection 4010V, Bodl. 2877-20, 33; Cambridge-T-S 16-61, 85.

that be contrary to his wishes." [6] In one instance, the woman is promised the retention of a servant whom the husband brought from his father, probably one sufficiently wanting in charms to set the wife at ease.[7]

The matter of domicile is often governed by a set of special clauses with greater restrictions than the Talmudic law prescibes. At times it is specified in the ketubah that "they shall dwell together in NN" [8] or more simply, "to reside in NN" [9] or " a dwelling in a Jewish neighborhood" [10] or a fuller clause reading "that he shall not compel her to move from one territory to another against her will, and if he do compel her to move from one territory to another against her will he shall pay her all that he has obligated himself and free her immediately by a legally valid bill of divorcement." [11]

Talmudic law formulated a clause in the ketubah by which the husband frees his wife from oath or vow in connection with the payment of her ketubah. But according to Talmudic law, the husband can at any time impose an oath or a vow on his wife that she has stolen none of his belongings while she was keeping house for him or working in his business.[12] The annoyance of such a thing to a woman is self-evident, and to avoid it a ketubah clause was introduced in some localities which read, "That she be trusted in all kinds of food and beverage of the household supply, and that he or his heirs may not demand from her oath or vow,

[6] Bodl. 2877-20, etc.
[7] Adler Collection 4010V.
[8] ibid.
[9] Adler Collection, Damascus 1706 and 1747.
[10] Yemenite ketubah ed. Gaster, MGWJ, Vol. 54.
[11] See Sephardic ketubah.
[12] Shabuot 45a, Ket. 85b, 87a.

neither a grave oath nor a light oath nor even a *Herem*, on the grounds of mere suspicion — not even as an addition to an oath which he may legally be entitled to impose on her." [13]

We are referred back to Talmudic times when we speak of the next special clause, dealing with the support of step-daughters. The widow or the divorcee was often left to care for her daughters herself, either because the father refused to care for them or because his estate was too poor to support them or because the daughters remained unmarried after attaining majority, when their support out of their father's estate comes to an end.[14] Not so frequently as the daughters, sometimes even the sons were left to the care of their mother.[15] It was natural that on her remarriage, she would demand from her second husband that he support her children. Therefore, even in tannaic days, we find a ketubah clause specifying "that I shall support your daughter for five years."[16] Cautious husbands would write "that I support your daughter for five years, so long as you are with me." According to the first clause the daughter must be supported even after her mother is divorced; according to the latter only so

[13] Ketubah ed. Abrahams, Bodl. 2877-16, 20, Cambridge, T-S 16-61, 85.

[14] The assumption made by Tos. Ket. 10, 2 that the case represents a minor girl seems to point to the supposition that the wife was divorced, and in accordance with the Talmudic rule (Ket. 102a-b, 'Erubin 82b) the daughters went with her, hence their need for support. If the mother were widowed, the minor girl would be supported out of her father's estate.

[15] Tos. ibid., Ket. 51b.

[16] Ket. 101b, Tos. Ket. 10, 2. The Mishna seems to imply definitely that this clause was written, either in the ketubah or the *Shetare Pesikata*, but Talmud Ket. 102b and Gittin 51a imply that it was a verbal agreement.

long as the mother remains with him.[17] This clause continued through the Talmudic period, and a remnant of it is found even in a post-Talmudic ketubah, which reads, "Furthermore has this 'Ali taken upon himself .... to have the two daughters of his wife Hosan, daughters of S'ei ... with him, and to support them until they are married."[18]

The clause as given in the post-Talmudic ketubah has already included a number of legal points in which the Talmudic clause was distinctly weak. It specifies that their support will continue so long as they are with him, their step-father, and so long as they are unmarried. The Talmudic clause made it possible for the step-daughter to continue getting the cash value of her support from her step-father after her marriage, while she was getting her maintenance from her husband, and if she had two step-fathers who had agreed to support her, she was getting twice the cash value of her support while she was being maintained by her husband.[19] This 'Ali has cleverly specified support but no cash value of support, and only so long as the step-daughters remain unmarried.

When such a clause is included in a writ, or even if it is expressed verbally and confirmed by a *Kinyan* or legal formality of conveyance, it becomes binding upon the father or his estate in a degree superior to the ketubah provisions, for it is like a note of indebtedness.[20] And the step-father is not entitled in return for his support of the step-daughter to any rights over

[17] Mishna Ket. 101b.
[18] T-S, 20-30.
[19] Ket. ibid.
[20] Yad, Ishut 23, 17.

her, her labor, or her earnings,[21] for nothing is promised in return.

As against the husband's care of his wife's children, the woman was often called upon to care for her husband's children. Whereas such a situation was often dealt with by mere verbal and informal agreements between the pair, it was sometimes stipulated in the marriage writ as a special ketubah clause. We find such a clause in a Damascus ketubah of 1706, which is probably one instance of many that are not known to us. Likewise, the wife was often called upon to care for her mother-in-law, or at least to tolerate her in her house — as an Egyptian ketubah of the thirteenth century specified,[22] "And the above-named bride agreed to have her mother-in-law live with her in one house."

Post-Talmudic days witnessed an antagonism to the Talmudic law which gives the husband the right to divorce his wife at his pleasure even without the formality of a court procedure.[23] The unfair disadvantage to the wife was a positive social evil. Two remedies were necessary, to prohibit divorce without the wife's consent, and to require court action in the matter of divorce. Both of these developed simultaneously, the first as an enactment of R. Gershon, the second as an unformulated social institution.[24] But the best safeguard was found in the ketubah clause which read, "That at no time may he or his agent divorce her, except with her

[21] Tos. Ket. 10, 2.

[22] T-S 24.9

[23] Although Targum Jonathan translates Deuter. 24, 1 "And he shall write her a bill of divorcement before a court," the need of a court for divorce is not assumed by Jewish law, altho it was probably executed before a court even in Tannaitic days. See Mishna Gittin 1, 1.

[24] See Responsa of Asheri, 42, 1.

consent and through a just (another word for Jewish) court." [25]

To prevent cases of wife desertion, *'Agunot*, post-Talmudic ketubot resorted to various ketubah clauses. One clause reads, "That he shall not take a sea voyage or go to a distant land unless he leave her a bill of divorcement conditional upon a specified time for his return and maintenance, and that he shall not leave her as a result of a quarrel for longer than ten consecutive days." [26] The Sephardim in Palestine insert in their ketubot the clause, "That he shall not go beyond Aram-Zobah or Beyroot or No-amon or any distance on the ocean, unless he leave her a bill of divorcement conditional upon a specified time of his return, together with a supply of food."[27]

A special clause is sometimes introduced to guard against the husband's taking too many liberties with the wife's dowry articles to the point of endangering their safety. Thus one ketubah states, "That he shall not sell or surrender as a pledge any article of her belongings except with her consent."[28] A Karaitic ketubah of the eleventh century phrases it thus, "That he has taken it upon himself to watch her dowry as he does his own belongings, and he shall alter them in no way without the knowledge and consent of his wife." [29] For fear that he might compel her to consent to his designs, the ketubah further provides that "The groom

[25] Damascus ketubah 1706 and Livorno 1787 of the Adler Collection.

[26] Damascus ketubah ibid.

[27] Luncz in *Yerushalayim* 1, 7.

[28] Luncz ibid. and Damascus ketubah 1706 of Adler Collection.

[29] Karaitic ketubah of 1028 and Genizah fragment T-S 16.236.

has agreed not to accept as a gift any part, large or small, of the mohar, mattan, or dowry, nor to persuade her to give him any part thereof. From now on such a gift is declared void and such conveyance naught — like unto a broken potsherd that is of no value." [30]

Often the special clause deals with the observance of religious rites by the husband or the wife. Foremost among them is the specification that the wife observe ritual cleanness and that the husband do not approach her for sexual contact unless he ascertain that she has performed the ritual ablution. Laxity in the observance of ritual purity is reported by Maimonides for his day [31] — which prompted him to enact a *Takanah*, "That any Jewish woman who does not immerse in the water of a ritual bath after counting seven days of cleanness, as is the law for Jewish daughters. . . shall be divorced without the payment of her ketubah or any of the terms of the ketubah." [32] He also records the fact that such provisions were being entered into the ketubah in his day.[33] The Genizah has since brought to light some of those ketubot referred to by Maimonides. The clause in composite form reads: "We have given warning to the bride that whenever she do not

[30] Livorno 1787, Tunis, Damascus, etc. of the Adler Collection.

[31] Responsa, I, 149. Schechter in *Genizah Specimens*, JQR, 13, p. 218f concludes from the fact that *tebilah* is not mentioned in the ketubah which he edits there, that even Rabbinites were lax in it. The inference is only a negative one and goes beyond the testimony of Maimonides, who merely complains of a substitute for the ritual immersion which is not wholly proper.

[32] Responsa of Maimonides ibid., where the *Takanah* is dated 1187-8. A Genizah MS, T-S, K-13 dates it 1175-6. Cf. Abrahams, *A Formula and a Responsum*, Jews' College Jubilee Volume, 1906, pp. 101f.

[33] Responsa, I, 116.

count seven days of cleanness after the menstrual flow has ceased and hereafter immerse in a place fit for ritual bathing and do not separate from her husband before that time, she shall lose all that is due her from her husband and shall leave him without aught. We have also given full warning to the groom thereon. . ."[34] One instrument contains the simpler formula, "We have legally bound the bride to the promise that she will take a ritual bath whenever she terminates menstruation."[35] And another ketubah fragment specifies that the bride will forfeit the ketubah if she do not light the Sabbath candles.[36]

Greater need for such clauses was felt in marriages between Rabbinites and Karaites. One writ specifies "That he (Rabbinite) shall not compel . . . his wife (Karaite) to stay with him in the house where the Sabbath candle is lit or to eat the fat of the rump, or to desecrate her own holidays, but she shall observe together with him also his holidays."[37] Another has the following list of rites, "That he shall not bring to the house where she is with him as his wife the fat of the rump, kidneys or liver,[38] nor the meat of a female animal with dead foetus within her body, nor a pregnant animal,[39] nor the bread of Gentiles, their wine, and

[34] Bodl. 2877.20, 33; T-S, 16.61, 85.

[35] Ketubah ed. Abrahams, Jews' College Jubilee Volume.

[36] T-S, 16.85.

[37] Ketubah ed. Schechter, JQR, 13. See Mann, *The Jews in Egypt and Palestine under the Fatimids*, II, p. 212.

[38] *Eshkol Hakofer*, A-232, *Gan Eden, Shehita*, 21, *Aderet Elijahu, Shehita*, 18-20. Cf. Ibn Ezra and Nahmanides ad Lev. 3, 9.

[39] The foetus makes the animal unclean, according to the Karaites, while the Rabbinites declare the foetus as slaughtered together with its mother. See *Aderet Elijahu, Shehita* 10. The pregnant animal may not be slaughtered, according to the

their abominations. Neither shall he light candles on the Sabbath eve, nor shall fire be in his house on the Sabbath day,[40] nor shall he lie with her on Sabbath and holidays in the manner of lying on week days, nor shall he force her to desecrate the holidays of the Lord which are established by the sight of the new moon and the appearance of spring in Palestine,[41] for she is of the Karaites and upon their faith. . . . "[42] Another ketubah specifies similar terms and adds that "If he act contrary to any of these terms, he shall pay a hundred drachmas, to be divided equally between the poor of the Karaites and those of the Rabbinites."[43] A Karaitic ketubah made out in Jerusalem also specifies that "They shall not eat the meat of oxen and sheep in Jerusalem until the Altar of the Lord is established."[44]

The Karaitic ketubah also adds the clause, "That they shall not go before a Gentile court in forfeiture of the judgments of the Torah,"[45] because Karaitic halakah prohibits suing before a Gentile court. This pro-

Karaites, because the mother and the child are thereby slaughtered together. See *Aderet Elijahu,* ibid.

[40] The Rabbinites prohibit lighting of a candle on the Sabbath; the Karaites prohibit the burning of a candle on the Sabbath even though it was lit before the Sabbath. Hence the prohibition of being in a room where a Sabbath candle is burning. See *Aderet Elijahu,* Sabbah, 7, 17-20. The prohibition against cohabitation is conceived on the basis of it being an un-Sabbath-like mode of life. See *Aderet Elijahu,* Sabbath, 11.

[41] Ibid. *Kiddush Ha-Hodesh,* 11, 36. Karaitic ketubah ed. Luncz.

[42] Mann, *The Jews in Egypt and Palestine, etc.,* Vol. II, pp. 211-12.

[43] Mann ibid., p. 212.

[44] See Ketubah ed. Luncz.

[45] Ibid. See also Karaitic ketubah ed. Gaster and Mann, ibid. p. 212.

hibition was not recognized in rabbinic halakah and, therefore, we have as an instance a rabbinic ketubah clause which reads, "And this deed of mohar shall be valid and trusted and honored wherever it shall be presented and read in accordance with law and by court action whether a Jewish or a Gentile court,"[46] and many ketubot refer to marriage agreements made between the husband and the wife before a "Christian Court" or notary public. It is true that prohibitions against suing in Gentile courts are found even among the Rabbinites. As an instance, R. Simeon b. Zemah Duran, an authority of the fourteenth century, speaks with much seriousness of his enactment "That all affairs and claims and demands between husband and wife shall not be brought by either to be judged by the Gentile courts, but by the Jewish courts."[47] However the rabbinic authorities recognized this to be more a matter of local political expediency than a matter of universal Jewish halakah.[48]

In conclusion, a few instances may be cited of material that has entered into the ketubah either as part of or as whole ketubah clauses, which reflects the social life of Jewish communities in the remote or recent past. One Egyptian ketubah fragment of the year 1111 describes the groom as a freed slave;[49] another of unknown date and place gives the bride the status of wife and freed slave combined.[50] A rather recent ketubah — Corfu, 1846 — records the fact that the bride was seduced by the groom prior to the marriage.[51] The

[46] *Ketubah Jerushalemit,* ed. Berliner.
[47] TShBZ, II, 292, 8.
[48] But see *Hoshen Mishpat, Dayyanim,* 26, 1 f.
[49] T-S, 24.5.
[50] T-S, J-3-Z.
[51] Gaster Codex 1668.

financial dependence of the couple at the time of the wedding is related in a series of provisions in the ketubah, that the groom's father or the bride's father or mother shall support them for a period of time after the marriage;[52] that the groom's father holds himself responsible for the dowry, since the groom is too young and dependent upon him;[53] that the groom shall receive instruction in Hebrew after the marriage at the expense of one of the parents;[54] that the wedding expenses shall be paid by the bride's parents or the groom's parents or, as one ketubah has it, out of the interest on an investment made by the bride's mother on behalf of the couple.[55] Sometimes the husband offers to clothe his wife out of his earnings; sometimes he lets her clothe herself out of her own earnings.[56] The contact of the Jew with his environment is also often recorded in the ketubah. A ketubah is dated by Napoleon;[57] succession is determined according to the law of the country;[58] Schlomo is called Solomon;[59] and the ketubah is registered in the *kehillah* office in the vernacular.[60]

What a distance between the lower Nile in the fifth century before the common era and the upper Rhine in

[52] M. D. Davis, *Shetarot*, London 1887, p. 33.

[53] Ketubah of Corfu 1764, Adler Collection.

[54] M. D. Davis, ibid.

[55] ibid., and p. 300.

[56] Damascus ketubah 1706 of the Adler Collection and the Sephardic custom as reported by Luncz.

[57] Metz, 1810.

[58] A Yemenite ketubah reads, "All matters of support and clothing in accordance with the non-Jewish law," and many ketubot refer the matter of property rights and succession to a non-Jewish contract made between the couple.

[59] Ketubah of Metz, ibid.

[60] Ketubah of Corfu 1764 in the Adler Collection.

our own twentieth century! The ketubah has gone through it all. Adjustment to environment, yielding to conditions — and what a variety of conditions — has been its problem for these many years, even as it has been the problem of the people it united in marriage; and yet for these twenty-five centuries how essentially faithful it has remained to Jewish form and content!

APPENDIX A

THE CHANGING CONCEPTION AND STATUS OF THE BETROTHED*

A MISHNAH in Ketubot (IV. 4) reads: "The father has the legal right to give his daughter in marriage by means of money, writ, and marital intercourse; to him belongs what she may find or earn; he also annuls her vows and receives her divorce; but he has no right to the fruit of her property during her life. When she marries, the husband's rights exceed those of the father in that he enjoys the fruit of her property during her life. Furthermore, he has the obligation of her support, ransom, and burial."

The Tosefta (IV. 1-2, cited Ket. 47a) reads: "In some respects the father's rights exceed those of the husband and in others the husband's rights are superior to those of the father. The husband eats the fruit of her property during her life, while the father does not. The father's rights exceed those of the husband in that the husband has the obligation of support, ransom and burial......while the father has not."

One can easily see that the mishnah and the tosefta represent one tradition, a comparison between the authority of the father and that of the husband. The comparison seems to be between two persons having authority over the same woman but not at the same time, that is, the authority of the father as long as the woman belongs to him, compared with the authority of the husband when she is transferred to him. The dividing line between these two realms of authority is the moment of nuptials, not betrothal, as is indicated by the word ניׂשאת in the mishnah. In other words, the period of betrothal which by custom was of twelve months' duration is definitely considered as belonging to the realm of the father's authority. This interpretation is natural enough and, furthermore, has the sanction of all commentators and is supported by what is implied in the scattered references made to the mishnah by the amoraim. It gives a series of halakic dicta which agree fully with the later halakah.

*Reprinted from JQR, N.S., Vol. 14, pp. 483-99.

(1) The father does not enjoy the fruit of his daughter's property either before or after betrothal. The Talmud Babli presents this (Ket. 47a) as the prevalent view, though R. Jose b. R. Judah contests it. The Yerushalmi gives this halakah as uncontested but allows the father to demand the right of the fruit (28d). Both Talmudim agree that the right of fruit is not an inherent right that goes with the guardianship over the woman, but a special provision by the court in exchange for something else, either for the ransom (Babli) or for the burden of caring for the property (Yer.). And the father is denied the right of fruit because he would do that service for his daughter without any special inducement or compensation.

(2) The father never owes support to his daughter. Legally this principle was established by R. Eleazar b. Azariah who inferred it from the text of the *Ketubat benin dikrin* and *Benan nukban* (49a). But it appears that this legal measure had to be modified, for, besides the moral obligation to support a daughter which is pointed out by R. Meir and R. Judah (*ibid*), besides the legal duty of supporting her at least until the age of six (65b), the court at Usha enacted a definite legal obligation for parents to support minor sons and daughters (49b).

(3) If the daughter is made captive the father does not owe her or the community the payment of her ransom. The later halakah, though not explicit, would seem to agree with that ruling of our mishna, for ransom, according to the Babli, is in exchange for the right to the fruit of the woman's property; and since the right to the fruit is denied the father, he is free from the obligation of ransom. The Talmud, though, does assume that the father would redeem his daughter from captivity without the compulsion of a specific legal obligation (47a).

(4) The father is not obligated to provide burial for his daughter whether she died after betrothal or as an infant. Nothing in later halakah or amoraic legislation modifies this evident ruling of the mishna. Logic should require the father to have the obligation of burial, for the obligation of burial falls upon him who is heir to her property (47b, 81a); nevertheless, the amoraim seem never to have formulated this logical point into a law.

(5) Turning to the rights and obligations of the husband, the mishna teaches that the husband is not entitled to the fruit of his wife's property until nuptials. That too agrees with the later halakah (b. Yeb. 31b). The enjoyment of fruit natural-

ly would depend upon the transfer of the dowry into the husband's keeping, and the transfer, in late tannaitic days, took place about the time of nuptials (48b).

(6) The husband owes his wife support only from the time of nuptials, not during the period of betrothal. Logic supports this halakah. Sustenance begins with the woman's coming to her husband's house, or nuptials. In a slightly modified form, this halakah is reflected in a mishna of R. Akiba's days, termed "The First Mishnah" (57a), which states that when the twelve months which constitute the betrothal period are over the woman is entitled to support from her husband even though the nuptials were not yet solemnized. If clothing may be treated as part of sustenance, there is direct evidence from a mishnah (67a) that the husband is not expected to clothe his wife during the betrothal period.

(7) The husband has the obligation of paying ransom for his wife only after nuptials, not during the period of betrothal. There is nothing in later halakah on the question of the husband's duty to pay ransom for his wife during the betrothal period save a supposed tannaitic tradition that the payment of ransom is given him in exchange for the right of fruit (47b) and since, as was said, he does not enter upon the right of fruit until nuptials, the obligation of ransom should not begin until nuptials.

(8) The husband's obligation to pay burial expenses for his wife applies only after nuptials, not prior to it. Here too the later halakah has nothing to say but to connect burial with the right of succession, and since succession begins with nuptials (53a) it is to be understood that the obligation of burial begins with the nuptials as well.

(9) The mishnah teaches us through these laws that the betrothed is part of her father's not of her husband's family. This, of course, is the general impression conveyed by all late tannaitic and amoraic halakah.

These nine points enumerated as contained in the halakic teaching of this mishnah and as corroborated by later halakah present a multitude of more evident and less evident difficulties. With reference to the first point, we ask, how is it possible that the father is entitled to all gain by her labor or to anything which she may find but not to the fruit of her property? Why is the view of R. Jose b. R. Judah omitted in the Mishnah? The reasons given in the Babli and the Yerushalmi for this law are evidently artificial. With reference to the second point, the difficulties are self-evident. How is it possible that a father shall not have the legal obligation to support his minor children? Who else shall support them? R. Eleazar b. Azaria's inference from the text of the ketubah must be faulty and the fallacy, to my mind, lies in the fact that he saw a parallelism between the *Ketubat benin dikrin* and the *Ketubat benan nukban*, rather than the parallelism between the *Mazon ha'ishah* and the *Benan nukban* clauses.

Let us for a moment consider this inference of R. Eleazar b. Azariah. The ketubah clauses as reported in the Mishnah (52b) read as follows: "The male children which thou shalt bear unto me shall inherit thy ketubah above their share of inheritance among their brothers." This is termed the *Benin dikrin* clause and specifies that when the woman dies before the husband, her dowry which goes to the husband as the legal successor must finally, at the death of the husband, revert to her sons. The next clause is the *Benan nukban* clause which reads: "The female children which thou shalt bear unto me shall live in my house and shall be supported out of my estate until they are married." The *Mazon ha'ishah* clause following next in order reads: "Thou shalt live in my house and be supported out of my estate as long as thou livest in widowhood in my house." R. Eleazar b. Azariah conceives a parallelism between the first and the second clauses, the first providing for the sons and the second providing for the daughters. Hence, he argues, as the inheritance provided for the sons in the first clause applies only after the death of the father, so the sustenance for the daughters provided in the second clause applies also to the time after the father's death. Finding no provision for the daughters during the father's lifetime, he concludes that there is no legal obligation on the father to support his daughters.

On examination, however, we see that while the first part of the second clause resembles the first clause, the second part resembles the third clause. There is no more reason for grouping the first two clauses together rather than the last two. In fact for halakic purposes the two last clauses are always grouped together—*Mazon ha'ishah we-ha-banot.*—There are very few legal elements in common between *Ketubat benin dikrin* and *Ketubat benan nukban*, but support for the widow and support for the female orphans run parallel throughout the halakah. And we are, furthermore, forced by the logic of the case to group the last two rather than the first two clauses together. The first clause provides for the instance where the wife dies first, while the last two clauses provide for the case where the husband dies first. This fact is noted in the few remnants we have of these clauses in the later keutbah. One edited by A. Berliner, in *Kobez 'al Yad* IX, 4, under the title "Ketubah Yerushalemit," Krakau, 1893, has this introductory phrase to these clauses ואם ח״ו יפטר זה פל׳ קודם לזאת פלנית תהא פלנית יושבת בביתו וניזונית ומתפרנסת. More evidently is this point brought out in a ketubah as yet not edited (T-S. 12.659 verso), which fell into my hands in the Cambridge University Library, containing the clauses of the mishnah, and reading: ועוד אתנון ביניהון.... חה תיזלין לבית עלמין.... ון יירתון כסף תובתיך... איזל לבית עלמי קדמיי(כי).... לגוברין יהודאין ואנת... This evidently contains the *ketubat benin dikrin* and *ketubat benan nukban* and *mazon ha'ishah* and clearly draws the line of distinction between the first and the last two clauses, the first applying to the case of her prior death, the last two applying to the case of his prior death. With this the whole argument of R. Eleazar b. Azariah falls to the ground. The ketubah assumes that the father will support his daughters as a legal duty, but guarantees them support from the estate after his death, for there is no legal duty upon the heirs to support the minor orphan girl. Later authorities could not contradict the ruling of R. Eleazar b. Azariah, but found themselves in difficulties in declaring the father free from the obligation of supporting his minor children, and therefore they applied themselves to finding a basis for the obligation on the father either on moral grounds or by a direct enactment.

The third point seems quite as untenable as the second. It sounds cruel for a law by which people live to permit a father to throw the burden of ransom for his minor daughter upon good people in the community. And what shall we say of the fourth point permitting the father to let his little girl lie unburied after she died?

There is nothing inherently illogical in the other halakic points enumerated above, but certain weaknesses in their transmission through the later halakah are evident. Thus, later halakah says the husband is not entitled to the fruit of his betrothed's property and supports this statement by the fact that the date is not inserted in the marriage contract, the *shetar kiddushin*. Early evidences, from Philo and from the papyri, prove beyond doubt that the *shetar kiddushin* did contain the date (see JQR., N.S., XIV, p. 274). The transfer of the dowry upon which the right of fruit is dependent did not always take place at or after nuptials, but sometimes before nuptials according to the testimony of a late tannaitic text (48b). Perhaps in earlier days it took place at betrothal. According to the *Mishnah*

Rishonah, after the lapse of the twelve months' period, the husband had to support his betrothed even though the nuptials had not yet been held. Perhaps earlier than that the twelve months' waiting did not matter. In the obligation to pay ransom the difference between nuptials and betrothal is not logical. The tannaitic text (47b) which connects ransom with the right of fruit is altogether unreliable, as is evident from the emendations in it and from the variant in the Yerushalmi. It is the same text which connects burial with succession. While in itself a weak support for the law supposed to be contained in our mishnah, namely that the husband does not owe his wife burial until after nuptials, it begs the question. Why assume that the husband is not entitled to succession to his wife after betrothal? We have many other evidences in earlier tannaitic texts that the right of succession is vested with the husband from the moment of betrothal, in the earlier halakah. The later halakah is based upon a tradition submitted by R. Hiyya, an amora whose identity is not clear, and is found in none of the tannaitic texts.

The truth is that all the evident or hidden weaknesses pointed out in these laws which shift the husband's obligations to the time of nuptials may be concentrated in the one and the last point enumerated, namely that the law recognizes the betrothed woman as still belonging to her father. This is something which every now and then comes into conflict with the older law. In the older law the ketubah was given to the bride at betrothal, as was ably pointed out by Dr. A. Büchler in Lewy's *Festschrift*. This means that the dowry was transferred to and the obligations assumed by the husband from the time of betrothal.

With this critical examination of the later halakah and the interpretation of our mishnah as prompted by later halakah, we feel we have done with the negative side of our thesis, namely that the mishnah does not mean what commentators and even the amoraim or perhaps the redactor took it to mean. We approach now the positive task of finding the original intention of the halakah contained in our mishnah.

To find the intention of the halakah, we must first decide where we shall find the source of the halakah, whether in the mishnah or in the tosefta. We seem to have nothing to guide us in this decision save their estimated ages. The mishnah as we read it now (without the correction that I seek to introduce) must be dated after the time of R. Eleazar b. Azariah, for it is evident that R. Eleazar b. Azariah was the first to teach that the father has no legal obligation to support his daughters

(49a), while this mishnah implies this law as granted. The age of the tosefta may be traced very systematically and leads us to conclude that it preceded the mishnah.

The ear-marks of this tosefta are the יפה כח series. Thus, it starts with the comparison of the authority of the husband with that of the father, and goes over into a comparison of the power of the husband with that of the *levir*. This יפה כח series must be completed by one point which has been lost in the tosefta but which has been preserved in the mishnah Nedarim (X. 2) which reads: "If the father dies, the power (of annulling the vows of a betrothed maiden) is not conveyed to the husband; if the husband dies, the power is conveyed to the father. In this respect the rights of the father are above those of the husband; in another respect, however, the rights of the husband are superior to those of the father, namely the husband can annul the vows of his wife who is of age, while the father cannot annul the vows of a daughter who has attained majority."

That this mishna in Nedarim belongs to the יפה כח series is evident by the reference made in the mishna to that series. Should we assume that the mishnah itself is older, but that the reference to the series of יפה כח is a later addition to it, we would have to assume three layers of the halakah, first in the old mishna, then in the series, and third in the mishnah as it now appears. Such an assumption is hardly logical when there is nothing against believing the mishnah to be in its original form but to have been transferred to Nedarim out of a series that had existed independently. If the יפה כח series is as old as the halakah of the mishnah of Nedarim, then it is pre-Shammaitic, for the Hillelites and Shammaites use the halakah as a text (Tos. Ned. VI. 2-3). As in the case of the אין בין series so ingeniously treated by Professor Louis Ginzberg in Hoffmann's *Festschrift* under the title "*Zur Entstehlungsgeschichte der Mishnah,*" where the learned author proves that the series antedates the citation of these halakahs in the Mishnah and is the source for them, so do we feel that the יפה כח series is the source from which the Mishnayot in Ketubot and Nedarim have drawn.

With this assumption, we feel compelled to consider the opion of R. Jose b. R. Judah to be a later addition to Tosefta Ket. IV. 1, and in some MSS. (cf. Zukermandel *a. l.*) it is omitted. The words אף האב indicate that it is a marginal note, taken probably from Ket. 47a, but apparently for lack of space the scribe could not put down the full text of R. J. b. R. J.'s statement (האב אוכל פירות בחיי בתו) which would be more appropriate from the point of view of clarity of style. It will presently be shown also that R. J. b. R. J.'s view does not in the least contradict the halakah of the tosefta.

Another correction in the text of the tosefta which we are forced to make because of our conclusion is to omit the words כיון שנכנסה לחופה אע"פ שלא נבעלה in Tos. Ket. IV. 3. This distinction belongs to the time of the *Mishnah Aharonah* as is conclusively pointed out by R. Jacob Tam (Tosafot Yeb. 67b, *ad fin.*).

Taking this יפה כח series in and for itself with the addition to it from the mishnah of Nedarim, we find a distinct motive for the building up of that series, and that motive is most evident from the part contained in the mishnah of Nedarim. There we speak of the *arusah*, the betrothed, as having a double authority over her, her husband and her father. Out of this condition arose the attempt at a clarification of the balance of authority between the father and the husband, and the series whereof we spoke came into being—"In certain respects the father's power is greater, in other respects the husband's power is greater." *We speak therefore distinctly of the betrothed,* neither of the father's power before betrothal nor of the husband's power after nuptials. The original text of our halakah, which the mishnah of Ketubot cites, simply stated that the fruit of the woman's property belongs to her husband during the period of betrothal, that his obligations for the same period are support, ransom and burial. The word נישאת was not in the original text, for it spoke only of the betrothal period.

In this light, the mishnah reflects a true representation of the older halakah concerning the status of the *arusah.* All these legal points, the right of fruit, the obligations of support, ransom and burial are bound up with the ketubah. The last three are ketubah provisions, the first is most intimately bound up with the dowry which is a provision in the ketubah. Since we granted, with Dr. Büchler, that in older tannaitic times the ketubah was made out at betrothal, how could it be otherwise but that all these rights and obligations became effective at betrothal?

Furthermore, we have traces of that older law left in rabbinic literature. Tosefta Ketubot VIII. 1, records a line of reasoning of Rabban Gamaliel the Elder pointing to the difference between the betrothed and the wedded. He points to the formula contained in the first part of our mishnah זכאי במציאתה ובמעשי ידיה ובהפר נדריה, the husband is the legal owner of what his wife finds or earns, and he is empowered to annul her vows after nuptials, but not during the period of betrothal. The goal for which they argue is whether or not the betrothed woman shall be allowed to sell any part of her property. What would be more logical to mention in this connection than the fact that the husband is not entitled to the fruit of the property of his wife until after nuptials, had this been the early law as it is the later law? This omission, because so pertinent to the question on which they argued, proves conclusively that in Rabban Gamaliel's time the older law prevailed which gave the husband the right to the fruit of his wife's property from the moment of betrothal.

That the older law imposed upon the husband the duty of supporting his wife from the time of betrothal can be seen from the law of אכילת תרומה concerning which Ula says: "Biblically, the wife of a priest eats of the heave-offering from the time of the betrothal." (Ket. 57b) and his inference from the Bible is perfectly logical. Even in the time of R. Akiba, she was permitted to eat of the heave-offering before nuptials. A priest's daughter who is the wife of an Israelite is prohibited to eat of the heave-offering from the moment of betrothal even according to the later halakah (Yeb. 67b). Now the eating of heave-offering seems to be directly connected with the obligation of support, so that whenever she is entitled to eat of her husband's bread, she eats also of his heave-offering, if he is a priest.

There is very scant material in rabbinic literature on the husband's obligation to redeem his wife from captivity, so that it is almost impossible to trace different strata of the law in this connection. The only source for this obligation, the ketubah clause cited in the Mishna (51a), as we have seen, refers to the betrothal. Common sense also impels us to believe that the husband's chivalry should start with betrothal, not with nuptials.

The obligation to provide burial should be linked up with the law of defilement for the dead stated in the Bible (Lev. 21. 2-3). He who owes the woman burial, if he is a priest, may defile himself at her death. The father and brothers according to the Bible, may defile themselves at the death of the daughter and sister, provided she has no husband (אשר לא היתה לאיש). Knowing that the biblical conception of the *arusah* is that she belongs to her husband, and seeing that the same phrase indicates betrothal in Numbers 30. 6, even according to rabbinic admission (Sifre, a. l.), we should surmise that the right of the father and brother to defile themselves at the death of the daughter and the sister ceases at betrothal. A remnant of this teaching is left in the opinion of R. Jose and R. Simeon (Yeb. 60a) and

Targum Jonathan (Lev. *ibid.*). If we side with Maimonides (Yad, Abel, 2. 7) who probably bases himself on Yeb. 89b and Ket. 47b, connecting the whole matter of the husband's obligation to defile himself at the death of his wife with his right of succession to her property we are referred back to the question whether the husband's right of succession begins with betrothal or not; and, as said above, the author feels to have proven satisfactorily that the husband is admitted to the right of succession according to the earlier halakah immediately upon betrothal. (See p. 137, note 24). As for the inferences from the Bible cited in Sifre Leviticus (ibid.), no one can doubt that it represents an attempt on the part of later halakah to prove its law by the artificial application of the hermeneutic method of derivation of the school of R. Ishmael.

This older halakah giving the husband the right of fruit as well as the obligations of support, ransom and burial from the moment of betrothal, however, presents the difficutly of how to understand the relation between the betrothed in the more remote past. If the period of betrothal means the period of time that the woman remains in her father's house, though she legally belongs to her husband, how can we logically conceive of the husband enjoying the use of her property or of being obligated to support her while she is in her father's house?

A satisfactory attempt has not yet been made by any one to present a detailed outline of the development of the institution of betrothal among the Jews. Nor am I prepared to draw it here. But it appears evident that the institution has gone through radical changes. Probably in earlier biblical days there was no betrothal period at all; as a recent writer (Neubauer, *Beitrage zur Geschichte des biblishch-talmudischen Eheschlissungsrechts*) puts it, marriage was a cash transaction, the mohar was paid and the bride thereupon delivered to her husband. Marriages recorded in the Bible have no betrothal period to correspond in the least to that of Talmudic days. (Cf. Nowack, *Lehrbuch d. Hebr. Archaologie*, Bd. 1, p. 162). Yet the wedding feast lasting a week (ibid., p. 163) opened the first opportunity for the peculiar legal status of the *arusah*, namely, the married woman who was yet in her father's house. Whether this was the period indicated by the words בתולה מארשה (Num. 22. 23) or whether in Deuteronomic days there had already developed a betrothal period distinct from the days of feasting cannot be told with certainty, but there is no evidence to conclude that it was by nature similar to the Talmudic betrothal period, namely an intervening time between betrothal and nuptials when the husband goes about his business and the wife remains in her father's house. It probably was a prolongation of the betrothal into the nuptials, so that both blended together into a single ceremony of some duration. The same type of marriage is described in the Book of Tobit (VIII. 1, 20). Out of this arose the Talmudic betrothal period, simply a duration of time between the acquisition and the home-taking of the bride. In this light, the Talmudic betrothal period is merely a postponement of the time when the husband takes his bride to his home. But logically, the law could not deprive the husband of any of his rights in his wife because of the fact that he is required by custom to postpone the home-taking for sometime later. Hence it was that the older halakah treated the betrothal period as in no way different from the period following nuptials.

Exceptions to this rule began to develop gradually. The first exception was probably that of הפרת נדרים in which respect the betrothed was subjected to a double authority, the father and the husband. The Bible itself does not recognize this double authority, but the Shammaites and Hillelites, as we have shown above, already found it incorporated in the body of Jewish law. Following upon this came the curtailment of the husband's rights and the modification of his obligations during the betrothal period.

In Alexandria this was carried out by one sweeping move by the insertion in the ketubah of the modificatory clause or condition: כשתכנס לביתי תהא לי לאיתתו כדת משה וישר' (Tos. Ket. IV. 9), "when thou comest into my house shalt thou be my wife according to the Law of Moses and Israel." Thereby all obligations contained in the ketubah were shifted from betrothal to nuptials. It is only in this light that we can understand the account of Hillel the Elder of the Alexandrian ketubah, for how else shall we understand the insertion of such a clause and how else shall we account for the license which Alexandrian Jews permitted themselves to capture the wife of another? Is it likely that the clause was inserted to make such license possible? Is it possible that the Alexandrian Jews would make light of the sanctity of the marriage vow? It appears evident, therefore, that the Alexandrian Jews felt compelled, probably through foreign influence, to free the husband from all obligations until the wife comes to his house. But since by custom the ketubah was made out at betrothal, in order to shift the terms of the ketubah to the nuptials, they had to insert the clause: "When thou comest into my house....". Hillel took this to apply to the marriage clause as to the other clauses of the ketubah and rendered the decision that until nuptials she is really not even betrothed.

Palestine did not insert that clause and retained for a long time the usage of making out the ketubah at the betrothal. It could curtail the husband's rights and obligations during the period of betrothal only through single and isolated enactments. Thus, the betrothed woman was permitted to sell her private property without the husband's consent (Ket. VIII. 1); later, the right of succession and the right of fruit were taken away from him (time unknown, but at least after the termination of the time of the Shammaites and Hillelites). Then, the *Tosafot ketubah* was declared ineffective until nuptials (Ket. V. 1) and following upon this or about the same time, he was freed from the obligation of support for the duration of the twelve months of the betrothal period (Ket. 57a). Probably at the same time he was freed from the obligation of ransom and burial.

The author of the Mishnah finding a legal dictum of the יפה כח series which specified certain rights and obligations of the husband during the betrothal period, did not want to set it into his Mishnah in its original form because it was contrary to the halakah of his day. Therefore, he, so to speak, interpreted it by adding the word נישאת to it, making these obligations and rights apply only from the time of nuptials. Possibly the implication by the words יתר עליו הבעל that the father never has the duty of support, ransom and burial and the privilege of fruit was not intended by him; possibly it was. If it was, he has thrown in the weight of his authority on behalf of R. Meir against R. Jose b. R. Judah who maintains that the father is entitled to the fruit of his unmarried and unbetrothed daughter. The scribe who has quoted the opinion of R. J. b. R. J. in connection with the tosefta misunderstood the tosefta, which in reality deals only with the betrothed, neither with the father's rights before betrothal nor with the husband's rights after the nuptials.

APPENDIX B

Register of Published Ketubot and Allied Deeds

Much of this material is found in books intended expressly as *Shetarot* compilations either for halakic purposes or as guides for scribes. Of these the important ones are:

1. *Sefer Ha-shetarot,* R. Judah Barzilai, ed. Halberstam, 1898.
2. *Tikon Soferim,* R. Samuel Jaffe, Levorno, 1789.
3. *Sefer Lekal Hefez,* R. Eliezer Melli, Venice, 1552.
4. *Nahlat Shiv'ah,* R. Samuel Halevy, Koenigsberg, 1869.
5. *Ozar Ha-shetarot,* Asher Gulack, Jerusalem, 1926.

A variety of ketubot and other marriage instruments from various dates and places are found in the works cited. But in addition to these, marriage deeds are found in halakic, historical, and liturgical works, and more recently scholars have displayed an especial interest in the host of marriage deeds found in manuscript form in the various libraries and whenever the opportunity offered itself to them have published them in monographs or periodicals. We briefly present these in the order of their estimated dates:

1. Papyrus G. ed. A. H. Sayce and A. E. Cowley, *Aramaic Papyri Discovered at Assuan,* London, 1906, p. 68.
   The same is re-edited by A. E. Cowley, *Aramic Papyri of the Fifth Century B. C.,* Oxford, 1923, p. 44.
2. Papyrus 34, ed. E. Sachau, *Aramaische Papyrus u. Ostraka aus Elephantine,* Berlin, 1911, p. 126. (Recorded in Cowely, ibid. p. 55).
3. Hai Ketubah, Babylonia, 9th century, ed. A. Harkavey, *Hapisgah,* Vol. 3, p. 46.
4. Gershon Ketubah, Mayence, 1013, ed. B. Goldberg, *Kerem Hemed,* Vol. 8, p. 106.
5. Egyptian Ketubah, Miandrus, 1022, ed. Jacob Mann, *Jews in Egypt and Palestine under the Fatimids,* Oxford, 1922, Vol. 2, p. 94.
6. Palestinian Ketubah, dated 1026, ed. S. Asaf, *Hazofeh Lehakmat Yisroel,* Vol. 10, p. 28.
7. Karaitic Ketubah, Jerusalem, 1028, ed. A. M. Luncz, *Yerushalayim,* Vol. 6, p. 237.

8. Egyptian Ketubah, Fostat, 1030, ed. S. Poznanski, *Revue des etudes Juives*, Vol. 48, p. 173.

9. Shetar Erusin, Fostat, 1049, ed. Israel Levy, *Revue des etudes Juives*, Vol. 47, p. 301.

10. Karaitic Ketubah, dated 1081, publ. G. Margoliuth, *Catalogue of Hebrew and Samaritan MSS in the British Museum*, Vol. 3, p. 558.

11. Karaite-Rabbinite Ketubah, Fostat, 1082, ed. Solomon Schechter, *Jewish Quarterly Review*, Vol. 13, p. 220.

12. Levirate Ketubah, probably of the 11th century, ed. B. M. Levin, *Ginze Kedem*, Vol. 2, p. 42.

13. Proxy-Marriage Ketubah, France, 12th Century, Rashi, *Sefer Ha-pardes*, ed. H. L. Ehrenreich, Budapesth, 1924, p. 85

14. Maimonides Ketubah, Egypt, 12th century, *Yad Ha-hazakah*, Yibbum, 4, 31.

15. European Ketubah, France, 12th century, *Mahzor Vitri*, ed. S. Hurwitz, Berlin, 1899, p. 791. (Contains also a levirate ketubah, *shetar erusin* and *ketubah demirkasa*).

16. Marriage deeds, France, 12th century, *Sefer Ha-Itur*, Vol. 1, Warsau, 1885, Vol. 2, Wilna 1874. (Contains *Pesikatha*, *Tenai-ketubah*, *Ketubah demirkasah* and levirate ketubah.)

17. Saadya Ketubah, 12th century, ed. Moses Gaster, *Monatschrift f. d. Geschichte u. Wissenschaft d. Judenthums*, Vol. 54, under the title, *Die Ketubah bei die Samaritanern*. (Contains also Samaritan, Karaitic, Ymenite, Benai Israel and Sephardic ketubot, as well as a *Shetar erusin*, a *ketubah demirkasah*, and a ketubah for marriage by proxy.)

18. German Ketubah, Germany, 12th century, recorded in *Mishpete Ketubah*, R. Elazar b. Joel Halevi, ed. A. Sultzbach, Jahrbuch d. Juedisch-literarischen Gesellschaft, Vol. 3, Frankfurt A. M., 1905.

19. Egyptian Ketubah, Balbis, 1220, ed. Israel Abrahams, *Jews' College Jubilee Volume*, London, 1906, p. 105.

20. Levirate Ketubah, Austria, 13th century, *Or Zaru'a*, Isaac of Vienna, Zhitomir, 1862, Vol. 1, p. 641.

21. *Tena'im*, England, 13th century, ed. M. D. Davis, *Hebrew Deeds of English Jews before* 1290.

22. *Deed formula*, Europe, before 1336, photographed by Herman L. Strack on the concluding pages of his *Der babylonische Talmud...Muenchen Codx Hebraicus* 95, Leiden, 1912. (Contains, among others, ketubah, *ketubah demirkasah*, levirate ketubah, *tenai-ketubah*, and *Mattanah lehud.*)

23. Algiers Ketubah, Algiers, 14th century, Samson b. Zemah Duran, Responsa, Amsterdam, 1737, Vol. 3, p. 301.

24. Ketubah Jerushalmit, no date, ed. A. Berliner, *Kobez 'al Yad*, Vol. 9, Berlin, 1893.

25. Sephardic Ketubah, no date, ed. M. Grossberg, *Hebel Menashe*, London, 1900.

26. French Ketubah, Marseille, 1494, Buxtorf, *Grammaticae Chaldaicae et Syriacae*, Bazel, 1650, Vol. 3, p. 423.

27. English Ketubah, 18th century, Raphael Meldola, *Hupat Hatanim*, Lublin, 1872, pp. 28f.

28. Southern Russian Ketubah, Caucasia, 1864, ed. J. Tschorney, *Sefer Ha-masa'ot*, St. Petersburg, 1884.

29. Karaitic Ketubah, modern, contained in the Karaitic prayer book, Wilna, 1890, Vol. 4, p. 54.

30. In addition to the above, ketubah photographs are to be found in *The Jewish Encyclopedia*, Vol. 7, pp. 475-478 and in M. Gaster's monograph, *The Ketubah*, Berlin-London, 1923.

BIBLIOGRAPHY

A. STUDIES IN COMPARATIVE LAW.

APTOWITZER, V., *Zur Geschichte d. armenischen Rechts*, WZKM, 1907.

APTOWITZER, V., *Beitrage z. mosaischen Rezeption in armenischen Recht*, SKAW, 1907.

APTOWITZER, V., *Die syrische Rechtsbuecher u. d. mosaisch-talmudische Recht*, SKAW, 1909.

APTOWITZER, V., *Die Rechtsbuecher d. nestorianischen Patriarchen*, SKAW, 1910.

APTOWITZER, V., *Hammurabi and Syrian-Roman Law*, JQR, 1907.

BRUNS-SACHAU, *Syrisch-römisches Rechtsbuch*, Leipzig, 1880.

COOK, S. A., *The Laws of Moses and the Code of Hammurabi*, London, 1903.

FRIEDRICHS, K., *Das Eherecht des Islam*, ZVR, 1887.

KOHLER, JOSEPH, *Altsyrisches u. armenisches Recht*, ZVR, 1906.

KOHLER-PEISER, *Aus d. babylonischen Rechtsleben*, Leipzig, 1890.

KOHLER-UNGNAD, *Hammurabis Gesetz*, Leipzig, 1909-10.

MARX, VICTOR, *Die Stellung d. Frau in Babylonien, Beitrage z. Assyriologie*, Vol. 4, 1902.

MAYER, S., *Die Rechte d. Israeliten, Athener u. Römer*, Leipzig, 1866.

MEISSNER, B., *Beitrage z. altbabylonischen Privatrecht*, Leipzig, 1893.

MITTEIS, L., *Römisches Privatrecht*, Leipzig, 1908.

MUELLER, D. H., *Zur Terminologie im Eherecht b. Hammurabi*, WZKM, 1905.

MUELLER, D. H., *Zum Eherecht d. Tochter*, WZKM, 1905.

MUELLER, D. H., *Das syrisch-roemische Rechtsbuch u. Hammurabi*, WZKM, 1905.

MUELLER, D. H., *Die Gesetze Hammurabis in ihr Verhaltnisse z. mosaischen Gesetzgebung*, Wien, 1903.

NIETZOLD, J., *Die Ehe in Aegypten*, Leipzig, 1903.

PICK, H., *Talmudisches u. Assyrisches*, Berlin, 1902.

THURNWALD, R., *Die Stellung d. Frau in alten Babylonien, Blaetter f. vergleichende Rechtswissenschaft*, 1906.

SACHAU, E., *Syrische Rechtsbuecher*, Berlin, 1903.

WELHAUSEN, S., *Die Ehe b. d. Arabern, Nachricht v. d. k. Gesellschaft d. Wissenschaften zu Göttingen*, 1893.

WAHRMUND, L., *Ehe u. Eherecht*, Leipzig, 1906.

B. WORKS ON JEWISH LAW.

ANDREE, R., *Zur Folkskunde d. Juden*, Leipzig, 1881.
BENZINGER, J., *Hebraische Archaologie*, Freiburg, 1894.
BLOCH, M., *Der Vertrag nach mosaisch-talmud. Rechte*, Leipzig, 1893.
BLOCH, M., שערי תורת התקנות, Wien, 1897.
BUHL, F., *Die sozialen Verhaeltnisse der Israeliten*, Berlin, 1899.
EWALD, H., *Die Alterthuemer des Volkes Israel*, Leipzig, 1894.
FISCHER, L., *Die Urkunden in Talmud*, Berlin, 1912.
KRAUSS, S., *Talmudische Archaologie*, Leipzig, 1910.
LOW, L., *Gesammelte Schriften*, Szegedin, 1889-90.
MICHAELIS, *Mosaisches Recht*, Frankfurt A/M, 1793.
NOWACK, W., *Lehrbuch d. hebraische Archaologie*, Leipzig, 1894.
SAALSCHUTZ, J., *Das mosaische Recht*, Berlin, 1853.
SUVALSKY, I., חיי היהודי על פי התלמוד, Warsau, 1889.

C. WORKS DEALING WITH JEWISH MARRIAGE LAWS.

AMRAM, D. W., *The Jewish Law of Divorce*, Philadelphia, 1896.
APOWITZER, V., *Review of L. Freund's Zur Geschichte des Ehegüterrechts b. d. Semiten*, WZKM, 1909.
BERGEL, J., *Die Eheverhaeltnisse der alten Juden*, Leipzig, 1881.
BILLAUER, A., *Grundzuege d. babylonisch-talmudischen Eherechts*, Berlin, 1910.
BLAU, L., *Die juedische Ehescheidung, Jahrbuch des Landesrabbinerschule in Budapest*, 1911-14.
BLAU, L., *Zur Geschichte des juedischen Eherechts, Festschrift Adolph Schwartz*, Wien, 1917.
BUECHLER, A., *Familienreinheit u. Familienmakel....., Festschrift Adolph Schwartz*, Wien, 1917.
BUECHLER, A., *Das juedische Verlobniss, Festschrift Israel Lewy*, Breslau, 1911.
BUECHLER, A., *Die Straffe des Ehebruches ....*, MGWJ, 1911.
BUECHLER, A., *Das Schneiden des Haares als Starffe des Ehebrecher bei den Semiten*, WZKM, 1909.
BUCHHOLTZ, P., *Die Familie in rechtlicher und moralischer Beziehung nach mosaisch-talmudische Lehre, Breslau*, 1867.
DUSCHAK, M., *Das mosaisch-talmudische Eherecht*, Wien, 1864
ENGERT, T., *Ehe- und Familienrecht der Hebraer, Muenchen*, 1905.
FRANKEL, Z., *Grundlinien des talmudische Eherecht*, Breslau, 1860.

FREUND, L., *Zur Geschichte des Ehegüterrechts bei den Semiten,* SKAW, 1908.

FREUND, L., *Zur Geschichte der Ehegüterrechts bei der Auf-loesung der Ehe,* WZKM, 1907.

FREUND, L., *Ueber Genealogien- u. Familienreinheit in biblische u. talmudische Zeit, Festschrift Adolph Schwartz,* Wien, 1917.

GANZ, E., *Die Grundzuege d. mosaisch-talmudischen Erbrechts, Zeitschrift f. d. Wissenschaft des Judenthums,* Berlin 1823.

GEIGER, A., *Dispensation von der Schwigerehe u. Weigerung der Unmuendigen, Zeitschrift f. d. Wissenschaft des Juden-thums,* 1823.

HOLDHEIM, S., מאמר האישות, Berlin, 1864.

KLUGMANN, N., *Die Stellung der Frau in Alterthum,* Berlin, 1898.

KURREIN, A., *Die Frau im juedischen Volke, Bilin,* 1901.

LICHTENSTEIN, *Die Ehe nach mosaisch-talmudische Auffassung,* Leipzig, 1879.

LOW, L., *Eherechtliche Studien, Ben-hananja,* Vols. 2-5.

MIELZINER, M., *The Jewish Law of Marriage and Divorce,* Cin-cinnati, 1884.

NEUBAUER, J., *Beitrage zur Geschichte der biblisch-talmudischen Eheschliessungesrechts,* Leipzig, 1920.

NEUWIRTH, *Zum juedischen Eherecht, Juedische Monatshefte,* 1916.

PERLER, S., *Die juedische Hochzeit in nachbiblischer Zeit,* MGWJ, 1860.

STUBBE, CH., *Die Ehe im alten Testament,* Jena, 1886.

WEIL, S., *La Femme Juive,* Paris, 1874.

D. TEXT STUDIES.

COWLEY, A. H., *Aramaic Papyri of the Fifth Century B. C.,* Oxford, 1923.

EPSTEIN, J. N., *Notizen z. d. jeudisch-aramaischen Papyri von Assuan, Jahrbuch d. juedisch-literarischen Geselffschaft,* 1908.

FISCHER, L., *Glossen z. d. juedisch-aramaischen Papyri von Assuan, Jahrbuch d. juedisch-literarischen Gesellschaft,* 1910.

FUNK, S., *Die Papyri von Assuan als die aelteste Quelle einer Halacha, Jahrbuch d. juedisch-literarischen Gesellschaft,* 1909.

FREUND, L., *Bemerkungen zu Papyrus G,* WZKM, 1907.

MERX, A., *Documents de paleographie hebraique et arabe,* Leyden, 1894.

FRITSCH, E., *Juedische Rechturkunden aus Aegypten,* ZVR, 1912. (A full list of literature on the various papyri collections is here given.)

SAYCE-COWLEY, *Aramaic Papyri Discovered at Assuan,* London, 1906.

SACHAU, E., *Aramaische Papyri aus Elephantine,* Berlin, 1911.

SCHORR, M., *Altbabylonische Rechtsurkunden,* SKAW, 1907.

STAERK, W., *Die juedisch-aramaischen Papyri von Assuan,* Bonn, 1907.

E. STUDIES IN THE KETUBAH.

ADLER, E. N., *Aus einem Brief Elkan N. Adlers,* MGWJ, 1897.

ASAF, S., בטולה של כתובת בנין דיכרין, *Hazofeh,* 1926.

CZERNOWITZ, CH., *Das Dotalsystem nach mosaisch-talmudischen Gesetzgebung,* ZVR, 1914.

CZERNOWITZ, CH., תורת הנדוניא בדיני ישראל, in N. Sokolow's *Sefer Ha-yobel,* Warsau, 1904.

BUECHLER, A., *La ketubah chez les juives du Nord de l'afrique.* REJ, Vol. 50.

FRIEDMANN, אגרת תשובה על דבר הכתובה Wien, 1888.

FRANKEL, Z., *Analekten,* MGWJ, 1861.

KAUFMANN, D., *Zur Geschichte der Ketubah,* MGWJ, 1896.

SOURCES AND AUTHORITIES

תנ"ך — חמשה חומשי תורה, יהושע, שופטים, שמואל א', מלכים א', מלכים ב', ד"ה א', ירמיה, הושע, מלאכי, רות, אסתר.

ספרים חצונים — חוקי הבבליים מאת המורבי, בן סירא, ספר טוביה, צוואת אברהם, כתבי פילון היהודי, ספרי יוסיפון, ספרי און גליון.

תרגומים — תרגום אונקלוס, תרגום יונתן בן עוזיאל.

תוספתא — שביעית, פיאה, שבת, כתובות, גיטין, קידושין, בבא בתרא, סנהדרין, עדיות, בכורות.

בבלי — פיאה, שבת, מוע"ק, עירובין, תענית, פסחים, יבמות, כתובות, נדרים, נזיר, סוטה, גיטין קידושין, בבא קמא, בבא מציעא, בבא בתרא, סנהדרין, עדיות, שבועות, מכות, חולין, בכורות, ערכין, נגעים, נידה, אדר"נ, ד"א זוטא, שמחות.

ירושלמי — מעשרות, כלאים, פיאה, שביעית, שבת, עירובין, יבמות, כתובות, נדרים, נזיר, סוטה, גיטין, קידושין, בבא בתרא.

מדרש — מכילתא דר' ישמעאל, מכילתא דר' שמעון בן יוחאי, ספרא, ספרי במדבר, ספרי דברים, ספרי זוטא.
בראשית רבה, שמות רבה, במדבר רבה, דברים רבה, פסיקתא דר' כהנא, איכה רבה, ילקוט שמעוני.

הלכות — שאילתות דר' אחאי, הלכות גדולות, ספר בשר על גבי גחלים, הלכות דרב אלפס, ספר הישר לר' תם, ספר ראבי"ה, מחזור ויטרי, הרא"ש, פסקי רב מרדכי, ספר החינוך להרא"ה.

פוסקים — יד החזקה להרמב"ם, ספר העטור לר' יצחק בן אבא מרי, ספר המכריע לר' ישעיה די טראני הראשון, אור זרוע לר' יצחק מווינא, אורחות חיים לר' אהרן הכהן מלוניל, תולדות אדם וחוה לר' ירוחם, ארבעה טורים לר' יעקב בר' אשר, צידה לדרך לר' מנחם בר' זרח, שולחן ערוך לר' יוסף קארו, חילוקי דינים למהרש"ל.

שאלות ותשובות — תשובות הגאונים מאת הרכבי, שו"ת הגאונים מאת גינצבערג, שו"ת גאונים קדמונים, שערי צדק, חמדה גנוזה, תשובות גאוני מזרח ומערב, קובץ תשובות הרמב"ם, שו"ת הרשב"א, שו"ת מהר"ם בר' ברוך, שו"ת הרא"ש, שו"ת הריב"ש, שו"ת הרדב"ז, תשב"ץ, דברי ריבות לרי' אדרבי, נודע ביהודה לר' יחזקאל לאנדא.

פירושים והגהות — (על התורה) אבן עזרא, רש"י, רמב"ן.
(על המשנה) פירוש המשניות להרמב"ם, פירוש ר' שמעון משאנץ, תוס' יו"ט לר' יו"ט ליפמאן העללער.
(על ספרא) פירוש הראב"ד, פירוש הרש' משאנץ.
(על הבבלי) פירוש ר' חננאל, פירוש רש"י, הרשב"ם, חידושי הרשב"א, תוספות, תוס' רי"ד, פירוש הרא"ש, פירוש הר"ן, חידושי הריטב"א, שיטה מקובצת, ים של שלמה למהרש"ל.
(על הירושלמי) שיירי קרבן מר' דוד דעסא.
(על האלפס) השגות הראב"ד, ספר המאור לרז"ה, מלחמות ד' להרמב"ן, פירוש הר"ן, נמוקי יוסף.
(על הרמב"ם) השגות הראב"ד, הגהות מיימוניות, כסף משנה, מגדל עוז, לחם משנה.
(על הטור) בית יוסף, בית חדש, דרישה ופרישה.
(על שו"ע) הגהות הרמ"א, חלקת מחוקק, בית שמואל, ביאור הגר"א, פתחי תשובה.
(על שאילתות) שאילת שלום לר' ישעיה ברלין.
(על העיטור) שער חדש.

תערובות — אגרת רב שרירא גאון, ספר הערוך, ספר השטרות לרי' ברצלוני, משפטי כתובה לראבי"ה, חופת חתנים לר' רפאל מילדולא, נחלת שבעה לר' שמואל הלוי, מלא הרועים לר' יעקב צבי יאליש.

ספרי הקראים — אשכול הכופר לר' יהודה הדסי, גן עדן לר' אהרן הקראי, אדרת אליהו לר' אליהו בשייצי.

CRITICAL NOTES

INDEX

www.ingramcontent.com/pod-product-compliance
Lightning Source LLC
Chambersburg PA
CBHW032343280326
41935CB00008B/429

* 9 7 8 1 6 1 6 1 9 5 1 1 3 *